Mediterranean Cookbook

Arabella Boxer was born in 1934, in Scotland, of Scottish and American parentage. As a child, she lived first in Scotland, then in London, and spent the summers in the United States with her grandparents. She has travelled widely, and was Food Editor of *Vogue* from 1975 to 1991. She has also written extensively for the *Sunday Times Magazine* and the *Telegraph Magazine*. Her books include among others *First Slice Your Cookbook*, *The Sunday Times Complete Cookbook*, *Arabella Boxer's Book of English Food* and *A Visual Feast* with Tessa Traeger. In 1992 she won the Andre Simon Award and a Glenfiddich Special Award for Food Writing.

Arabella Boxer
Mediterranean Cookbook

GRUB STREET * LONDON

This edition published in 2021 by
Grub Street
4 Rainham Close
London
SW11 6SS
Email: food@grubstreet.co.uk
Web: www.grubstreet.co.uk

First published by J.M.Dent & Sons Ltd in 1981.
This edition is a re-issue of the Penguin edition first published in Great
Britain in 1983.

Cataloguing in Publication Data for this title is available from the British
Library

ISBN 978-1-911667-19-3

Printed and bound in India

CONTENTS

ACKNOWLEDGEMENTS

I should like to thank all my friends – and their friends – who were kind enough to help me with this book, by giving me meals, recipes, and advice, having me to stay, lending me books and so on. In particular: Eliane and Anthony Grigg, Janetta and Jaime Parlade in Spain; Valerie and Robert Goulet in Mallorca; George Bradford, Yves Coutarel, Sylvia Guirey, Elspeth Juda, Natasha Spender and Dee Wells in France; Bianca Cavaglieri, Bruno and Susie Palmarin in Venice; Harry Blackmer in Athens; Nuri Birgi, Mica and Ahmed Ertegun, Eva Neumann, Lyn Water and Erdogan Dinc in Turkey; my sister-in-law Rosemary Sayegh in Beirut; Sevin Akser, Edwina and Rodolfe d'Erlanger in Tunis; and Irene Arcoumanis, Cristina Cholmondeley, Alan Davidson, Alex Dufort, Min Hogg, Sarah Jones, Dorothy Lygon, Demetri Marchessini, Luisa McCubbin, David Plante, Dominique Rocher, Nikos Stangos, Eliane Stefanidis, Caroline Thrupp, Tessa Traeger, Day Wollheim, Richard and Rupert Wollheim at home; my sisters Sarah Stuart and Mary Anne Denham, and above all my niece Joumana Sayegh.

THE MEDITERRANEAN SEA

To write about the foods of all the countries that surround the Mediterranean could seem an impossibly ambitious task. Some fifteen countries border the sea, to say nothing of its many islands, and they span three continents. Yet when one starts to consider the matter it becomes clear that all these countries have a great deal in common, and the task seems simpler than at first imagined. It is as if the sea itself has imposed a strong unifying effect on the areas surrounding it. Different as the countries may be, in terms of race, politics, religion and culture, in the end we are forced to acknowledge that food is based on quite other matters. When I was a child, I used to study geography from an atlas that had two maps for each country, on facing pages. The first, in bright primary colours, represented all the man-made aspects of the country: the towns in degrees of importance, borders between the different regions, the ports, railways, shipping lines and similar points. The second map restricted itself to showing the country in its natural state; here we saw the mountain ranges, rivers, sea currents, even the rainfall was sometimes indicated. This form of differentiation has now been largely abandoned by modern text books, but it is as good a way as any of understanding, in the simplest possible terms, what affects our diet. Whatever new regulations the EEC may impose upon our country, our food production can only be altered within fairly narrow limits which were laid down in prehistoric times by our climate and the composition of our soil.

Once this has been accepted, the relevance of Mediterranean food as a concept becomes more meaningful. According to Fernand Braudel, the French historian whose *History of the Mediterranean at the Time of Philip II of Spain* is such an absorbing book, the area technically known as 'Mediterranean' can be clearly defined. It is the land lying between two roughly parallel borders: to the north, the northern limit of the olive tree; to the south, the northern limit of the palm grove. (Although isolated palms are often seen growing far north of this line, they never grow naturally, in clumps, above this point.) This area includes the southern half of Spain and Italy, and a narrow strip running along the shores of southern France, northern Italy, Yugoslavia, Albania, Greece, Turkey, Syria, Lebanon and Israel. The southern part comprises a broad coastal strip running along the shores of Morocco, Algeria and Tunisia, but for the purposes of this book I am also including Egypt, with its rich and varied cuisine.

If this area is studied on a map, it becomes apparent that it is not so large as at first imagined; indeed, it is just possible to visualize it as one huge country turned inside out, with the Mediterranean Sea like a huge inland lake, filling the vacuum in the centre and bringing all the surrounding countries together into a cohesive mass. Every sea has its own character, and any body of water as large as this cannot fail to have a strong effect on the countries round about. Its temperature, depth, degree of salinity all bring forces to bear, not only on the fish that swim in it, and on the islands, but on the surrounding climate, soil and vegetation. In fact, the climate of the Mediterranean lands is formed by two opposing factors which are constantly reacting against each other: the Atlantic Ocean and the Sahara Desert. The interplay between these two forces can be easily traced; from May until September the desert is responsible for the almost universal clear dry air, while from October to April the climate is dominated by the ocean, bringing grey mists and much rain.

To most Anglo-Saxons, influenced by summer holidays and tourist publicity, the Mediterranean has an unreal image, bathed in constant sunshine falling on calm seas. The reality is very different. A few years ago I spent Easter on the Greek island of Patmos; it was early April, and I have never been colder in my life. This was my first experience of the Mediterranean under wintry conditions, and I found it almost impossible to believe that this *was* the same island I had visited the previous August. Everything was grey – the skies, the sea, while the rolling hills dotted with small white-washed houses reminded me of parts of south-west Ireland, the only difference being that stone terraces replaced the Irish walls. Yet this same year, they had been swimming on the island at Christmas, only a few months previously. Similar Easter visits in later years, all nearly as cold, to Venice, Tuscany, Naples and even Tunis led me to believe that this is not the best time to visit the Mediterranean. It seems that the sea cools down slowly after the hot summer, often remaining warm until the beginning of January. When the cold weather does finally come, however, it takes an equally long time to warm up again. When spring comes, and this can vary widely, it happens very suddenly; within a matter of days the leaves burst out and flowers bloom, and all the vegetables start to ripen together.

Since all the Mediterranean countries have a basic similarity of climate, allowing for the obvious modifications of latitude, this in its turn causes a similarity of vegetation. In fact, most crops can be grown almost interchangeably throughout this whole area, and any differences are more likely to have been caused by religious or ethnic variations than physical ones. According to M. Braudel, this basic similarity of climate and vegetation has imposed its own unity on the countries bordering the Mediterranean. He claims that it has made it relatively easy for people to leave their homes in one country for another, so long as they are still within reach of the Mediterranean itself. It is only when they leave the region altogether that they become displaced and unsettled. (This does not of course apply to the Palestinians whose displacement was hardly voluntary.) Certainly in earlier times there was constant movement of peoples around and across the shores of the sea; the Greeks in particular settled in large numbers in many cities outside Greece. Almost all the large cities on the edges of the Mediterranean have, or had at one time, a sizable Greek community. Apart from the actual resettling of peoples, there was the constant traffic of cargo ships. Due to the necessity of taking on fresh provisions, crew and the cargo itself, the ships had to stop frequently. Nor was this only at the ports around the shores; the islands too made convenient, even necessary stops on the often hazardous trans-Mediterranean crossing. This endless to-ing and fro-ing of boats also caused a stream of commerce on a small scale, for each sailor would carry with him a small store of goods for sale or barter. In this way, as well as on the larger scale of imports and exports, foodstuffs would travel from place to place, and almonds from Provence, beans from Egypt and spices from Venice would find their way from one port to another.

Even more influential were the exchanges of goods caused as a result of the frequent conquests and reconquests of past centuries. The Moorish occupation of southern Spain, lasting as it did for seven hundred years, inevitably had a strong influence on the Spanish cuisine. This can still be seen in the almost Oriental love for very sweet things prevalent in Spain, unlike any to be found in the neighbouring countries on the northern shore of the Mediterranean. The Sardinian domination of Nice, lasting on and off for hundreds of years, is readily appreciated by anyone interested in food, for the Italian influence is still clearly visible, and the excellent cooking of Nice is in many ways closer to that of Genoa than of other French towns. In Trieste also, the fact that it was until the end of the First World War part of the Austrian empire is still very plain, and its cooking is an interesting combination of the central European/Slav cuisine with that of the Latin Mediterranean countries. An island such as Malta, occupied by different countries over the centuries and used as a stopping place for many more, must inevitably become a melting pot of different culinary traditions, and form a sort of individual cuisine of its own. Unfortunately the extreme poverty of most of the islands does not seem to have encouraged the growth of an interesting cuisine; it is hard to find any food of interest in Sardinia today, although some families still bake the traditional *carta di musica*, thin sheets of bread baked in a pizza oven.

Conquests outside the Mediterranean also had an important part to play. The Spanish conquistadores brought chocolate back from America; understandably enough this had a strong appeal to the sweet tooth that had been fostered by the Moorish occupation, and quickly acquired a lasting popularity. The potato, however, met with less success, and in any case was not suited to cultivation in the hot dry climate.

Another factor common to all the Mediterranean countries is the lack of pasture, due to the aridity. This has three important effects. First, there is an almost total lack of dairy produce. What produce exists is used largely as milk, and in lesser amounts, and only in certain countries, as butter. Cream does not exist and never features in the cooking. Oil is used as a substitute for butter, and sometimes even for milk. (In the south of Spain the peasants eat olive oil on their bread instead of butter, and even mix it with condensed milk for their children.) The second result of the absence of pasture land is the shortage of beef. Since it is almost impossible to fatten calves to maturity on the dry summer soil, they are almost always killed off and eaten as veal. Lamb is in any case the prevalent meat in this area. The absence of mature cattle gives rise to the third effect, caused originally by lack of pastures; this is the lack of manure. Although less immediately obvious, it also has a strong effect on the farming, since without it, it is impossible to cultivate the rich crops of the northern European countries.

Taken as a whole, the average diet of the Mediterranean countries, particularly in the east, is austere but supremely healthy. Based on grilled meat and fish, raw salads, bread, fruit, herbs and yogurt, it provides a limited but to me very appealing diet. It would be hard to suffer a liver attack or a cardiac condition in a true Mediterranean area, for the animal fats consumed by the north Europeans and the Americans simply do not exist. The potential monotony of such a limited diet is offset by the use of herbs on the northern shores of the Mediterranean, and spices in the south.

Each country has its own preference in these matters; the most rich and complex use of herbs is probably that to be found in Provence and the south of France. Throughout Italy, basil is the favourite herb, followed by oregano; in its dried form, the latter is used almost indiscriminately throughout Greece, sprinkled over everything from salads to meatballs. In true Greek food, however, such as is only found now in private houses or in the pages of old cookery books, the use of herbs was much more sophisticated. Dill was often added to dishes of white beans, in fricassees of lamb or chicken, and in the *avgolemono* sauce which goes so well with almost any basic food. Purslane was, and still is, popular in many parts of Greece, but this is perhaps closer to a salad vegetable than a herb. Another borderline vegetable, rocket, is widely used in Turkey, both as a substitute for lettuce in salads and as a garnish for fish. The Turks also use herbs with mastery; chervil, dill and parsley are all much in evidence in Turkish food. In the Middle Eastern countries, parsley and mint are used in vast quantities; almost every home dries its own supply of mint, which is then often used in preference to the fresh leaf, sprinkled over dishes of cucumber in yogurt for instance. Subtle mixtures of rose petals with various herbs and spices are blended by the Shi'ite tribes in south Lebanon, giving an indescribable flavour to certain dishes which is impossible to duplicate in the west.

As we reach the North African shores, the use of spices begins to dominate that of herbs. Cinnamon is the great favourite in Egypt, while coriander and cumin are also popular. Coriander is the most popular spice in Tunisia, and is often used in conjunction with cinnamon and dried buds of a variety of Damask rose. Another much used Tunisian combination is coriander, caraway, garlic and dried chillies, called *tabil*. Saffron is used here also, especially in fish dishes such as fish *couscous*, but in this case it is not combined with other spices, but used alone. *Harissa*, the fiery paste made from pounded chilli peppers, is used in moderation in Tunisia, again with *couscous*, but even more so in Algeria and Morocco, the other countries that used to make up the Mahgreb. Fresh herbs are also used in Morocco, where a day hardly passes without a glass of mint tea.

The three main crops of the Mediterranean are wheat, olives and vines. This has been so since ancient times; wheat grew in the western Mediterranean countries some ten thousand years ago, and has grown there widely ever since. The wheat most commonly cultivated is the hard durum wheat, high in gluten and ideal for making pasta, although a softer variety for making bread and pastry is also known in some parts. Its pattern of growth is different from our own, however, since the extremes of the Mediterranean climate have imposed their own effects, causing it to be regarded almost as a winter crop. It completes its growth by early spring in some parts, and is ready for harvesting by April in the south of Spain, and May or June in Egypt.

Apart from pasta and bread, the flour is used to make the many dishes of pastry and bread dough so popular in France and Italy, the pancakes and dumplings of Yugoslavia, and the paper thin *filo* pastry beloved of the Greeks, Turks and Tunisians. It also provides the semolina for making *couscous*, and the gnocchi of Italy. Secondary cereal crops include a short-grain rice, grown round Valencia in Spain, in the Camargue, north-eastern Italy and Egypt. This provides the Spanish paellas, the Italian risottos, the Turkish pilavs and many Middle Eastern dishes. Corn, or maize, is grown extensively in the Friuli area near Venice, and eaten as polenta throughout northern Italy. Before the importation of maize from America, polenta, which is one of the most ancient of foods, was made with millet.

The olive is also ancient, like many other aspects of the Mediterranean. The olive tree was well known to the ancient Egyptians and the Phoenicians, and is often mentioned in the Bible. It originated on the northern shores of the Mediterranean, probably in and around Greece. The spread of its cultivation round the shores of the Mediterranean was assisted by the colonization of the times; the Greeks brought the first olive trees to Provence some two and a half thousand years ago, while the Romans planted the first olive groves in Tunisia. (Olives are still grown there on a scale unlike any I have seen elsewhere, with parallel lines of olive trees stretching almost as far as the eye can see.)

There are more than sixty different varieties of olive tree. They grow to a considerable height – as much as sixty-five feet near the coast – and to an immense age; three hundred years is considered comparatively young. They start bearing fruit from their sixth or seventh year, but do not reach their full yield, some twenty to forty kilos, until about twenty-five years. They are harvested on alternate years, at times that vary according to the use for which the olives are intended.

The olive is a bitter fruit, and at no time can it be eaten straight off the tree. Lengthy immersion in brine and other processes are necessary before it becomes palatable. It changes colour gradually, from green through tan, violet, purplish-red to a glossy black, after which it starts to shrivel and lose its shine. The olives that are grown for eating, 'table olives' as they are called, are picked either green or glossy black sometime in October, while those for making oil are left on the tree until they start to shrivel, usually in November. There are many different sorts of table olives, and each country probably has its champions. The black Kalamata olives of central Greece are generally thought to be one of the best, while those of Provence are also delicious. Spanish olives are good eating too, especially those grown within a fifty kilometre radius of Seville, as far as can be seen from the top of the Giralda tower, according to local legend. Two sorts are grown here, the large 'queen' olive, and the smaller but superior 'manzanilla'. These last are mostly stuffed with red peppers for export, much of it for the English market. More interesting stuffings, made on a smaller scale since they necessitate stuffing by hand, are peeled almonds and fillets of anchovy. (The red pepper is now manufactured into a thick ribbon of paste, like a fat red noodle, so that it can be handled by machine.)

Olive oil is made from a different type of olive, after it has started to shrivel on the tree. This means that they are harvested later in the year – not until late November in Tuscany, for instance. The oil made around Lucca is thought by many to be the best in the world, but I have a slight preference for the Provençal oil, especially one made by Nicolas Alziari of Nice. Needless to say, the oils of Provence and Lucca are among the most expensive; less expensive but still good, certainly for cooking, are the Italian Sasso oil and the Spanish Carbonel, with a charming old-world picture of a flamenco dancer on its bright red tin. The first pressing of the olives yields a fruity green oil, quite thick and full of flavour, which is much prized by connoisseurs.

Sadly enough, the cultivation of olive groves is declining everywhere. Not only is the olive expensive and demanding to cultivate, since the fertilization is costly and most of the work, including the pruning and picking, must be done by hand, but people everywhere are turning to cheaper oils like corn and peanut. I fear that olive oil may in time become a luxury product instead of a basic food, as it has been for thousands of years. In Italy, the olive groves have diminished greatly, even since my first visit to Tuscany less than thirty years ago. No longer do stubby vines grow under the olive trees as they once did. (Since the shade of the olive tree is not dense, it permits cultivation of other crops – vegetables, vines or flowers – under its branches.) Encouraged by government subsidies, more and more farmers are turning to the cultivation of vines, which are both more economic and more adaptable to mechanization. As a result, the whole countryside is changing; even the vineyards are no longer pretty, since the vines are now trained on wires supported by concrete posts.

The other basic ingredient of the Mediterranean diet has of course been fish, but this is also becoming a luxury in many parts. In relation to its size, the Mediterranean has never been a rich fishing ground for a number of reasons. Firstly, the coastal shelf, which is so vital for the hatching of young fish, is extremely narrow, except in the Aegean and Adriatic, and along the coast of Tunisia. Secondly, the comparatively shallow depth of this sea limits its inhabitants; many of the Atlantic fish simply cannot exist at this depth. The Mediterranean is also much warmer than the Atlantic, and much poorer in vegetation. The shelf that divides the ocean from the sea, between Gibraltar and Tangiers, is very shallow indeed, and although there is a considerable intake of water here which helps to offset that lost in evaporation, there is little traffic in fish. (This narrow shelf also helps to explain the almost total absence of tides in the Mediterranean.) The second outlet, in order of importance, is into the Black Sea through the Bosphorus; water is taken in here, and some fish, although they prefer the richer, colder waters of the Black Sea. The third outlet, that of the Suez Canal, is an interesting example of the way in which man alters the natural order of things; although usually detrimental, this can at times be beneficial.

As a result of the opening of the Canal, the intake of water and fish at this point is starting to change the ancient pattern, and with the reduced salinity of the lakes, fish from the Red Sea are beginning for the first time to spread into the Mediterranean. Another interesting effect is that caused by the building of the Aswan Dam, for this has stopped the age-old influx of the Nile waters. These are, of course, now being put to valuable use in fertilizing the land, but this in turn means that the sea has suffered a substantial loss of food. One of the reasons why the Mediterranean is poor in plankton is explained by the existence of the Sahara, for this means that there are no rivers of any size flowing into the sea from its southern shores. Even on the northern shores, the rivers in the eastern basin are of little importance, and it is the rivers which bring much of the plankton into the sea. (For much of this information I am grateful to Alan Davidson's fascinating book, *Mediterranean Seafood*.)

These natural causes of the comparative poverty of the sea have been greatly aggravated in recent years by man's inherent thoughtlessness. Firstly by pollution, and secondly by over-fishing, he has almost succeeded in eliminating fish altogether. Staying recently in Bodrum, a small town in south-west Turkey, I was puzzled by the almost complete lack of fish in the market, while a few miles up the coast at Kusadasi there was a good selection. This was explained to me as a result of blasting, a horrific method of fishing which had been used at Bodrum some years previously, and the fish population has not recovered.

THE FOOD MARKETS

A visit to a food market is as good a way as any of learning about the local dishes. Some of the most beautiful markets, to my mind, are those of the south of France, stretching from Provence to the Italian border. The larger towns have a daily market, while the others share a mobile market which moves from place to place on different days of the week. Some of the old towns have covered market places, while others simply close a large street or series of streets, usually under shady trees, to traffic for the duration of the market. There is a very pretty covered market at Antibes, with panels of blue glass down the centre which cast a cool light over the produce. One of the most attractive and largest of the French markets is that at Toulon; it is renowned for its produce throughout a large area. Toulon is a naval base, a busy and attractive town with a large port running parallel to the town. The market takes place daily, except Mondays, in a long street called the Cours Lafayette which runs at right angles to the port. It is a broad street, with an avenue of plane trees running down the centre. A small square fish market is set at right angles to the rest, which sells only fruit, vegetables and flowers. Many of the stalls are quite specialized; one sells only onions, shallots and garlic, while another sells the three sorts of beans for making *pistou*: fresh pink and white haricots, and haricots verts. One little stall sells only lemons, laid out a half kilo at a time, on small enamel plates. Another, even smaller, sells fresh herbs – basil, chervil, parsley and coriander – each tied neatly in a small bundle.

The daily market at Arles is less picturesque, but full of interest. This takes place in the main street, running past the elegant façade of the Hôtel Jules César, where I once stayed years ago. This market is given a character all its own by the growing Algerian population in the region. There is as a result an emphasis on North African spices which one would not expect to find in a French provincial town, and many of the stalls are kept by black Africans. It is also an unusually varied market, selling meat, charcuterie, fish, cheese and bread as well as vegetables, fruit and flowers. The cheese stalls are always appealing; one of the local specialities is a large cream cheese called *brousse*, while another is the little St Marcellin cheese preserved in olive oil with herbs. A sort of layer cake of gorgonzola and cream cheese, here called *mascarpone*, reminded me of one I had seen in the Venice market in winter time. The Venetian version, called *torta di formaggio*, was in fact lighter and more delicious than the French. The charcuterie stalls are always full of interest; local specialities include the little *saucisson d'Arles* and the excellent *rosette* salami. French bread has become much more varied in recent years, due to a growing interest in health foods. No longer limited to baguettes and flutes of white flour, it now includes many different *pains de campagnes*, like a fat oval baguette in shape, made of mixtures of wholemeal and rye flour.

The market in St Tropez takes place on Tuesdays, in the Place des Lices. Many of the stalls are the modern mobile sort, like small trucks with one side that lets down to form a shop front. They sell vegetables, fruit, flowers, cheeses and objects made from the local olive wood. There is also a fish market, quite small, which is more picturesque; this takes place daily, just behind Senequier, the popular café on the harbour. This little market consists of five or six stalls selling the most beautiful fish, sparkling with freshness. They are mostly quite large, which makes me suspect that the restaurants have first choice and buy up all the one-portion fish, leaving the handsome but sizable *loups*, *daurades roses* and *royales*, large red mullets and *rascasses*. One can, however, buy mixtures of small fish especially for making bouillabaisse, including a large proportion of *poissons des roches*. The prices are high, pretty much the same as in the best London shops, and seem to vary little from fish to fish. Virtually the only inexpensive fish are mackerel and sardines.

One of the loveliest of the covered markets is in the old town at Nice, next to the flower market. This specializes in fruit and vegetables, with an emphasis on herbs. One stall sells eighteen different herbs, all fresh, including one marked '*pour les chats et chiens*'; this, I was told, is '*un medicament*'. All are marked '*non traités*', another sign of the growing interest in health foods. Beside the market is a *traiteur* and charcuterie, almost one hundred years old. Here they sell a fascinating variety of smoked, cured and cooked foods. Many of the dishes have an Italian aura, and remind us that until 1860 Nice was part of the kingdom of Sardinia, Piedmont and Liguria. A year after it was ceded to France, the rest of the kingdom became part of unified Italy, and the Italian influence can still be seen in many of the dishes, even in this one shop. There are dishes of lasagne and canneloni, fritters made from the flowers of courgettes and aubergines, and a dish called *porchetta* consisting of a skin of sucking pig filled with tripe in jelly. (*Porchetta* in Italy means simply roast sucking pig.) As well as pissaladière, here made without anchovies, there are large rectangular pizzas, a *fromage Corse maison* and a dish of brawn in jelly, set in a bowl and turned out under a crust of black peppercorns. The *jambon persillé* here is spectacular: regular cubes of pink ham set in a clear jelly, formed into a rectangular loaf shape and covered all over with a layer half an inch thick of bright green parsley. Tiny *jambonneaux* are also appealing; shaped like giant pears with the central bone protruding like a stalk, they are a sort of ham in miniature, covered with white breadcrumbs. On a second visit to Nice a year later, I found many Provençal dishes for sale: *tian* of courgettes, *tourte de blea* – a curious speciality of Nice in the form of a sweet pastry tart filled with a mixture of spinach beet, raisins and pine nuts – *lapin à la provençale*, *pintadeau à l'estragon*. Also, somewhat to my surprise, a Spanish paella called *riz à l'espagnole* and a *tabbouleh libanais*.

The Italian food markets are no less visually appealing than those of France; indeed, the Italians seem to have an almost unequalled mastery and feeling for the presentation of their food. Even the toughest-looking men in the fish market in Venice, armed with huge knives, can be seen laying out the fish on their stalls with all the delicacy of a painter arranging a still life. The Venice market is a particularly interesting one, especially the fish market, which is held under a covered building on the edge of the Grand Canal, near the Rialto Bridge. It is fascinating to watch the produce arriving early in the morning, much of it still by *sandallo*. (There is at this point a ferry service by gondola across the Grand Canal called a *traghetto*. Until recently, a cat who lived on the other side used to cross each morning, around midday, to eat the refuse from the clearing up of the fish market; it never crossed on Sundays, when there is no market.) Some of the large Mediterranean fish are extraordinary looking, if one is quick enough to catch sight of them before they are cut up for display on the stalls. Small species of shark called *palumbo* or *asia*, huge spotted *gatto di mare*, strange shaped *violino* – none of which have any equivalent in English. Giant spotted rays, skate, John dory, and monkfish are all quite startling to look at; the two last are very popular in Venice, and *filetto di san pietro* and *coda di rospo* are to be found on most restaurant menus. The range of shellfish for sale is extensive; many of them, like oysters, scallops, mussels, cockles and winkles are familiar enough to our eyes, but there are others like the razor shell or *cannolicchio*, which we are not accustomed to seeing offered for sale, and others, like the horny murex, here called *garunzolo*, which we are not used to seeing at all. There are a variety of clams for making *spaghetti alle vongole*; two of the best are the *tartufo di mare* and the *telline*. (These are well known in France as *praires* and *clovisses*.) There are also various octopus, cuttlefish and squid.

The vegetables and fruit are adjacent to the fish, and no less interesting, although less strange. As always, it is the specific attention to detail which fascinates me. One lady sells only artichokes, and she offers them in three different forms. The hearts and bottoms are neatly trimmed and laid under water, on beds of emerald green parsley, so that they shine like jewels. The hearts are also shredded, which she does with an amazingly sharp knife in mid-air, and sold for use in risottos, frittatas and salads, for they are tender enough to be eaten raw.

Also full of interest was a Tuscan market which I visited in late October, a better moment for seasonal foods than midsummer. The game stalls were impressive, although slightly daunting: huge chunks of wild boar, still complete with tusks and bristles, jostled with hares and rabbits, and a variety of small birds. The vegetable stalls were still as alluring as in summer, or even more so, since now there were some four or five different fungi, ranging from the giant *porcini* to the delicate *ovoli*, in shades of pink and orange. Sacks of courgette flowers were on sale for making fritters, and baskets of wild green leaves which have been gathered in the fields. An unusual dark purplish leafed cabbage called *cavolo nero* is much in evidence at this time; it is the main ingredient for a favourite Tuscan winter soup called *ribollita*. Another widely used leaf is *bietolle*, or beet; this is puréed and mixed with ricotta for filling ravioli and canneloni. It is sold both at vegetable stalls and at the dairy food stalls, where it is already cooked and squeezed into neat round handfuls, side by side with the ricotta. I had hoped to find a colourful market at Naples but was disappointed; the old market was demolished some years ago and has not been replaced.

The most interesting Spanish market that I have visited is the Mercado di San José, in Barcelona. This takes place daily, in a huge covered market just off the Ramblas. Apart from the impressive range and quality of its produce, the thing that most struck me about it was that the fish market was entirely run by ladies, and I do not use the word 'lady' by chance. No fish wives these, but superior looking matrons such as one might find running a Women's Institute sale in aid of the Red Cross; complete with hair-do's, dark glasses, pearl earrings and twin sets protected by white plastic aprons, they were immensely efficient. Many of the butchers' stalls were also run by women, and it gave me a strange shock to see them handling huge sides of meat. Another interesting aspect of the fish market, whose produce was quite as good as any I have seen, was the presence of all the 'baby' specimens of normally large fish which the Spanish love to eat. Here were baby soles, small hake, minute eels, tiny crabs and the minuscule gobies known as *chanquetes*. I also saw wild asparagus for sale in the vegetable section, with its elusive slightly bitter taste, and some fascinating stalls selling a mixture of dried and crystallized fruit, nuts and seeds. Here were the strange *chufas*, from which the popular almond-flavoured drink called *horchata di chufas* is made and sold in the streets.

In contrast to these large urban markets was one I visited last summer in a small fishing village in Turkey. Sariyer is on the Asian side of the Bosphorus, almost as far as one is allowed to go before reaching the Black Sea. (The final stage of the Bosphorus is a military zone, and landing is not permitted.) It is easily reached by steamers which ply up and down from the Galatea Bridge, zigzagging from side to side, and it makes an ideal place to get off for a couple of hours before returning to Istanbul. The small village is like one huge market. Fish are everywhere, swimming live in tanks: tunny and bonito, blue fish, red mullet, mackerel and sardines. The vegetables are even more impressive, since due to some abnormality in the soil, they grow to gigantic sizes. I counted as many as seventeen different vegetables, and even the radishes were as large as squash balls, yet with no loss in quality. Water was playing constantly over the fruit and vegetable stalls, so that they sparkled and glistened with colour. A few small restaurants beside the harbour offer a limited but superlative menu. Here I ate a blue fish for the first time, within sight of the Black Sea from whence it probably came. It was one of the best fish I have ever eaten, and I regretted all the times I had been offered it in New England seafood restaurants and rejected it. As I was eating it, a huge Russian ship came steaming past, and I felt, although this was not the case, that I had never been further from home.

The North African markets vary widely; those devoted to selling vegetables, grains and spices are fascinating, but I feel that the livestock markets are best avoided. Although I have fond memories of ravishing markets in Morocco, particularly in a small town called Asilah where we spent a summer, these were entirely of fruit, vegetables, eggs, grains and spices. When I wandered into a butcher's shop one day I was dismayed to find a whole camel's foot, complete with hoof, sitting on the counter. In Tunisia my feelings were similar. Although the soukh in Kairovan was vastly appealing, I found myself at one point in the poultry area of the Tunis market, where I was appalled to see an old man plucking a live chicken, held by the neck. Later he plunged it head down in a bucket of water, while he had a cup of tea.

Less upsetting, but less worthy of note, was a fish market I chanced upon in Split. Since it was the only market apart from a supermarket that I had been able to find in Yugoslavia, I fell upon it with fervour, only to discover it consisted of sixteen stalls, all selling sardines. Since it is hard to tell one sardine from another at the best of times, this seemed a good example of the degree of personal choice that is considered reasonable in a communist country; hardly a paradise for shoppers.

1   SOUPS

The most typically Mediterranean of soups is the bouillabaisse. This can only be found in its true form in and around Marseilles, since it must include a large proportion of *poissons des roches* which are only found in this locality. Attempts to make a bouillabaisse outside the Mediterranean are to my mind mistaken; there are other fish soups which are more adaptable and just as delicious. In fact, I prefer the simple *soupe aux poissons*, the *bourride*, and the *aigo-saou*, all of which can be made relatively successfully with other fish. There are excellent fish soups to be had all along the north coast of the Mediterranean, with infinite small variations. In Barcelona, I ate one which included chopped hard-boiled eggs; in parts of France, small amounts of vermicelli or thin spaghetti are sometimes added, while in Genoa, fresh basil is included.

Basil is the most important ingredient in the delicious *soupe au pistou* of the Côte Niçoise. This is a thick vegetable soup, similar to a minestrone but made with summer vegetables which should include three different sorts of fresh beans, and flavoured with a last-minute addition of a pounded paste of basil, garlic and pine nuts. Minestrone exists in myriad forms up and down both Italian coasts; in some areas it includes pasta, in others rice, while in some parts it is made with vegetables alone. In Genoa, the much loved basil is added. A favourite soup of mine is the Tuscan winter soup called *ribollita*; this is made with a minestrone of the day before, reheated (*ribollita*) with a local variety of purplish cabbage called *cavolo nero* cooked in it, and poured over home-made bread. Many of the Italian soups are strictly seasonal, as is the bean soup made in Tuscany with the new season's haricot beans and the first pressing of the olive oil, in autumn and early winter.

Since many of the Mediterranean countries are relatively poor, soup has formed a basic diet for many of its peoples. This category includes the many hearty soups made with dried beans, chick peas and lentils which are so popular in Spain, France, Italy, Greece and the Middle East, to say nothing of the North African coast. Another reason for their popularity is due to the strict traditions of fasting which exist in most of these countries, whether Roman Catholic, Greek Orthodox or Moslem. In Spain, a solid mixture of chick peas and spinach with potatoes and hard-boiled eggs is traditionally eaten during Holy Week, when little fresh food is allowed, while in Greece a thick lentil soup is customary. The Greek Lenten fast is broken after the midnight service on Easter Saturday with a soup called *mayeritsa*; this is made with the innards of a baby lamb or kid, which is itself roasted, usually on a spit or in a bread oven, for lunch the following day. Another delicious soup for breaking a fast is the Moroccan *harira* which is made daily during Ramadan, and eaten at sunset.

Although less well known than the fish soups, a series of soups which to me typify the food of the Mediterranean are the garlic soups of Spain and Provençal France. The simplest and most austere is the Spanish *sopa de ajo*; this is made with garlic, bread and water, sometimes with eggs cooked in it. It can be surprisingly delicious, considering the simplicity of its ingredients, and is very healthy. In Provence, the garlic soups called *aigo boulido* are only slightly more complex, with additions of Provençal herbs, and sometimes eggs, cheese, potatoes or fish. Here also they are much relied on as a restorative during and after illness.

Cold soups do not figure much in this part of the world, except in Spain. Gazpacho, once the midday meal of the poorest peasants, basically a liquid salad with pieces of bread soaked in it – has now become one of the most popular Spanish dishes with all classes, both at home and abroad. Another delicious iced Spanish soup is the *sopa de ajo blanco*: a purée of pounded almonds and garlic mixed with iced water, and with added grapes or cubes of melon. In Provence, an iced purée of fresh tomatoes is sometimes served, scented with fresh basil.

AIGO BOULIDO WITH CHEESE   **France**

This French version of garlic soup is slightly less austere than the Spanish one, but is still simple and wholesome.

12 cloves garlic
2 pints/1·2 litres water
1 sprig thyme
½ bay leaf
1 clove
2 teaspoons sea salt

black pepper
10 slices dry French bread
1½–2 oz/40–50 g grated cheese:
   gruyère or emmenthal
1 tablespoon olive oil

Peel the cloves of garlic, leaving them whole. Put them in a saucepan with the water, thyme, bay leaf, clove, sea salt and black pepper. Bring to the boil and boil steadily, half covered, for 20 minutes. Meanwhile lay the bread slices on a baking sheet, cover them with grated cheese and put in a moderate oven just until the cheese melts – about 5 minutes at 150°C/300°F/Gas Mark 2. Transfer them to a hot tureen, sprinkle the tablespoon of olive oil over them, then pour on the soup through a strainer. Cover and stand for 5 minutes before serving. Serves 4.

AIGO BOULIDO WITH EGGS   France

There are many versions of garlic soup throughout Spain and the Provençal area of France; this is one of my favourites.

1 large mild onion
6 tablespoons olive oil
3 leeks, sliced
3 cloves garlic, chopped
½ lb/225 g tomatoes, skinned
   and chopped
2½ pints/1·5 litres water

sea salt and black pepper
½ bay leaf
2 sprigs thyme
a pinch saffron
12 thin slices dry French bread
4–6 eggs (1 per person),
   poached

Chop the onion and cook slowly in the oil till starting to soften. Add the sliced leeks and continue to cook slowly. When all is lightly coloured add the chopped garlic and the skinned and chopped tomatoes. Stir well, then leave to stew gently for 5 minutes. Add the hot water, sea salt and black pepper, bay leaf, thyme and saffron. Boil fast, uncovered, for 15 minutes. Lift out the solid part of the soup with a slotted spoon and lay in a heated tureen. On this, lay the bread which has been very lightly toasted in the oven. Poach the eggs and lay on the bread. Adjust the seasoning of the liquid soup, throw away the bay leaf and thyme, and spoon over the eggs. Serves 4–6.

AIGO BOULIDO WITH POTATOES   **France**

1 large mild onion	½ bay leaf
6 tablespoons olive oil	2 sprigs thyme
3 leeks, sliced	a pinch saffron
3 cloves garlic, chopped	3 medium potatoes, peeled and
½ lb/225 g tomatoes, skinned	thickly sliced
and chopped	3 tablespoons chopped parsley
2½ pints/1·5 litres water	4–6 eggs (1 per person),
sea salt and black pepper	poached

Make as for *aigo boulido* with eggs, adding the peeled and thickly sliced potatoes together with the water and herbs. Omit the French bread, and sprinkle the chopped parsley over the cooked vegetables in the tureen. Lay the poached eggs directly on the vegetables, and pour the soup over. Serves 4–6.

AIGO-SAOU   **France**

This is a Mediterranean fish soup, but quite different from a bouillabaisse; more like an *aigo boulido* (garlic soup) with fish, it can be made with almost any white fish, unlike the bouillabaisse which demands rock fish.

2–2½ lb/1 kg mixed white fish:	1 bay leaf
sea bass, bream, John dory,	1 sprig thyme
monkfish, grey mullet, etc.	1 stalk celery
1 onion, chopped	sea salt and black pepper
3 tomatoes, skinned and	4 tablespoons olive oil
chopped	3½ pints/2 litres water
3 medium potatoes, peeled and	French bread, sliced and dried
chopped	in the oven
2 cloves garlic, minced	rouille (see page 32) or aïoli
3 stalks parsley	(see Sauces, pages 244–5)
2 stalks fennel	

Wash the fish; leave them whole if fairly small, but cut in two or three pieces if large. Put them in a deep pan with the chopped onion, tomatoes, potatoes and garlic, and the herbs wrapped and tied in the celery stalk. Add sea salt and black pepper and pour the oil over all.

Pour on the water and bring to the boil rapidly; boil fast, as for a bouillabaisse, for 20 minutes.

This is traditionally served like a bouillabaisse, with the fish on one dish, and the soup poured over pieces of dried bread in a tureen. Since I have a dislike of bones in fish soup, I prefer to fillet the fish, break it up into smallish pieces and lay it in the tureen. I then pour the soup over it, after discarding the herbs, and serve the dried bread separately, with a bowl of *aïoli* or *rouille*. Serves 6–8.

SOPA DE AJO   Spain

This is the simplest of all garlic soups, and can be restoring and delicious in spite of its austerity. Although made with large amounts of garlic, it does not make one smell of it for days, since the cloves are not actually eaten.

2 pints/1·2 litres water   *8 slices dry French bread*
sea salt   *4 eggs*
20 cloves garlic, peeled   *black pepper*

Put the water in a pan, add sea salt to taste, and the whole peeled cloves of garlic. Bring to the boil and simmer for 30 minutes. Meanwhile toast the bread very gently in the oven and lay in 4 soup bowls. When the soup has finished cooking, lift out the garlic with a slotted spoon and discard. Poach the eggs in the soup and lay one in each bowl. Taste the soup, add black pepper and more salt if needed, then pour slowly through a strainer onto the eggs. Serve immediately. Serves 4.

SOPA DE AJO BLANCO   Spain

Like many Spanish soups, this is delicate in flavour, almost bland; it has a subtle taste that may well not be appreciated by those accustomed to highly flavoured dishes.

¼ lb/100 g almonds, skinned   *4 tablespoons olive oil*
2 cloves garlic, chopped   *1 pint/600 ml water*
1 teaspoon sea salt   *6 ice cubes*

| 2 tablespoons white wine vinegar | 5–6 oz/150–175 g white grapes, peeled and seeded or the same amount of cubed melon |

If you have the patience to skin the almonds yourself, the flavour will be better and it will cost less. Simply pour boiling water over them, then lift out a few at a time and slip the skins off between the fingers. Replenish the boiling water as needed, for they will become hard to skin as they cool. Chop them by hand or in a food processor. Add the garlic and sea salt and chop or process again. Turn into a mortar and pound until fairly smooth, adding the oil. At this point I return it to the food processor and add the water, but it can be done in the mortar if it is big enough. Add 6 ice cubes and chill. Just before serving, stir in the vinegar and the peeled and seeded grapes, or the melon cubes. Serve in chilled bowls. Serves 4.

AVGOLEMONO SOUPA   Greece

A light summer soup, this is equally good made with meat or fish. It is sometimes served with small meatballs in it. If you do not have quite enough stock, you can cook the rice separately, in salted water, and add it to the soup, thus avoiding loss by evaporation.

| 2 pints/1·2 litres chicken, veal or fish stock | 2 eggs |
| 1½ oz/40 g rice | juice of 1 large lemon (3–4 tablespoons) |

Bring the stock to the boil and shake in the rice. Keep boiling steadily until the rice is cooked. Beat the eggs with the lemon juice in a small bowl. Stir a ladleful of the boiling soup into the egg/lemon mixture, beating with a small whisk, then return to the pan. Whisk for 3–4 minutes over very low heat, without allowing it to boil. Serve immediately; serves 4.

AVGOLEMONO SOUPA WITH MEATBALLS   **Greece**

1¾ pints/1 litre veal stock
2 eggs
juice of 1 large lemon

meatballs:
½ lb/225 g minced veal
1 oz/25 g soft breadcrumbs

1 tablespoon grated onion
1 tablespoon chopped parsley
sea salt and black pepper
1 small egg, or ½ large egg,
   beaten

Make the meatballs while the stock is heating. Mix the minced meat with the crumbs, grated onion, chopped parsley, sea salt, black pepper and beaten egg. Form into balls the size of large marbles. When the stock boils, drop them in, bring back to the boil, then lower the heat and simmer for 15 minutes. Lift out all the meatballs with a slotted spoon and place in a heated tureen. Beat the eggs with the lemon juice in a small bowl, stir in a ladleful of the boiling soup and beat with a small whisk. Remove the pan from the heat and stir in the egg/lemon mixture. Stir constantly for 3 minutes, replacing over gentle heat towards the end but without allowing it to boil. Pour over the meatballs and serve immediately. Serves 4–5.

BEAN SOUP   **Greece**

This recipe is in fact Greek, but it is very similar to others made around the Mediterranean coast, particularly in Spain, France and Tuscany.

½ lb/225 g dried white beans,
   Greek, Italian or Spanish
2 pints/1·2 litres cold water
6 oz/175 g onions, chopped
6 oz/175 g carrots, chopped
2 stalks celery, chopped

3 tablespoons olive oil
½ lb/225 g tomatoes, skinned
   and chopped (optional)
sea salt and black pepper
2 tablespoons chopped parsley

Soak the beans for 3–4 hours. Drain, cover with the cold water and bring slowly to the boil. When it reaches boiling point, skim the surface, and add the chopped onions, carrots, celery and the oil. Simmer gently for about 50 minutes, adding the tomatoes, if used, after 25 minutes. Only add sea salt and black pepper at the end of the cooking. Stir in the chopped parsley just before serving. Serves 5–6.

TUSCAN BEAN SOUP   Italy

Among Tuscan specialities are their exquisite white beans, and this soup is a suitably simple way of preparing them. It is particularly delicious when made with the fresh beans, before drying, in summer, or with the first pressing of the olives in November, using the green virgin oil.

¾ lb/350 g cannelini beans	2 cloves garlic
2 pints/1·2 litres cold water	3 tablespoons olive oil
sea salt and black pepper	4 tablespoons chopped parsley

If using dried beans, soak them for a few hours. Drain, cover with the water and bring slowly to the boil. Simmer gently until soft; this depends on the age of the beans, and will probably take 45–60 minutes for dried beans, or 20–25 minutes for fresh beans. When soft but not broken, lift out half the beans with a slotted spoon and reserve, while you purée the rest of the soup in a food processor, or by pushing through a medium food mill. Return the purée to the cleaned pan and reheat, adding lots of sea salt and black pepper. Put the reserved whole beans back in the pan and mix gently. Chop the garlic and fry gently in the oil until it starts to change colour; be very careful not to burn it. When pale golden, stir in the chopped parsley and remove from the heat. Stir into the soup and stand, covered, for 5 minutes before serving. Serves 4–5.

BOUILLABAISSE   France

This famous dish, more truly typical of the Mediterranean than any other, can only be found in its true form within a relatively small radius of Marseilles. It is not, as is often supposed, a soup but a main dish; a composite soup-plus-fish-dish, needing nothing either before or after. Since it demands a large proportion of *poissons des roches*, which do not exist outside the Mediterranean, I feel there is little point in giving an alternative 'English' version. An excellent *bourride* can be made with Atlantic fish, and a passable *soupe aux poissons*, but not a bouillabaisse. For the sake of interest, and for those planning to visit the Mediterranean, I give here an authentic recipe which I was given by a French cook living in Provence. A purist, he was emphatic about two points: (1) *'Sans poissons des roches – jamais'*. (2) The bread must be merely dried in the oven, never toasted.

4–5 lb/2–2½ kg *fish, mostly*
poissons des roches, and at
least 6–8 different sorts:
rascasse, wrasse, red mullet,
weever, conger eel, bream,
stargazer, bass, John dory,
monkfish
2 *large onions, thinly sliced*
2 *leeks, white parts only, finely*
chopped
2¼ lb/1 kg *tomatoes, skinned,*
chopped and drained
6 *cloves garlic, chopped*
1 *large handful parsley,*
coarsely chopped
1 *piece dried orange peel*
1 *branch each thyme and*
fennel
1 *bay leaf*

2–3 *cloves*
12 *black peppercorns*
6 *whole allspice*
1 *dried chilli*
½ pint/300 ml *best olive oil*
1 *handful sea salt*
1 *coffeespoon saffron threads*
1 *slightly stale French loaf,*
sliced and dried in a low
oven

rouille:
2 *dried chillies*
2 *pinches sea salt*
1 *coffeespoon saffron threads*
1 *head garlic*
2 *slices bread, crusts removed*
a little milk
¼ pint/150 ml *olive oil*

Wash the scaled and gutted fish and cut them in pieces about 3 inches/7·5 cm across. Cut the conger eel and monkfish in 1½-inch/3-cm slices. Put them all in a large pan and add the thinly sliced onions, finely chopped leeks (white part only), skinned, chopped and drained tomatoes, garlic, coarsely chopped parsley, orange peel, thyme, fennel, bay leaf, cloves, peppercorns, allspice and chilli. Pour over them the olive oil and sprinkle with the sea salt. Mix well, then leave for 1 hour to marinate.

Meanwhile make the *rouille*: pound the chillies with the salt and saffron till reduced to a paste. Add the peeled and finely chopped garlic, then the bread which has been soaked in milk for 10 minutes, then squeezed dry. When blended, start to add the oil very slowly, pounding all the time, as if making an *aïoli*. When amalgamated smoothly, put aside.

Boil a large pan of water, and pour it, boiling, over the fish until they are just covered. Put over a high flame and cook fast for 10–12 minutes. (It must boil hard to amalgamate the oil and water.) After 10 minutes, lower the heat and add the saffron. Lift out the fish and lay on a heated serving platter; keep warm. Pour the soup into a large tureen, and add half a tablespoonful to the *rouille* to thin it slightly. Have the dried bread on a separate dish and serve the 4 foods separately. Each guest, armed with soup plate, spoon and fork, helps himself first to some fish, a few pieces of bread, a little of the *rouille* (it is very strong), and pours some of the soup over all. This will serve 6 easily; it is not worth making it for a smaller number.

CHICKEN AND YOGURT SOUP   Syria

This nourishing soup with its pleasant tart flavour has become a favourite in our home.

2 oz/50 g barley	sea salt and black pepper
2 oz/50 g butter	1 large carton (¾ pint/350 ml)
1 large onion, chopped	yogurt
2 large leeks, chopped	1–2 tablespoons lemon juice
2½ pints/1·5 litres chicken	4 tablespoons chopped parsley
stock	

Soak the barley for 2–3 hours. Heat the butter in a heavy pan and cook the chopped onion and leeks for 10 minutes, without allowing them to brown. Add the drained barley and the heated stock. Bring to the boil, add sea salt and black pepper, and simmer for 1 hour. Beat the yogurt until smooth, then add a ladleful of the hot soup and mix well. Return to the pan, stir, and cook gently for 2–3 minutes, keeping it well below boiling point, or the yogurt will separate. (If you don't mind serving the soup less than hot, it is safer not to replace it over the heat after adding the yogurt.) Add sea salt and black pepper and lemon juice to taste. Sprinkle with chopped parsley. Serves 6.

CHORBA   Yugoslavia

This is an excellent and substantial soup with a slightly hot sour taste, particularly good on cold winter evenings. It is a meal in itself, and I sometimes serve a bowl of boiled rice with it, and a green salad to follow.

2 lb/900 g pie veal
2 pints/1·2 litres cold water
2 teaspoons sea salt
1 bay leaf
3 stalks parsley
a small handful celery leaves
1 medium onion, coarsely chopped
1 green pepper, cut in large pieces
1 tomato, skinned and coarsely
    chopped

1 small chilli pepper, deseeded
    and finely minced
1 oz/25 g butter
2 tablespoons flour
½ teaspoon paprika
2 eggs, beaten
3 tablespoons white wine
    vinegar
¼ pint/150 ml sour cream

Cut the meat in small neat pieces. Put it in a deep pot and cover with the cold water. Bring to the boil and skim well until only a white foam rises to the surface, adding a little extra cold water to compensate, and to facilitate the skimming. Then add the sea salt, bay leaf, parsley, celery leaves, chopped onion, green pepper, tomato and chilli. Bring back to the boil, lower the heat, and simmer for 1½ hours. Lift out the pieces of meat and keep warm. Discard the herbs, and lift the vegetables with a little of the soup into a blender or food processor. Reduce to a purée. Strain the liquid part of the soup. In a clean pan, melt the butter and stir in the flour. Cook for 1 minute, then add the paprika and the puréed vegetables, stirring till blended. Add the liquid soup gradually, and simmer for 3–4 minutes, stirring, till absolutely smooth. (It can always be returned to the blender at this stage if necessary.) Put the meat back into the soup and simmer for 4–5 minutes. Beat the eggs, add the vinegar and beat again. Pour a ladleful of the hot soup into the eggs and mix well. Return this to the pan and blend with the rest of the soup, without allowing it to boil. Finally add the sour cream and stir for a moment or two till all is smooth and hot. Serves 5–6.

COUSCOUS SOUP

This is not a genuine Mediterranean soup, but simply one I invented to use up the remains of a chicken couscous.

1 leek
1½ oz/40 g butter
1 carrot
1½–2 pints/900–1·2 litres
    chicken stock

¼ lb/100 g courgettes
¼ lb/100 g tomatoes
2–4 oz/50–100 g cooked
    chicken, chopped
6 tablespoons cooked couscous

Slice the white part of the leek and cook in the butter for 5 minutes. Chop the carrot and add to the leek with the heated stock. Cover and simmer for 10 minutes. Chop the unpeeled courgettes and add to the pan with the skinned and chopped tomatoes. Cook gently for 10 minutes, then add the chicken and the couscous. Simmer gently for 3 minutes, then serve. Have a small bowl of harissa (see Sauces, page 246) on the table, if you like. Serves 4.

GAZPACHO   Spain

Gazpacho is a good example of a basically simple dish that has been complicated and 'improved' by foreign cookery writers and restaurateurs. Each time I go back to Andalusia, I order gazpacho in a good restaurant to remind myself how it should really be: a dull-looking, pinky-grey liquid, quite smooth, with a slightly tart almost fizzy taste. Neither thick nor thin, it is served very cold, and only comes to life when the garnishes are added. These consist invariably of 6 bowls: chopped tomato, green pepper, onion, cucumber, hard-boiled egg and little cubes of brown bread, sometimes fried in oil. Immensely refreshing, it is like a liquid form of salad.

1 lb/450 g tomatoes
½ lb/225 g green peppers
½ cucumber
2 oz/50 g white bread, 2–3 days old
½ Spanish onion
3 tablespoons white wine vinegar
2 tablespoons olive oil
⅓ pint/200 ml iced water
sea salt and black pepper
6 ice cubes
a little extra iced water

garnishes:
2 tomatoes, skinned
½ green pepper
¼ Spanish onion
¼ cucumber, peeled
2 hard-boiled eggs
2 slices stale white bread, crusts removed
1½ tablespoons olive oil

Skin the tomatoes and cut in quarters. Remove stalks and seeds from the peppers and cut in chunks. Peel the cucumber and cut in sections. Have the bread torn in pieces and soaked in water for 1 hour, then squeezed dry. Cut the onion in pieces. Put all in the blender in batches, mixing the different ingredients each time with the vinegar, oil and iced water. Pour into a large bowl, add salt and pepper and ice cubes, and chill for a few hours.

Before serving, prepare the garnish. Chop the vegetables finely and pile each in separate bowls. Chop the eggs also, and cut the bread in dice and fry till golden brown in the oil. Serve the 6 bowls on the table. Chill the bowls or soup plates also. Thin with a little extra iced water before serving. Serves 8.

HARIRA   Morocco

This is the soup with which the daily fast during Ramadan is broken at sunset, and I cannot think of any nicer way of breaking it. There are many different recipes, varying according to the locality, but I find this version perfectly delicious, especially an hour or so after making.

¼ lb/100 g chick peas
1 large onion
3 tablespoons sunflower seed
  oil
1 stalk celery with leaves,
  chopped
6 tablespoons chopped parsley
1 teaspoon ground turmeric
1 teaspoon ground cinnamon

1½ lb/675 g tomatoes
2 tablespoons chopped
  coriander leaves
¼ lb/100 g brown lentils
2 pints/1·2 litres chicken or
  veal stock
sea salt and black pepper
2 oz/50 g vermicelli or other
  soup pasta

Soak the chick peas overnight. Next day, chop the onion and cook gently in the oil with the chopped celery and chopped parsley. Add the spices and cook steadily for 12 minutes. Meanwhile skin the tomatoes and cut in quarters. Put them in the food processor (or blender) and process briefly with the coriander leaves. Add to the pan and stir to mix well. Bring back to the boil, lower the heat, and stew gently for 5 minutes. Then add the soaked and drained chick peas and the washed lentils. Cook for another 5 minutes, then add the hot stock, and sea salt and black pepper to taste, and simmer gently, covered, until the chick peas are cooked. This will probably take 1½–2 hours. Add the vermicelli (or soup pasta in the shape of large grains of rice) and cook for about 10 minutes more, until the pasta is done. I like to let this cool slightly before serving. Serves 6–8.

HOLY WEEK SOUP (POTAGE DE SEMANA SANTA)   Spain

This substantial soup is made during Holy Week, when the Lenten fast is at its most rigorous.

¾ lb/350 g chick peas
½ bay leaf
2 stalks parsley
2 pints/1·2 litres water
1 lb/450 g spinach

½ lb/225 g potatoes
1 clove garlic
½ tablespoon olive oil
2 hard-boiled eggs
sea salt and black pepper

Soak the chick peas overnight, then put in a pressure cooker with the bay leaf and parsley. Cover with 2 pints/1·2 litres fresh cold water (unsalted), bring to the boil and cook until soft. This will take from 20–30 minutes under pressure, or 1–1½ hours in an ordinary saucepan. Meanwhile, boil the spinach for 5 minutes in lightly salted water, drain and chop. Boil the potatoes in their skins, drain, and when cool enough to handle, peel and chop. Chop the garlic finely and cook for a few moments in the olive oil, without allowing it to burn. Chop the hard-boiled eggs. When the peas are soft, add sea salt and black pepper and stir in the chopped spinach, potatoes, fried garlic and chopped eggs. Serves 5–6.

KISSHIK SOUP   Syria, Lebanon

This is the Middle Eastern version of trahanas. Since it is finer in consistency it needs shorter cooking and is indeed an almost 'instant' food.

1 small onion, finely chopped
1½ tablespoons olive oil
1 clove garlic, minced

3 oz/75 g kisshik (or trahanas)
1½ pints/900 ml water or light
   stock

Cook the onion in the oil until it starts to colour, then add the minced garlic, then the kisshik. Stir round to mix well and cook gently for 2–3 minutes, then add the heated stock. Stir constantly while it comes to the boil, simmer for a moment or two, then serve. Serves 4.

(If using trahanas instead of kisshik, allow 10 minutes gentle cooking after adding the liquid, as the Greek form is coarser than that of the Middle East.)

Kisshik soup is sometimes served with small unfilled kibbeh balls in it; for this version, follow the recipe for the kibbeh shell mixture on page 143, making it in half quantities. Make small balls no larger than walnuts and add to the kisshik soup once it comes to the boil. Simmer gently for 10 minutes and serve. When adding kibbeh balls, it is probably better to increase the liquid to 1¾ pints/1 litre, to allow for reduction.

LATTUGHE RIPIENE IN BRODO   Italy

This dish of stuffed lettuce leaves in broth is a speciality of Genoa, and is quite lengthy to prepare. When there are no Genoese present, however, it can be simplified considerably, and still remains a most excellent dish.

Brains and sweetbreads are often hard to find in England, and I have made this soup successfully without. I sometimes make much smaller lettuce rolls, and don't bother to make a ragú specially, unless I have some already from another dish.

8 large lettuce leaves
1 small onion
1 clove garlic
1 stalk celery
½ carrot
1 stalk parsley
1½ oz/40 g butter
7 oz/200 g minced veal
2 oz/50 g calves' brains,
    blanched (optional)
2 oz/50 g sweetbreads,
    blanched (optional)
1 tablespoon flour

1½ pints/900 ml veal or
    chicken stock
2 oz/50 g soft breadcrumbs
a little milk
1 egg yolk
2 tablespoons grated parmesan
½ tablespoon chopped
    marjoram
sea salt and black pepper
grated nutmeg
4 tablespoons ragú bolognese
    (see Sauces, page 250), if
    available

Blanch the lettuce leaves for 2 minutes in boiling water; drain. Chop the onion, garlic, celery, carrot and parsley to a fine hash (this can be done successfully in a food processor). Stew gently in the butter until all is lightly coloured, then add the chopped meats. Stir around until they are pale golden, about 2–3 minutes, then add the flour and

¼ pint/150 ml of the stock. Cook gently for 15 minutes, or until the stock is completely absorbed. Put the contents of the pan in a food processor and process until smooth; alternatively, pound in a mortar. Add the breadcrumbs which have been soaked in milk for 10 minutes then squeezed dry, the egg yolk, grated parmesan, marjoram, sea salt, black pepper and nutmeg. Process (or pound) until all is a smooth homogenous mass. Place a mound like a small egg on each lettuce leaf, roll up and tie with fine string. Put the remaining meat stock in a broad pan and bring to the boil. Add the stuffed lettuce leaves and simmer for 10 minutes. Lift them out, untie string, and serve in soup plates, 2 per person, with the stock poured over them and a teaspoonful of *ragù bolognese* which has been heating in a small bowl over hot water, on top of each one. This makes a substantial first course for 4 people.

MAYERITSA Greece

This is the soup which is eaten after the midnight service on Easter Saturday in the Greek Orthodox Church, after the long Lenten fast. It is made with the intestines of a baby lamb or kid, which is then eaten in its turn, roasted whole, for lunch the following day. It is not possible to make *mayeritsa* in its true form in this country, since baby animals are not killed at such an early age. I give the recipe all the same, for interest, with a modified version for use in England. Both recipes were given to me by Greek friends, one in Greece and one living in London.

the liver, heart, spleen, lungs and entrails of a baby lamb or kid	*sea salt and black pepper*
	4 tablespoons olive oil
	4 eggs
6–7 spring onions, chopped	*2 lemons*
a bunch of dill, chopped	*⅓ pint/200 ml cold water*

Clean all the innards very well indeed, turning the entrails inside out under a running tap. Then form them into a plait. Put them all in a deep pan and cover with cold water. Bring slowly to the boil, skimming constantly while the scum rises. Simmer gently until the liver no longer has any blood (20–30 minutes). Then take out the meats and chop very finely. Return them to the pan with the chopped spring onions, chopped dill, sea salt, black pepper and olive oil. Bring back to the boil and simmer until it has reduced by half, probably about 1 hour. Separate the eggs, beat the yolks with the lemon juice, then fold in the stiffly beaten whites. Stir in ⅓ pint/200 ml cold water, then add slowly to the soup. Serves 6.

A MODIFIED FORM OF MAYERITSA

lamb stock, made with:
1 lb/450 g stewing lamb
1 onion, halved
1 carrot, halved
1 stalk celery

1 lamb's liver
1 lamb's heart

2 lamb's kidneys
4 spring onions, chopped
3 tablespoons chopped dill
sea salt and black pepper
2 eggs
juice of 1 lemon

Make a well-flavoured stock 1 day in advance by simmering the stewing lamb and flavouring vegetables in 3 pints/1·75 litres water for 2 hours, or 45 minutes in a pressure cooker. Strain the stock and leave to cool. Chill overnight, and next day remove all fat from the surface.

Put the stock in a deep pan with the liver, heart and kidneys. Bring slowly to the boil, skimming until no more scum rises, and simmer gently for 25 minutes. Take out the meat and chop it finely; strain the stock. Reheat, adding the chopped meats and chopped spring onions, also the chopped dill, sea salt and black pepper. Simmer gently for 1 hour. Beat the eggs with the lemon juice, stir in a little of the simmering soup, then return to the pan. Stir over a very low heat for 2–3 minutes, without allowing it to boil, then serve. Serves 6.

MELOKHIA   Egypt

This soup, which is almost a national dish in Egypt, is made from the leaves of melokhia, a sort of mallow. It is probably the same plant that was formerly cooked as a vegetable in England in Elizabethan times, and is still eaten in Italy, where it is called mazzocchi. The soup can also be made with the dried leaves, which are easily found in shops selling Eastern goods; they are light as a feather, and packed in plastic bags. They make a good soup, not unlike a spinach soup, in a very short time, but it lacks the strange glutinous quality of that made from the fresh melokhia.

½ oz/15 g dried melokhia
2 pints/1·2 litres chicken or
   veal stock
1 large clove garlic

1 teaspoon whole coriander
   seeds
1 teaspoon sea salt
1 tablespoon sunflower seed oil

Put the melokhia leaves in the food processor or blender and process until finely chopped. Bring the stock to the boil and shake in the melokhia. Cook gently for 20 minutes, half covered. Chop the garlic and crush in a mortar with the coriander seeds and the sea salt. Heat the oil in a small pan and cook the pounded seasonings for 1–2 minutes, being very careful not to let the garlic burn. When the soup has finished cooking, stir in the fried spices and simmer for another 2 minutes, stirring almost constantly. Serves 4.

MINESTRONE   Italy

This delicious soup never fails to revive and stimulate one, even during the gloomiest winter months. It can be served as it is, with grated parmesan and fresh olive oil floating on the surface, or with a more elaborate garnish, like a pistou without the basil, which is not obtainable until early summer.

1 large mild onion
2 leeks
4 tablespoons olive oil
2 stalks celery
1 large carrot, halved
6 oz/175 g spinach beet or
   chard
¼ lb/100 g string beans
2 courgettes
2½ pints/1·5 litres light stock
sea salt and black pepper
¼ lb/100 g cannelini beans
2 oz/50 g macaroni, broken up
   into short lengths

garnish I:
2 tablespoons olive oil,
   preferably virgin oil
4 tablespoons chopped parsley
2 oz/50 g freshly grated
   parmesan

garnish II (optional):
2 tomatoes, halved
2 cloves garlic, chopped
1 oz/25 g pine kernels
1½ oz/40 g grated parmesan
4 tablespoons olive oil

Chop the onion and the white part of the leeks coarsely. Stew them gently in the oil in a heavy pan until they start to soften. Slice the celery and the halved carrot; add to the pan and cook for 6–8 minutes. Cut the spinach beet or chard across in 1-inch/2·5-cm strips, and cut the string beans in short lengths. Add both to the pan and cook another 5 minutes. Cut the unpeeled courgettes in ½-inch/1-cm slices and add to the rest. Stew all gently for 5 minutes then pour on the heated stock. Add sea salt and black pepper, cover the pan and simmer for 50–60 minutes. Have the dried beans soaked overnight and cooked till tender in boiling unsalted water. When the cooking time is up, add them to the soup, bring back to the boil and throw in the macaroni. Simmer till the latter is tender, about 15 minutes.

Minestrone is best made in advance, either a few hours or the previous day. When ready to serve, reheat slowly. If serving with the first garnish, simply pour in the fresh oil just before serving, stir in the parsley and serve the grated cheese separately. If serving with the second garnish, prepare it while the soup is cooking. Grill the halved tomatoes until slightly blackened, then cool. Remove the skin, squeeze out the pips and juice, chop, then pound in a mortar. Add the chopped garlic and pound again. Then add the chopped pine kernels and pound till smooth. Add the grated cheese and pound to a smooth paste, adding the oil very slowly. When ready to serve, spoon this paste into the hot tureen, and stir in a ladleful of the hot soup. Mix gently, then pour in the rest of the soup and stand, covered, for 5 minutes before serving. Serves 6–8.

RIBOLLITA   Italy

This Tuscan speciality is one of my favourite winter soups; traditionally made with minestrone left over from the day before, I often make it from scratch, which involves starting one day in advance. In Tuscany, it is made with a purplish cabbage called *cavolo nero*; chard is the best substitute I can suggest.

¼ lb/100 g cannelini beans
1 large onion
2 large carrots
3 stalks celery
1 head fennel
½ lb/225 g courgettes
½ lb/225 g tomatoes
4 tablespoons olive oil
2 cloves garlic

2 pints/1·2 litres chicken stock
sea salt and black pepper

next day:
6–8 slices dry white bread,
    home-made if possible
1 lb/450 g chard, spinach beet
    or green cabbage
a little extra olive oil

Start one day in advance. Put the dried beans in a pan, cover with cold water and bring to the boil. Turn off the heat when they reach boiling point, cover the pan, and leave for 1 hour. Chop the onion, carrots, celery, fennel, unpeeled courgettes and skinned tomatoes. Heat the oil in a large pan and stew the vegetables gently for 8–10 minutes. Add the chopped garlic towards the end. Heat the stock and add to the pan, along with the drained beans. Simmer gently for 1 hour, or until the beans are tender. Add salt and pepper – do not add salt before this stage for it toughens the beans – and leave overnight.

Next day, have some deep soup plates – one per person – heated, with a thick slice of bread in each. Cook the chard, spinach beet or cabbage in boiling water, drain, and chop coarsely. Pile on top of the bread in the soup plates. Reheat the minestrone and spoon over the bread. Have some fresh olive oil, virgin oil if possible, in a small jug on the table, so that each person may pour a little over their soup if they wish. Serves 6–8.

SOUPE AU PISTOU   France

This is a French version of the delicious vegetable soup, like a summer minestrone, which both Genoa and Nice claim as their own. Since I have given the Genoese recipe for pesto (the sauce alone), I give a Niçois recipe for the soup. It can only be made in its true form for a few weeks during midsummer, since it demands three sorts of beans, leeks and large quantities of basil, and these various ingredients are not all available together for very long. The beans are *haricots frais* – the same beans that we only find here in their dried form, but can grow easily in our gardens – ideally a combination of *haricots blancs* (in white pods), *haricots roses* (in mottled pink pods), and *haricots verts* (string beans). Since this is virtually impossible to do in England, we are forced to compromise, substituting onions for leeks and a combination of dried beans (soissons or cannelini) and fresh broad beans for the *haricots frais*.

2 leeks, or onions when leeks
  are unavailable
4 tablespoons olive oil
2 small carrots
1 small turnip
2 pints/1·2 litres hot water
½ lb/225 g shelled white and
  pink haricots frais or
  ½ lb/225 g shelled white
  haricots frais, or ¼ lb/100 g
  dried soissons or cannelini
  beans and 6 oz/175 g shelled
  broad beans

6 oz/175 g string beans
½ lb/225 g courgettes
½ lb/225 g tomatoes
2 oz/50 g shell pasta
sea salt and black pepper

pistou:
¾ pint/350 ml loosely packed
  basil leaves
2 cloves garlic
4 tablespoons pine kernels
2 oz/50 g grated parmesan
6 oz/175 ml olive oil

Chop the leeks (white parts only), or the onions. Heat the oil in a large pan and cook them gently for 5 minutes. Chop the carrots and turnip coarsely and add to the pan. Cook for 2 minutes, then add the hot water and the haricot beans. (If using dry beans, they must be soaked overnight and pre-cooked for 20 minutes beforehand.) Cook gently for 45 minutes, then add the shelled broad beans (if used) and the string beans cut in short lengths, the unpeeled courgettes cut in chunks, and the skinned and coarsely chopped tomatoes. Add pasta also at this stage. Add sea salt and black pepper and simmer for 30 minutes.

Meanwhile prepare the pistou. Chop the basil leaves and pound in a mortar. Add the finely chopped garlic and pound again. Add the pine nuts and continue pounding, then add the grated cheese. When all is reduced to a fairly smooth paste, start to add the oil, drop by drop. Continue to pound until all the oil is amalgamated, and the whole well blended into a fragrant oily mixture. When the soup is ready, put the pistou in the bottom of a hot tureen and pour the hot soup over it. Stand, covered, for 5–10 minutes before serving. Serves 6–8.

If fresh basil is not available in sufficient quantities, I sometimes make an alternative using fresh marjoram or oregano. Since this is a strong herb, I make it in smaller quantities. The result is not the same of course, but is still very good. Pound 1 chopped clove garlic in a mortar, add 2 tablespoons pine kernels, then 2 heaped tablespoons chopped marjoram leaves, and finally 2 tablespoons grated parmesan. When smooth, add 2 tablespoons olive oil gradually, and stir the resulting purée into the finished soup.

SOUPE AUX POISSONS   **France**

I like this typically Mediterranean soup even better than bouillabaisse; having been sieved, it retains all the flavours of the fish without the endless bones. In Marseilles, this would be made with a mixture of tiny *poissons des roches* sold expressly for soup; these might include *rascasses, rougets de roches, wrasses, girelles, serrans,* pieces of *congre,* and some *favouilles,* the tiny crabs which abound in this region. Even away from the Mediterranean, we can still make an approximation of this delicious soup however, since the other flavourings – the fennel, dried orange peel, the saffron and finally the *rouille* – are both strong enough and so individual as to give a genuine Mediterranean flavour to the soup, whatever fish it may be composed of.

2–2½ lb/1 kg mixed fish: red or
  grey mullet, monkfish, conger
  eel, etc.
¼ pint/150 ml olive oil
1 leek, white part only,
  chopped
1 medium onion, chopped
2 cloves garlic, chopped
2 tomatoes, peeled and crushed
2 stalks fennel
1 bay leaf

1 piece dried orange peel
sea salt and black pepper
3½ pints/2 litres water
2 packets saffron
2 oz/50 g vermicelli or
  spaghettini (optional)
sliced French bread, dried in
  the oven
grated parmesan
rouille *(see page 32)*

Wash the fish and cut in similar-sized pieces. Heat the oil in a heavy casserole and cook the chopped leek (white part only) and onion. When they start to colour, add the chopped garlic and the skinned and crushed tomatoes. Put in the fennel, bay leaf and orange peel, stir round briefly, then leave to stew gently in the oil for 12–15 minutes, stirring now and then. Lay the pieces of fish on this base, sprinkle with sea salt and black pepper and leave for 2 or 3 minutes. Heat the water and pour on, bring to the boil quickly, then boil hard for 15 minutes, as for a bouillabaisse. When the time is up, remove the large pieces of bone and push the rest of the soup through a coarse sieve or medium-fine food mill. (Alternatively, it can be poured through a muslin and squeezed, to express all the liquid.) Reheat, adding the saffron. When it reaches boiling point, add the vermicelli or spaghettini, if used.

Cook for 8–12 minutes, adjusting the seasoning, until the pasta is cooked. Pour into a large tureen to serve, accompanied by a plate of sliced French bread dried in the oven, and bowls of grated parmesan and *rouille*. Spread the *rouille* on pieces of bread and drop into the soup, sprinkled all over with the grated cheese. Serves 6–7.

ICED TOMATO SOUP   France

Cold soups do not figure much in the Mediterranean cuisine, so this fresh-tasting purée of tomatoes scented with basil is all the more welcome.

2 lb/900 g tomatoes	sea salt and black pepper
½ pint/300 ml strong chicken stock	2 tablespoons chopped basil
	4 ice cubes

Skin the tomatoes and cut into quarters. Put them in a pan with the cold chicken stock. Bring slowly to the boil and simmer gently for 20 minutes, adding sea salt and black pepper. Cool slightly, then put in the food processor or push through a coarse food mill. Stir in the chopped basil and leave to cool completely. Chill for a few hours in the refrigerator, and serve with an ice cube in each bowl. Serves 4.

TRAHANAS SOUP   Greece

This is a Greek peasant soup made from *trahanas*, a form of dried wheat mixed with yogurt or goats' milk. *Trahanas* can be bought in Greek Cypriot shops, either in packets or in plastic bags; the Greeks prefer the plastic bags, but I find the powdered form in packets easier to use. It makes a most delicious soup, full of vitamins and quick to make, with a flavour of oatmeal combined with lemon. *Trahanas* is a useful thing to have in the store cupboard, together with some chicken stock cubes.

1½ pints/900 ml light chicken stock	3 oz/75 g trahanas
	sea salt and black pepper

Heat the stock – use a stock cube if you have no real stock to hand – and shake in the powdered *trahanas*, stirring constantly while it comes to the boil. (If using the *trahanas* in rolls, sold in plastic bags, these must first be soaked in water for 30 minutes, then squeezed dry and broken up as smoothly as possible to avoid lumps.) Simmer gently, half-covered, for 10–15 minutes. Add sea salt and black pepper as required. Serves 4.

YOGURT SOUP WITH MEATBALLS   Turkey, Middle East

This is the only hot yogurt soup that I have come across; it exists in various forms in parts of Turkey and throughout the Middle East, and probably originated in Iran. The yoghurt must first be stabilized to prevent it separating. The egg tends to separate slightly, as the soup must simmer in order to cook the rice and meatballs; the little strands of egg are hardly apparent in the finished dish, since it is thick with green leaves, rice and chick peas, but if this upsets you it can easily be left out. The little meat balls can be made with beef or lamb, or small unfilled *kibbeh* balls (see pages 143–5) can be used.

meatballs:
½ lb/225 g finely minced lamb
  or beef
1 small onion, grated
sea salt and black pepper
¼ teaspoon dried mint

soup:
1¼ pints/750 ml yogurt
1 tablespoon flour
1½ pints/900 ml light chicken
  or beef stock, hot

1 egg, beaten (optional)
4 tablespoons rice, washed
¼ lb/100 g spinach
1 bunch spring onions
4 tablespoons chopped
  coriander leaves, or parsley
4 tablespoons chopped dill
¼ pint/150 ml cooked chick
  peas (2 oz/50 g uncooked)

First make the meatballs: mix the minced meat with the grated onion, adding sea salt and black pepper and a little dried mint. Form into small balls about the size of large marbles: it will make about 16. Put aside.

Tip the yogurt into a heavy pan and beat with a whisk until smooth. Shake in the flour and continue to beat till amalgamated. Heat gently, stirring constantly in the same direction, until the yogurt has thickened slightly – this is quite a slow process. Then add the hot stock gradually, continuing to stir until all is blended. Beat the egg in a small bowl, if used, and stir in a little of the soup. Return to the pan and stir into the soup. Then add the washed rice and the little meatballs. Bring back to simmering point and cook for 10 minutes, stirring often. Have the green leaves prepared in advance: cut the spinach leaves off their stalks if at all tough, and chop quite finely, either in a food processor or by hand. Chop the spring onions, using the best part of the green leaves as well as the bulbs. Chop the coriander leaves, substituting parsley when coriander leaves are not available, and the dill when in season. After the 10 minutes are up, add the greens to the soup together with the cooked (or tinned) chick peas. Bring back to simmering point and cook gently for another 5 minutes. This is a most excellent thick soup, full of nourishment, but it should be served fairly soon after making or it will thicken still further. Serves 4–6.

Small *kibbeh* balls can be substituted for the meatballs as a variation; simply make the *kibbeh* shell mixture in half quantities (see pages 143–5), form into small balls like walnuts, and add to the soup with the rice.

The custom of serving small snacks, either hot or cold, with drinks before a meal is almost universal in Mediterranean countries. In bars and restaurants these are usually served like aperitifs, while in the home they may equally well be eaten at the table. They provide an adaptable series of dishes, usually eaten cold or shortly after cooling, and can easily be added to in order to accommodate an unexpected guest. In this way they fit in with Eastern rules of hospitality, by which a guest must always be offered food and drink.

The English and Americans have never really felt the need for a first course except when eating in restaurants; while Americans often serve snacks with drinks, the English almost never do this either, except at a full-scale cocktail party. A French family, on the other hand, rarely sits down to a meal of a single course; there will almost always be something, however simple, to start with.

In many Mediterranean countries, it is not done to drink alcohol without eating anything; this is particularly true when drinking ouzo, raki, arak, or whatever form the local variety of pernod takes, and foreigners who do this are often eyed askance. Even the simplest bar in Greece or Spain will offer little dishes of olives, nuts or fried shrimp, while in the large bars, especially in Spanish towns, the array of tapas may run to as many as thirty dishes. Many of their clients make their evening meal in this way, standing or sitting at the bar, and eating a variety of little dishes with their sherry. The choice of tapas in a Spanish home or small restaurant would certainly not be as extensive as this, but it might still include thin slices of Serrano ham, fried shrimps or prawns, little hot cheese croquettes, sliced spicy sausage, and of course olives. In France one would be likely to find some tapenade or anchoïade on little squares of bread, thin slices of salami, small squares of pissaladière, and a dish of radishes with butter and salt. In Greece, olives are invariably served with drinks before a meal, possibly accompanied by a dish of *taramasalata*, some *dolmades*, and a few pistachios. In Turkish restaurants, the first course is often the best part of the meal, with bean dishes in variety, purées of aubergine sometimes mixed with yogurt, dishes of fried squid, small *boreks* filled with cheese or minced meat, and mussels deep fried in batter. Throughout Tunisia small pastry *briks*, similar to the Turkish *borek*, are served as aperitifs filled with minced meat mixed with herbs, while the *brik à l'oeuf* is more often served as part of a meal, or a light meal in itself. In the Middle East, *hommous* is invariably served as an aperitif, sometimes accompanied by a smoky purée of aubergines blended with *tahini* (sesame seed paste), and eaten with pieces of hot pitta bread. In Lebanon, grilled chicken wings make a tasty snack, while a mixture of minced meat with cracked wheat called *kibbeh* is formed into small balls for eating with the fingers. A typical Egyptian hors d'oeuvre might consist of *foul medames*, *hamine* eggs, a lemon pickle and an Arab salad.

ANCHOÏADE   France

This purée of anchovies and garlic makes a good salty snack to serve with drinks, when spread on thin slices of French bread. It makes a useful dish to serve instead of a first course, while watching meat cook on a barbecue, or over an open fire.

¼ lb/100 g fillets of anchovies	3 tablespoons olive oil
a little milk	2 teaspoons white wine vinegar
2 cloves garlic, chopped	thin slices French bread

Rinse the tinned anchovies and soak in milk for 10 minutes. Rinse again and squeeze out the water. Chop by hand or in a food processor, then pound in a mortar till reduced to a thick paste. Add the chopped garlic and pound again. When well blended, add the oil gradually, continuing to pound, then the vinegar. Toast the bread slices lightly on one side, then spread with the paste. Grill for 2–3 minutes, until golden brown. Serve immediately. Makes about 20 pieces.

AUBERGINE PURÉE   Turkey

There are many different Turkish dishes based on a purée of aubergines; this is one of the simplest and best. It has a refreshing tart flavour, and mixes well with other dishes. Do not be tempted to make it in a food processor, or by sieving; it does not want to be too smooth.

2 lb/900 g aubergines
1 tablespoon olive oil
juice of 1 lemon

1 clove garlic (optional)
sea salt and black pepper

Grill the aubergines until they are charred and blackened all over, and soft to the touch; this may take as much as 45 minutes. Cool briefly, then hold them by the stem and peel off the skin with the other hand, using a small sharp knife. Cut the flesh in pieces. Mix the oil and lemon juice in a soup plate or shallow dish, beating with a fork. Put in the aubergines, one at a time, and pull them into shreds using 2 forks. Mash the shredded pulp into the oil and lemon and stir in the crushed garlic, if used (I find it equally good either way), and add a little sea salt and black pepper. Cool, then chill for 1–2 hours before serving. Mix once more just before serving. Serves 3 alone, or 4–5 with other dishes.

AUBERGINE PURÉE WITH YOGURT   Turkey

Another Turkish aubergine meze, this is equally delicious.

1½ lb/675 g aubergines
1 medium green pepper
3 tomatoes
2 tablespoons olive oil

4 tablespoons lemon juice
1 large clove garlic
sea salt and black pepper
⅓ pint/200 ml yogurt

Grill the aubergines, either under the grill or over an open flame, until the skin is blackened and charred all over. Do the same thing with the pepper and the tomatoes; this will take much less time. When cool enough to handle, pull the skin off all the vegetables, scraping away every little bit with a small knife. Mix the oil and lemon juice in a shallow dish, beating well with a fork. Mash the vegetables into it, using 2 forks, and add the crushed garlic, and sea salt and black pepper to taste. Blend briefly in the food processor or blender, add the yogurt and blend again. Adjust seasoning, adding a little more lemon juice if needed, or salt or pepper. Tip into a shallow dish and chill for an hour or two before serving, with hot flat bread. Serves 4 alone, or 6 with other *mezes*.

BABA GHANNOUJ
Syria, Lebanon

This is a favourite *meze* in the Arab countries of the Middle East. The grilling of the aubergines over an open flame (when possible) gives a delicious smoky flavour which blends perfectly with the subtle taste of *tahini*.

1 lb/450 g aubergines
¼ pint/150 ml tahini *(sesame seed paste)*
⅓ pint/200 ml lemon juice
sea salt and black pepper

2 cloves garlic, crushed
olive oil
½ tablespoon finely chopped parsley

Grill the aubergines slowly, under the grill or over an open fire, turning them over and over until the skin is charred and blistered, and the flesh soft to the touch. Cool slightly, then peel away the skin and purée the flesh either in a food processor or blender, or by pushing through a food mill. Turn into a bowl and add the *tahini* and lemon juice alternately, beating with a wooden spoon. Add sea salt and black pepper to taste, and stir in the crushed garlic. Taste, and add more *tahini* or lemon juice as required; it is impossible to give exact measurements since so much depends both on the quality of the aubergines and on personal taste. Ideally, it should be a perfect blend between the two flavours, sharpened by garlic and lemon juice. To serve, spoon onto a flat dish and make a few swirls on the top. Pour a thin trickle of olive oil into the whirls, and sprinkle with a very little finely chopped parsley. Accompany with hot flat bread, and serve either with drinks or as a first course. Serves 5–6.

BEAN CAKE   **Greece**

This is a popular *meze* throughout much of the eastern Mediterranean.

1 lb/450 g dried white beans	*1 teaspoon sugar*
2 medium onions	*3 tablespoons lemon juice*
7 tablespoons olive oil	*6 spring onions*
2½ pints/1·5 litres hot water	*5 sprigs dill or a few chives*
sea salt and black pepper	

Soak the beans overnight. (The Egyptians use dried broad beans, but haricot beans can be used if these are not easily available.) Next day, drain them and chop the onions. Heat 4 tablespoons of the olive oil and cook the chopped onions until golden. Add the hot water and bring to the boil. Cook steadily until the beans are soft and the liquid absorbed. Push through a medium food mill and add sea salt and black pepper to taste, a little sugar, the rest of the olive oil and the lemon juice. Stir well, then spoon onto a flat dish and form into a round cake with a flat top, smoothing it well with a palette knife dipped in hot water. Spread a little extra oil and lemon juice over the top to prevent a hard crust forming, and cover with cling-film wrap. Cool at room temperature, but do not chill unless making a day or two in advance; in this case, remove from the refrigerator an hour or two before serving. Before serving, decorate the top with thinly sliced spring onions and feathery sprigs of fresh dill; if dill is not available, use a few spiky chives to contrast with the round onion slices. Serves 6–8, with other dishes.

BEANS PLAKI   **Greece**

This is typical of the sort of bean dish flavoured with dill which you find so often in Greek tavernas, as part of the *mezes*. It is also popular in Turkey, but differs from the Italian cold bean dishes which are made with beans boiled in water and dressed with a vinaigrette after cooking. Both are good, and have their own character. Ideally the beans should be the fat white broad beans which can be found in Greek shops, but the dish can be made successfully with Italian cannelini beans.

½ lb/225 g dried white beans
1 pint/600 ml water
1 medium onion, coarsely
  chopped
1 medium carrot, cut in
  quarters lengthwise then
  sliced

2 stalks celery, sliced
3 tablespoons olive oil
sea salt and black pepper
2 tablespoons chopped dill, or
  parsley

Soak the beans for several hours, then drain and cover with 1 pint/600 ml fresh water. Bring very slowly to the boil, without adding salt. When it finally simmers, skim the surface and add the onion, carrot and celery, also the olive oil. Simmer gently, half-covered, until the beans are soft but not broken. The timing will depend on the beans; the large Greek beans may take 1½–1¾ hours, while the cannelini beans will probably be tender in 45 minutes. When they are soft, remove from the heat and stir in salt and pepper. Cool, and stir in the chopped dill or parsley. Do not chill. Serves 4, or 6, with other dishes.

BROAD BEANS IN THEIR PODS   France, Italy

This delightfully simple hors d'oeuvre is served in early summer in Provence and parts of Italy. In France, the beans are simply served, in their pods, with a bowl of sea salt. In Tuscany, they are accompanied by some pecorino cheese, while in Genoa, sardo (a salty white cheese from Sardinia) is the usual accompaniment. Each guest simply shells the beans and eats them raw, with sea salt, or a small piece of salty cheese.

CALVES' BRAINS VINAIGRETTE   Turkey

This is a popular meze in eastern Turkey, where the choice is not great.

2 sets of calves' brains
2 tablespoons white wine
  vinegar
sea salt
a few lettuce leaves

3–4 tablespoons olive oil
juice of 1 lemon
black pepper
2 tablespoons chopped parsley

Wash the brains very well under cold running water, carefully pulling off all the pinkish-red membrane which covers them. Leave them for 1 hour in a bowl of cold water with 1 tablespoon of the vinegar. Wash again before cooking. Bring some water (just enough to cover the brains) to the boil in a pan with sea salt and the rest of the vinegar. When it boils, drop in the brains and poach very gently for 8 minutes; turn off the heat and leave them to cool in the liquid. Later, pat them dry and cut in thick slices. Lay them on a bed of lettuce leaves and pour over a sauce made by beating the oil and lemon juice together, with a little black pepper. Sprinkle with very finely chopped parsley and serve at room temperature. Serves 4.

CAPONATA   Sicily

This dish of chopped aubergines, tomatoes, celery and olives in a sweet/sour sauce is one of my favourite *mezes*.

1 lb/450 g aubergines	*1 tablespoon capers, drained*
1 small onion	*black pepper*
approx. ¼ pint/150 ml olive oil	*1 tablespoon sugar*
3 stalks celery	*2 tablespoons white wine*
½ lb/225 g tomatoes	*vinegar*
12 green olives, stoned	

Cut the unpeeled aubergines in cubes about ½ inch/1 cm square. Lay them in layers in a colander, sprinkling each layer with salt: weigh down with a plate and leave for 1 hour. Chop the onion and cook gently in 2 tablespoons of the olive oil in a sauté pan. Cut the celery in dice and add to the onion when it starts to colour. Skin and chop the tomatoes and add to the celery after a few moments. Cook gently until thickened, adding the stoned olives, capers, black pepper, sugar and vinegar (do not add salt at this stage). In a broad pan, heat the remaining oil. Dry the aubergines in a cloth and sauté in the oil, turning them over as they cook. When they are brown and soft, lift them out with a slotted spoon and mix with the rest of the vegetables. Mix well, pour into a shallow dish and leave to cool; do not chill. Serves 4–5, or more with other dishes.

CROSTINI   Italy

These hot hors d'oeuvre are quickly made, and are usually based on a combination of cheese and anchovies, fried chicken livers, or a salty spread like anchoïade or tapenade. They are useful to serve with drinks while waiting for a joint of meat to cook over the fire, or on a barbecue.

CROSTINI I

10 slices French bread
1 mozzarella cheese, sliced

5 flat fillets anchovies, soaked
  in 3 tablespoons milk

Toast the bread on one side under the grill, then turn over and lay a slice of mozzarella on each slice. Replace under the grill, and toast until the cheese melts. Remove, and top each one with a half fillet of anchovy, rinsed in cold water and dried.

CROSTINI II

½ lb/225 g chicken livers
½ oz/15 g butter
½ tablespoon olive oil
½ clove garlic
2–3 leaves sage

black pepper
approx. ½ tablespoon lemon
  juice
10–12 slices French bread
½ tablespoon chopped parsley

Chop the livers, discarding any discoloured bits. Melt the butter with the oil and cook the finely chopped garlic for a moment, until it starts to colour, then add the chopped livers. Cook them briefly, adding the chopped sage, over a brisk heat until they have lost their pinkness; this will only take about 3 minutes. Sprinkle with freshly ground black pepper and a squeeze of lemon juice. Have some slices of French bread lightly toasted, under the grill or in the oven. Spoon the livers onto them and sprinkle with finely chopped parsley. These are best served at table, as the livers tend to fall off the bread.

GRILLED CHICKEN WINGS   **Lebanon**

These are often served as part of a mixed hors d'oeuvre. The little joints, slightly charred, are also good served with garlic sauce (see Sauces, page 246), but in this case omit the garlic from the marinade.

2 lb/900 g chicken wings, joints only, without breast	*juice of 1 lemon*
4 tablespoons olive oil	*1–2 cloves garlic*
	sea salt and black pepper

1–2 hours before cooking, line the grill pan with foil and rub with oil. Lay the chicken wings on it and pour over the oil and lemon juice. Crush the garlic and spread over the chicken, and sprinkle with sea salt and black pepper. Turn over once or twice while marinading, then grill slowly, allowing about 8–10 minutes on each side. They should be well browned, almost slightly blackened in places, and just cooked through inside. Serve as part of a mixed hors d'oeuvre, or alone with garlic sauce (see note above). Serves 4 as a first course, or 6–8 with other dishes.

DOLMADES   **Greece**

These little stuffed vine leaves are familiar to anyone who has travelled in Greece or Turkey; they are often tinned, but are far better when made at home. They make a perfect accompaniment to drinks, particularly ouzo or raki, or part of a selection of hors d'oeuvre.

½ lb/225 g onions	*sea salt and black pepper*
¼ pint/150 ml olive oil	*about 30 vine leaves, freshly picked or preserved in brine*
¼ lb/100 g risotto rice	*juice of 1 lemon*
½ pint/300 ml boiling water	*½ pint/300 ml hot water*
3 tablespoons pine kernels	

Chop the onions and cook gently in 4 tablespoons of the olive oil in a sauté pan. When softened and pale golden, add the washed rice (I use Italian arborio or cristallo rice) and stir around for 2–3 minutes. Pour on the boiling water, add the pine kernels, sea salt and black pepper, and bring back to the boil. Simmer gently until the water is absorbed, about 6 minutes. Turn the stuffing onto a plate and leave to cool.

Meanwhile prepare the vine leaves. These can be bought in packets or tins, or picked fresh from the garden. If using preserved leaves, pour off the brine and soak the leaves in a basin of cold water. Separate them carefully, then drop them into a pan of boiling water and blanch for 5 minutes; drain. If using fresh leaves, blanch for 10 minutes in boiling water, then drain. Lay a heaped teaspoonful of stuffing in the centre of each leaf, roll it up and squeeze gently in the hand so that it does not unroll. When all the filling is used up, take any unused leaves and lay them in the bottom of the clean sauté pan. Lay the stuffed leaves on them and pour over them 4 tablespoons olive oil, 2 tablespoons lemon juice, and ½ pint/300 ml hot water. Lay a small plate over the vine leaves to weigh them down lightly, and cover the pan. Bring to the boil and simmer gently for 45 minutes, checking once or twice that they are not boiling dry. (Add more boiling water if necessary.) Leave to cool in the pan. To serve, lay the dolmades on a flat dish and sprinkle with a little more lemon juice. Serve at room temperature. Serve with drinks, or as part of a mixed hors d'oeuvre. This makes enough for 8–10 people; it can be made in half quantities if preferred.

ESCALIBADA   Spain

This Spanish dish is similar to numerous Italian and French dishes of vegetables in oil, yet the smoky flavour of the grilled vegetables renders it almost closer to the Tunisian *salat meschoui*.

1 lb/450 g aubergines	4 tablespoons olive oil
1 lb/450 g mixed red and	sea salt and black pepper
yellow peppers	1 tablespoon chopped parsley

Grill the aubergines slowly, until the skin is blackened and the flesh soft to the touch. This will take 25–35 minutes, depending on size. Do the same thing with the peppers; this will be much quicker, since they are hollow. Cool both vegetables until they can be handled, then peel off the skin, scraping away every speck. Cut the flesh in strips, discarding all the seeds from the peppers. Mix both lightly together, and pour over the oil. Sprinkle with sea salt and black pepper and leave to cool; do not chill. Sprinkle with chopped parsley before serving. Serves 3–4 as a first course, or 5–6 with other dishes.

FALAFEL   **Israel**

These little balls of chick peas ground up with spices and herbs and
deep fried are a very popular Israeli dish, as a meze or snack. They are
also much loved in Egypt, where they are made with dried broad
beans. I find them absolutely delicious, and have a slight preference
for the Israeli version, since I love chick peas. They make a perfect hot
snack for serving with cocktails before a meal, or part of a mixed hors
d'oeuvre.

½ lb/225 g chick peas, or dried
  broad beans
1 large mild onion, cut in
  pieces
1–2 cloves garlic, chopped
1½ oz/40 g white bread, crusts
  removed

3 tablespoons chopped parsley
½ teaspoon ground cumin
½ teaspoon ground coriander
¼ teaspoon baking powder
sea salt and black pepper
frying oil

Soak the chick peas or beans for 48 hours, then drain and rinse. Put
them in a food processor and process until reduced to a fine purée. (If
you have no food processor, this will involve first chopping or mincing
the peas or beans, then pounding them for several hours in a mortar.)
Add the onion, cut in chunks, and the garlic finely chopped. Process
again until blended, scraping down the sides and starting again several
times. Have the bread torn in pieces and soaked for 10 minutes in cold
water, then squeezed dry. Add to the mixture and blend again. Finally
blend in the herbs and spices, baking powder, and sea salt and black
pepper to taste. Turn into a bowl and leave for 1 hour before using.

Heat a pan of oil while you are forming the *falafel*; these can be
made in little balls about 1 inch/2·5 cm across, or slightly flattened.
Deep fry for 3 to 4 minutes, turning once, until golden brown. Serve
hot. This makes quite a lot, enough for about 15 people as a snack with
drinks, but it can be made in half quantities. These also make good
picnic food, especially if they can be kept hot, although they are never
quite so delicious as just after cooking.

FAVA   Greece

This is a very popular Greek dish, and is found in many of the better tavernas. Basically a thick purée, it is usually served either warm or after cooling, but never chilled. Thicker than a soup, it is eaten sprinkled with chopped onion and with a little olive oil poured over it.

1 lb/450 g yellow split peas, or
   yellow lentils
2½ pints/1·5 litres water
2 medium onions
6 tablespoons olive oil
sea salt

garnishes;
1 small onion, finely chopped
a small jug olive oil

Wash the peas (or lentils) and put them in a pan with the cold water. Do not add salt. Bring to the boil and skim. Add the coarsely chopped onions and 6 tablespoons olive oil. Cook slowly till soft, about 1 hour, adding sea salt towards the end. Purée in a food processor or push through a medium food mill. Serve either warm, as a thick purée, or after cooling, when it will set to a solid mass, with a bowl of finely chopped onion and a small jug of olive oil on the table. *Fava* is a simple but excellent hors d'oeuvre, which can be eaten alone or with other dishes. Serves 6.

FOUL MEDAMES   Egypt

I give two versions of this much loved Egyptian bean dish which makes a useful and sustaining meze. The first has a nice sharp fresh taste, but when spring onions are not readily available the second version can be made, which is also good. The amounts of garlic used are a matter of personal choice; in Egypt, it is used liberally, but I prefer it in moderation. *Foul* is often served accompanied by *hamine* eggs (see Eggs, page 85), but since these are not one of my favourite dishes, I prefer to serve it alone, or with plain hard-boiled eggs.

FOUL MEDAMES I

½ lb/225 g dry foul (dried foul
  beans), soaked overnight
3 tablespoons olive oil
sea salt and black pepper
1–3 cloves garlic, crushed

2 tablespoons spring onions,
  chopped
2 tablespoons parsley, chopped
2 tablespoons lemon juice

Cook the beans in a pressure cooker in unsalted water, allowing
anything from 20 to 40 minutes; test after 20 minutes. (In an ordinary
pan, allow 1–2 hours, testing after 1 hour.) Drain, tip into a bowl and
stir in the olive oil and sea salt and black pepper to taste. Allow to
cool, then stir in the crushed garlic, chopped spring onions, chopped
parsley, and finally the lemon juice. Serves 4 alone, or with hard-
boiled eggs, or 6 with other *mezes*.

FOUL MEDAMES II

½ lb/225 g dry foul (dried foul
  beans), soaked overnight
1 medium onion, finely
  chopped
1–3 cloves garlic

2 tablespoons olive oil
sea salt and black pepper
2 tablespoons parsley, chopped
1½ tablespoons lemon juice

Cook the beans as for *foul medames I*. Drain, tip into a bowl and allow
to cool slightly. Cook the chopped onion and the minced garlic in the
oil until they are softened and lightly coloured. Stir into the beans,
adding sea salt and black pepper to taste, and chopped parsley and
lemon juice. Serve after cooling; do not chill. Serves 4 alone or with
eggs, or 6 with other *mezes*.

HARICOTS VERTS NIÇOIS   France

Nice has a tradition for these sort of dishes of lightly cooked vegetables
dressed with olive oil and sliced leeks or onion. They make a bridge
between the cooking of Provence and that of Italy, and provide some
of my favourite first courses.

1 leek
3 tablespoons olive oil
½ lb/225 g tomatoes, skinned
and coarsely chopped
1 clove garlic, crushed

sea salt and black pepper
a pinch of sugar
3 tablespoons water
¾ lb/350 g string beans

Slice the white part of the leek and cook gently in the oil in a sauté pan. When it has softened and lightly coloured, add the tomatoes, skinned and coarsely chopped, and the crushed clove of garlic. Stir around until coated with oil and well mixed, then add sea salt and black pepper, the pinch of sugar, and 3 tablespoons water. Cover the pan and simmer gently for 12 minutes, stirring now and then. Meanwhile trim the beans, leaving them whole, and cook till just tender but still slightly crisp in boiling salted water, then drain well. When the sauce is ready, add the beans and stir gently over low heat till all is amalgamated and hot. Add more salt and pepper as needed, then turn into a shallow dish. Serve if possible soon after cooling; at all events, do not chill. Serves 4 as a first course, or 6 with one or two other dishes.

HOMMOUS BI TAHINI   Lebanon

The first time I tasted hommous was when I was staying in my sister-in-law's house in Beirut, some twenty years ago. I found it strange at first, but grew to love it and eventually became totally addicted. It keeps well in a covered carton in the refrigerator, so it may be worthwhile making in double quantities.

½ lb/225 g chick peas
approx. ¼ pint/150 ml tahini
approx. ½ pint/300 ml lemon
juice

sea salt and black pepper
1–2 large cloves garlic, crushed
olive oil, or sesame seed oil
paprika

Soak the chick peas overnight then cook in a pressure cooker until soft, without adding salt. This may take anything from 20–45 minutes, depending on the quality of the peas; I suggest testing after 20 minutes. If using an ordinary saucepan, allow 1–2 hours. When they are soft, drain them, reserving the liquid. Purée the peas in a food processor, adding a little of the cooking stock, or push through a food mill (this is hard work). Add some sea salt, and stir in *tahini* and lemon juice alternately, tasting before it is all incorporated. The strong taste of the *tahini* must not be allowed to dominate totally that of the chick peas. All this can be done speedily in a food processor, or more slowly by hand in a large bowl. Stir in the crushed garlic, more sea salt, black pepper and thin with a little of the cooking liquid if necessary. (The rest can be used for soup.)

To serve, spoon onto a flat dish and make some whirls on the surface with the back of a wooden spoon. Pour a thin trickle of oil, either olive or sesame seed, into the whirls, and sprinkle with a little paprika. Serve with hot flat bread, with drinks, or as a first course. Serves 5–6.

LEEKS NIÇOIS

France

This excellent dish is to be found in Nice and the surrounding area. It is particularly good served soon after cooking, before completely cold.

2½ lb/1·15 kg thin leeks	½ teaspoon sugar
1 large onion	2 cloves garlic, crushed
4 tablespoons olive oil	2 tablespoons parsley
1 lb/450 g tomatoes	½ tablespoon lemon juice
sea salt and black pepper	

Trim the leeks, leaving them whole. Clean them well, then drain and pat dry. Slice the onion and cook gently in the oil in a broad heavy pan until it starts to colour. Add the leeks, turning them over and over in the oil. Add the skinned and chopped tomatoes, sea salt and black pepper, sugar and crushed garlic, and cover the pan. Cook slowly for 10–15 minutes, until the leeks are tender, moving them round from time to time so that they cook evenly. When tender, lift them out with a slotted spoon and lay on a flat dish. Boil up the sauce till reduced and tasty. Turn off the heat, add parsley and lemon juice, and spoon over the leeks. Leave to cool somewhat before serving, but do not chill. Serves 4 as a first course, or 6 with one or two other dishes.

MIXED PEPPER SALAD   Yugoslavia

Peppers are enormously popular in Yugoslavia, both the sweet bell peppers and the hot chilli ones. This mixed pepper dish is one of the best.

1½ lb/675 g peppers, mixed   4 tablespoons olive oil
   red, yellow and green   sea salt and black pepper

Grill the peppers, preferably over an open fire, until the skins have charred and blistered. Cool slightly, then peel away all the skin and cut the peppers in strips. Lay them in a shallow dish and pour over the oil, mixing lightly, and adding sea salt and black pepper to taste. Serve at room temperature. Serves 3–4, or 4–5 with other dishes.

SALAT MESCHOUI   Tunisia

This dish is similar to the Spanish *escalibada*, in that it is like a cold vinaigrette of vegetables which have been previously grilled. This gives a subtle smoky flavour, and makes them soft and tender. It is usually served at room temperature, as a first course, but in very hot weather I like to serve it chilled.

1½ lb/675 g large ripe tomatoes   1 tablespoon capers
3 large cloves garlic   juice of ½ lemon
1 mild onion   sea salt and black pepper
¾ lb/350 g green peppers   ½ teaspoon ground coriander
1 celery heart, with leaves   2 tablespoons olive oil
½ preserved lemon, chopped   5 black olives
   (see Pickles, Preserves and
   Spice Mixtures, page 264)
   (optional)

Grill the whole tomatoes, either under the grill, over the fire, or over a gas flame, until the skins have blackened and blistered all over. Repeat this process with the garlic cloves stuck on the end of long skewers, and the onion and green peppers. When all the vegetables are charred, scrape away the blackened skins with a small knife, and wash away the seeds of the tomatoes and the peppers. Chop all by hand to a fine hash and mix with the chopped celery, including the leaves, and the preserved lemon, if used. Add the drained and rinsed capers. Put the lemon juice in a soup plate and add a little sea salt and black pepper, and the ground coriander. Add the oil and beat with a fork till blended. Mix with the purée and spoon into a shallow dish. Garnish with the black olives. Serve after cooling, or chilled. Serves 4 as a first course, with crusty bread.

TAPENADE   France

This is one of those delicious salty Provençal spreads, usually eaten on slices of toasted French bread, which go so well with drinks. It is also excellent with hard-boiled eggs, either used as a stuffing, or served simply with the halved eggs lying in a shallow dish of the *tapenade*. Some versions are made with olives alone, but I prefer this one which also contains tunny fish and anchovies.

6 oz/175 g black olives, stoned	1 tablespoon mustard powder
6 oz/175 g capers, drained	⅓ pint/200 ml olive oil
3 oz/75 g anchovy fillets	2 tablespoons brandy
2 tablespoons milk	½ teaspoon mixed spices: black
3 oz/75 g tunny fish, drained of	pepper, ground cloves,
its oil	nutmeg or mace

Put the stoned olives in a food processor (or blender) with the capers, the anchovy fillets which you have soaked in the milk for 10 minutes, then drained, the tunny fish and the mustard. Process till a smooth paste. (Alternatively, this can be done by pounding in a mortar and sieving.) Turn into a bowl and gradually stir in the oil as if making mayonnaise. Finally add the brandy and the spices. (Salt will not be necessary.) Pile into a jar, cover closely, and store in the refrigerator where it will keep for several weeks. To serve, cut thin slices of French bread and toast lightly under the grill or in the oven. Spread with *tapenade*, and serve with drinks, or as a first course. To serve with eggs, see page 88.

TARAMASALATA

Greece

Taramasalata is a dish of Greek, or possibly Turkish, origin which has become immensely popular all over the world. It was originally made with *tarama*, the preserved roe of the grey mullet, but in the last twenty years smoked cod's roe has become more generally used. The original *tarama* was quite hard, which explains the instructions to pound continually which are found in old recipes. Since my Greek and Anglo-Greek friends all disagree on the best way to make *taramasalata*, I am forced to give at least two versions to avoid offending any of them. One assures me that it should be made with just smoked cod's roe, onion juice, olive oil and lemon juice, and that additions of breadcrumbs or mashed potato were invented by restaurants to 'stretch' the expensive *tarama*. Others insist that a little soaked bread should be added, but it is generally agreed that potato makes it heavy. A third school of thought, fostered by modern cookery writers like myself, adds cream cheese; this makes a delicious light fish pâté, but it cannot be claimed as authentic, since cream cheese just doesn't exist in Greece.

TARAMASALATA I

1 lb/450 g smoked cod's roe	black pepper
3 tablespoons lemon juice	5–6 tablespoons olive oil
2 teaspoons onion juice (made in a garlic press)	2 tablespoons yogurt (optional)

Scrape the roe out of its skin into a bowl and cover with the lemon juice. Leave for an hour to soften. Then put in a food processor, or a mortar, and process (or pound) until reduced to a smooth purée. Add the onion juice and black pepper and process (or pound) again, then finally add the oil gradually, continuing to work until it is all smoothly amalgamated. This is hard work in a mortar, but quickly achieved in a processor. I like to add a little yogurt to lighten the mixture and render it a little more bland, but this is purely personal, and not orthodox. Some people add a drop of cream for the same reason. Serves 4–6.

TARAMASALATA II

As above, but add a handful of soft white breadcrumbs, previously soaked in water for 10 minutes then squeezed dry, to the cod's roe before adding anything else.

TARAMASALATA III

½ lb/225 g smoked cod's roe
2 tablespoons lemon juice
1½ tablespoons olive oil
¼ lb/100 g cream cheese

black pepper
1 tablespoon yogurt
(sometimes)

Scrape the roe out of its skin and put in the food processor. Cover with the lemon juice and leave for a little to soften. Process until smooth, adding the olive oil and scraping down the sides once or twice. Add the cream cheese and process again. Add black pepper to taste. If using a firm cream cheese like Philadelphia, a spoonful of yogurt will be necessary to thin it; if using a lighter cheese, or a low fat cream cheese, this will not be necessary. Chill for an hour or two before serving with hot flat bread. Serves 3–4.

SALADS

Each of the countries bordering the Mediterranean has its own particular salads. In Spain they are usually very simple, composed for the most part of lettuce, sometimes with tomatoes added, in a dressing of olive oil and lemon juice. In Provence and the Côte Niçoise, salads are among the most popular of summer dishes, either served on their own as a light meal, or as an hors d'oeuvre. The more complex salads like the *salade niçoise* are ideal for a light lunch, or as the first course for a more formal meal. Another popular salad in the south of France is the *salade mesclun*, a mixture of tiny green leaves grown locally by the country people. It was originally composed of wild green leaves, but is now made from cultivated plants – dandelion, chicory and rocket – with corn salad and lettuce thinnings sometimes included. *Salade mesclun* commands a high price in the markets, and an even higher one in the restaurants. It is an ancient dish, and another is the *salade au chapon*; usually made with one or two forms of chicory, this has a piece of dry bread rubbed with garlic and olive oil concealed within it. Salads rarely accompany the main dish in France, while those that follow it are almost invariably green, sometimes made with lettuce alone, or composed of a mixture of different green leaves. In winter, corn salad (*mâche*) is always popular.

In the north of Italy, the choice of salad vegetables in the markets is the most tempting I have seen anywhere, but I am not enamoured of the habit prevalent in all but the grandest restaurants of leaving you to mix your own dressing. As I struggled to do this with a modicum of success recently in a small restaurant in Venice, I was enraged to see an old and favoured customer presented with a large jug of the new season's green olive oil, which he poured over a green salad. When you are lucky enough to find one, the Italian dressings are very simple;

just olive oil with a touch of lemon juice and the minimum of seasonings – no garlic. The Italians have a passion for salads made from wild green leaves; these are offered for sale daily in the markets, freshly gathered from the fields and hedgerows and piled loosely into sacks. The cultivated salad plants also include many that were formerly unknown to me; these vary from region to region, both in their popularity and their name. One of my favourites is the spiky green leaf that looks exactly like grass clippings; very popular in Tuscany where it is called *barba di capucino*. It is also found in Milan where it is known as *venti quattro hora*. A delicious Tuscan salad is made of these mixed with sliced peeled tomatoes. Another popular Tuscan leaf is called *orecche di lepre*, since the small oval leaves do indeed resemble hares' ears. The Italian mixed salads are enormously varied, often including yellow peppers, spring onions, celery, cucumber, radishes and tomatoes as well as a wide mixture of green leaves. Rocket is a popular salad leaf, since the Italians have a great fondness for a bitter touch in their salads; this explains the popularity in winter time of the red lettuces called *trevigiana* or *radicchio* – actually a form of chicory – particularly in the Veneto area.

I cannot write fairly of salads, or indeed of much else, in Yugoslavia, since in the course of two visits I failed to find even one good restaurant. The only salad that springs to mind is one that would have been better forgotten; called Serbian salad, it consisted of chunks of red and green hot chilli peppers, complete with seeds – nothing else.

Greek salads are excellent, but not even the most ardent Grecophile could call them varied. Their summer salad is almost always the same, at least in the tavernas: a mixture of tomato, cucumber and onion with black olives and crumbled feta cheese, sprinkled with dried oregano. The most popular winter salad is one of cooked dandelion leaves, cooled and dressed with oil and lemon juice.

Turkish salads are extremely good, at least in my experience; here rocket is often used as a substitute for lettuce, and the salads are usually a finely chopped mixture of this with cucumber, tomato and onions. As we move further east, through Syria to Lebanon and Israel, the salads change their character and become more complex, often containing a grain such as *burghul* (cracked wheat), and quantities of chopped fresh herbs. In the North African countries, salads do not figure in the way that we know them. Their equivalent lies in the number of dishes of vegetables, usually cooked and dressed with oil, lemon juice and spices after cooling, that are served at the start of a meal, or as side dishes. An unusual dish of this sort found in Morocco is one of grated carrots, sweetened with sugar and rose water. A good salad can be made in North Africa on Middle Eastern lines, using *couscous* instead of *burghul* and adding green leaves like rocket and purslane, but this is not authentic.

ARAB SALAD   Egypt

This is basically a Greek salad with one or two extra additions. In Egypt it is often served as an hors d'oeuvre, along with one or two other dishes – possibly some *foul medames, hamine* eggs and a lemon pickle.

¾ lb/350 g tomatoes, skinned and chopped
½ cucumber, unpeeled and chopped
½ large mild onion, chopped

1 bunch watercress
a pinch of shatah (pounded red pepper) or a dash of Tabasco
5 tablespoons olive oil
2 tablespoons lemon juice

Mix the chopped tomatoes, cucumber, onion and watercress sprigs. Mix the *shatah* or Tabasco with the olive oil and lemon juice, pour over the salad and toss. Serves 4.

AVOCADO, TOMATO AND MOZZARELLA SALAD   Italy

This makes a perfect first course for a light summer meal. It is quick to prepare, and both appetizing and nourishing.

2 avocados
4 tomatoes
1 Italian mozzarella cheese
6 tablespoons olive oil

1½ tablespoons white wine vinegar
sea salt and black pepper
1 teaspoon dried oregano

Cut the avocados in half, skin them and remove the stones. Cut each half in thin slices and lay in the centre of a flat dish. Skin the tomatoes and slice them. Cut the mozzarella in half and slice also. Lay alternate slices of tomato and mozzarella around the avocado. Mix the oil and vinegar in a small jug and pour over all, then sprinkle with a little sea salt, freshly ground black pepper and dried oregano. Serves 4 as a first course.

CARROT SALAD

This unusual sweet salad is served either as a first course, usually with one or two other dishes, or as a side dish. (Rose water can be bought from chemists' shops.)

1 lb/450 g young carrots, grated
4 tablespoons lemon juice
1½ tablespoons rose water

a pinch of salt
1 tablespoon sugar
½ teaspoon ground cinnamon

Pile the grated carrots in a bowl. Mix the lemon juice and rose water, add the salt, sugar and cinnamon, and pour over the carrots. Toss and serve. Serves 4.

GREEK COUNTRY SALAD

This is the very essence of Greek salads, in its simplest and to my mind most delicious form.

1 lb/450 g tomatoes
6 oz/175 g feta cheese
12 black olives
black pepper

5 tablespoons olive oil
¼ teaspoon dried oregano
(rigani)

Cut the tomatoes (unpeeled) in quarters and pile in a bowl. Chop the feta in small cubes and scatter over the tomatoes. Add the olives, sprinkle with black pepper, dress with olive oil, and scatter oregano over all. This makes the perfect accompaniment to *souvlaki*, or any grilled meat for that matter, with flat bread. Serves 4.

COUSCOUS SALAD   France

The French became devotees of couscous as a result of their years of sojourn in the countries of the Mahgreb, and they invented dishes using it in ways unknown to the Arabs. This salad is similar to the Lebanese tabbouleh, which is made with burghul (a form of crushed wheat).

10–12 oz/300 g cold cooked
    couscous
3 tablespoons olive oil
sea salt and black pepper
1 bunch spring onions, sliced
¼ cucumber, peeled and diced

2 tomatoes, skinned and
    chopped
1 chilli, or 2–3 dashes Tabasco
1 tablespoon lemon juice
2 tablespoons chopped
    coriander, or flat parsley

Stir the oil into the couscous, breaking up any lumps. Add sea salt and black pepper to taste. Stir in the sliced spring onions, using the young green leaves as well as the bulbs. Peel the cucumber, cut it in dice, and stir in. Skin and chop the tomatoes and add to the couscous. Chop the chilli, if used, very finely indeed, being careful to discard all the seeds, and stir into the salad. (The chilli can be first blanched for 3 minutes in boiling water, if a less hot flavour is desired.) Stir in the lemon juice and the chopped coriander or parsley. Serves 5.

DANDELION SALAD   Greece

This is the most popular winter salad in Greece; it is also found in Turkey.

a large bunch dandelion leaves
salt

3 tablespoons olive oil
1½ tablespoons lemon juice

Cook the well-washed leaves in a little boiling salted water for 5–6 minutes, until tender. Drain and cool. Dress with the olive oil and lemon juice and serve at room temperature. Serves 4.

SALADE D'ENDIVES FRISÉES AU CHAPON   France

An excellent salad for a rustic meal, rather than an elegant dinner party.

1 thick slice of a dry French
  loaf
1 large clove garlic
3½ tablespoons best olive oil
1 curly endive

1 batavia, or escarole
sea salt and black pepper
1 tablespoon white wine
  vinegar

Dry the bread lightly in a cool oven, without actually toasting it. Rub it on both sides with a cut clove of garlic, and sprinkle ½ tablespoon of the best olive oil – preferably a green 'virgin' oil – over it. Put this 'chapon' in the bottom of the salad bowl and pile the washed and drained leaves on top, using only the inner pale green ones. Make a dressing in the normal way with sea salt and black pepper, the remaining olive oil and the white wine vinegar. Mix well, then pour over the salad. Toss well, mixing the chapon with the leaves, then stand for 5 minutes before serving, to allow the flavour to develop. Serves 4.

FATTOUSH   Lebanon

This is a most refreshing dish for hot weather; juicy and tart, it makes a perfect light lunch for a summer day, or it can be served as a first course, or as part of a mixed buffet. Purslane can be bought during the summer months from Greek Cypriot shops, as can flat parsley; purslane is sometimes sold under the name 'continental watercress'.

1 flat bread
1 bunch spring onions, chopped
1 small cucumber, or ⅔ of a
  large one, peeled and
  chopped
½ lb/225 g tomatoes, skinned
  and chopped
2 cloves garlic, crushed
1 heart of a cos lettuce,
  shredded

½ bunch purslane, when
  available
¼ pint/150 ml chopped parsley,
  flat if possible
¼ pint/150 ml chopped mint
sea salt and black pepper
¼ pint/150 ml olive oil
¼ pint/150 ml lemon juice

Toast the bread, cool slightly, then break in pieces about 1 inch/2·5 cm square. Lay them in a salad bowl and cover with the chopped spring onions, the chopped peeled cucumber, the skinned and chopped tomatoes, and the crushed garlic. Leave for 10 minutes for the bread to absorb the juices, then add the shredded lettuce heart, the tender tops of the purslane and the chopped parsley and mint. Sprinkle with sea salt and black pepper. Put the oil and lemon juice in a jug and beat with a wire whisk until blended, then pour over the salad and toss. Serves 4.

SALADE MESCLUN   France

There seems little point in giving a detailed recipe for this, since we are unable to obtain the mixture of tiny leaves with which it is made, unless we grow them specially in our gardens. It is composed of a mixture of minute green leaves, usually chicory, dandelion and rocket, sometimes also including corn salad and lettuce thinnings. This is sold already mixed in all the markets in the south of France, and is served alone, always as a first course, with a strong, almost harsh dressing of olive oil with a lot of garlic. Garlic-flavoured croûtons, like the *chapon* in the *salade d'endives frisées* (above), are sometimes served with it. Although it is extremely healthy, I am not over-fond of this salad, finding it rather too strong, bitter and expensive for what it is.

SALADE NIÇOISE   France

The original *salade niçoise* was composed of raw vegetables – tomatoes, onions and green peppers – with hard-boiled eggs, black olives and anchovies. Nowadays string beans and boiled potatoes are usually added, while tinned tunny fish is used either instead of, or as well as, the anchovy fillets. I tend to compromise between the old and new versions, using string beans but no potatoes, and tunny fish either alone or with anchovies.

4–5 large lettuce leaves
3 tomatoes, cut in quarters
1 green pepper, cut in strips
½ Spanish onion, cut in half
 rings
6 oz/175 g string beans, boiled
 and cooled
3 hard-boiled eggs, halved

1 lb/450 g tinned tunny fish,
 drained
8 anchovy fillets (optional)
sea salt and black pepper
¼ teaspoon Dijon mustard
6 tablespoons olive oil
4 large basil leaves, cut in
 strips

Line a large bowl with the lettuce leaves. Lay the quartered tomatoes and pepper strips in it, and cover with the semi-circular onion rings. Lay the whole string beans over this, and surround with the halved eggs. Divide the tunny fish into chunks and arrange in the centre of the bowl. If using anchovies, cut them in half and scatter over the dish. Put the sea salt, black pepper and mustard in a small bowl and mix with the olive oil (I don't use any lemon juice or vinegar with this salad). Pour over the dish at the table and mix well, adding the basil. Serves 5–6 as a first course, or 4 as a light main dish.

PROVENÇAL RICE SALAD   France

This makes a good accompaniment to cold meat. It looks pretty served in a bowl lined with lettuce leaves.

½ lb/225 g long grain rice
sea salt and black pepper
3 tablespoons olive oil
1 tablespoon white wine
 vinegar

2 green peppers
½ lb/225 g tomatoes
8 black olives, stoned
a few lettuce leaves (optional)

Cook the rice as usual, drain, rinse under cold running water and drain again. Tip into a bowl and add sea salt and black pepper, olive oil and vinegar. Grill the peppers until the skin is charred and blistered; pull it off and cut them in strips, discarding all the seeds. Skin the tomatoes and cut, first in half, and then in semi-circular slices. Drain for a few minutes on a sloping surface to allow the juice to run off. Mix the peppers, tomatoes and olives lightly with the rice and serve soon after cooling. Serves 4.

PURSLANE SALAD   Greece

Another very popular Greek salad. Purslane can be found in Cypriot shops under the name of continental watercress; it is easily recognized by its plump fleshy stalk with a rosette of leaves at the top.

1 bunch purslane
olive oil

lemon juice or white wine
vinegar
sea salt and black pepper

Pinch the top 2 inches/5 cm off the purslane stems and pile in a salad bowl. Dress with olive oil and lemon juice or vinegar, in the usual way, adding sea salt and black pepper.

TABBOULEH   Lebanon

This Lebanese dish is like the essence of health foods; it is composed mainly of parsley, and is therefore rich in minerals and vitamin C. *Burghul* is a form of crushed wheat available from health food stores. It is important to get the correct grain: English cracked, kibbled or crushed wheat will not do for this salad.

In the Lebanon this is served as a first course or as part of a buffet, and small crisp lettuce leaves are often served on the side, to scoop it up with.

2 oz/50 g burghul
2 bunches spring onions,
  chopped
2 tomatoes, skinned, chopped
  and drained
3 oz/75 g parsley (1 pint/600 ml
  when chopped)

4 tablespoons chopped mint
sea salt and black pepper
4 tablespoons olive oil
4 tablespoons lemon juice
a few lettuce leaves

Wash the burghul and soak it for 30 minutes in cold water. Drain and squeeze dry. Put in a bowl and mix with the chopped spring onions, squeezing between the hands. Skin the tomatoes, chop and drain off the juice, then stir into the burghul. Stir in the chopped parsley and mint, and add the sea salt and black pepper. Stir in the olive oil and lemon juice. Line a bowl with lettuce leaves and pile the *tabbouleh* into it. Serves 4.

TOMATO AND FENNEL SALAD   **Italy**

This is a popular salad in Italy; the crisp texture of the fennel contrasts well with the soft juicy tomatoes. Prepare an hour before serving.

1 lb/450 g tomatoes, skinned
   and sliced
2 medium heads fennel
sea salt and black pepper

4 tablespoons olive oil
½ tablespoon white wine
   vinegar

Skin the tomatoes and slice thinly. Trim the coarse outer leaves off the fennel, then cut in thin slices. Arrange the two vegetables on a flat dish, each covering one half. Sprinkle with the black pepper and spoon the oil and vinegar over both. Only add salt, if wanted, just before serving. Serves 4–6.

TOMATO AND MOZZARELLA SALAD   **Italy**

One of my favourite first courses.

1 lb/450 g ripe tomatoes
2 Italian mozzarella cheeses
3 tablespoons olive oil
1 tablespoon white wine
   vinegar

sea salt and black pepper
2 tablespoons basil leaves, cut
   in strips

Skin the tomatoes and slice thinly. Slice the mozzarella also. Lay on each side of a large flat dish. Mix the oil and vinegar and sprinkle over. Scatter a little sea salt and quite a lot of freshly ground black pepper over all, then scatter the basil over the dish. Serves 4 as a light first course.

TOMATO AND FETA SALAD   **Greece**

Make as for tomato and mozzarella salad, substituting feta for mozzarella, and omitting the salt and vinegar.

TOMATO AND PEPPER SALAD   Spain

1 lb/450 g tomatoes, skinned
   and sliced
1 lb/450 g green and yellow
   peppers

sea salt and black pepper
3–4 tablespoons olive oil
½ tablespoon white wine
   vinegar

Skin the tomatoes and cut in slices. Grill the peppers until the skins are blackened; peel away when cool. Cut in strips and mix with the tomatoes. Sprinkle with sea salt and black pepper and dress with olive oil and vinegar. Serves 4–6.

A TURKISH SALAD   Turkey

Turkish salads are much more varied than Greek ones; a typical Turkish salad might consist largely of rocket, with spring onions, cucumber, green pepper and sometimes tomatoes. The rocket is shredded, and the other vegetables finely chopped and piled on it. A simple dressing of oil and lemon is poured over it, and the whole tossed together. All the salads I have eaten in Turkey have been similar to this, and very good. In an old Turkish cookery book I found a recipe for a salad dressing including nuts and soaked bread, similar to a sauce tarator, but I have never actually seen this served with salad myself.

TZATZIKI   Greece

This excellent Greek dish is also well known in the Middle East, where it is the inevitable accompaniment to dishes of roast lamb, while in Greece it usually accompanies souvlaki. A similar dish, cucumber raita, is served in India, as a cooling contrast to hot curries.

1 pint/600 ml yogurt
1 cucumber
2 large cloves garlic, crushed
sea salt and black pepper

½ teaspoon dried mint, or 1
   tablespoon chopped fresh
   mint (optional)

Beat the yogurt until smooth. Peel the cucumber and slice, chop, or grate coarsely. Stir into the yogurt, adding the crushed cloves of garlic, sea salt and black pepper. Tip into a bowl and chill for 2–3 hours before serving. Sprinkle with dried or fresh mint, if liked, before serving. (In the Middle East, this is invariably served with a scattering of dried mint, for most families dry their own mint, and use it in preference to fresh.) Serves 6.

VENETIAN WINTER SALADS   Italy

The Italians, especially the Venetians, are extremely fond of bitter salad leaves, and they grow a wide variety of them to last through the winter months. Most of these are varieties of chicory, hence their bitter taste, and they do not develop their true flavour until after the first frost. In the Venice market one February I found a wide choice of leaves, far removed from what one might find in an English green-grocer. These included a plain red *radicchio*, a blotchy green and red *radicchio*, a pretty striped red and white *trevisio*, corn salad and tiny green leaves called simply *salatina*. There were various sorts of lettuce, and shredded artichoke hearts which are also used in salads at this time of year, being a tender winter variety. Although I am not quite so enamoured of bitter leaves as the Italians, I like a proportion of them mixed with milder ones, and particularly loved a salad I had in the home of a gondolier which was a simple combination of green lettuce and plain red *radicchio*, dressed with olive oil and a touch of lemon juice.

Mediterranean egg dishes are for the most part variations on one of the following themes: the omelette, *oeufs au plat* and *piperade*. Yet each of these can vary considerably, according to local tastes. The most exquisite omelette, the only true omelette in fact, is of course the French one. In Mediterranean France this often contains a regional filling: a few spoonfuls of ratatouille, some garlic-flavoured croûtons or some fried aubergine. The Spanish tortilla is a very different matter. If you are expecting a soft French omelette you will be disappointed, for the tortilla will seem solid and leathery, but if you consider it as something quite other, its merits will become apparent. Much the best of the tortillas to my mind is the *tortilla de patates*, and I find this infinitely better eaten warm, or even cold, rather than hot. It makes an admirable picnic dish, and is relatively easy to transport. The Egyptian *eggah* is another dish of this sort; a firm omelette containing a generous proportion of other food, either cooked meat or vegetables. The leek *eggah* is a particularly good example. Similar to the *eggah* is the Tunisian *tagine*, not to be confused with the Moroccan *tagine* which is a totally different dish. This again has a solid base; my favourite is based on spinach with tiny meatballs and hard-boiled eggs, all encased within a mass of beaten raw eggs and baked in the oven until firm. In Greece, a *frittata* type of omelette is made by pouring beaten eggs over lightly stewed purslane in a frying pan, and cooking until set.

Oeufs au plat, or baked eggs, are very popular in Spain where much of the cooking is done in individual earthenware dishes. The simply baked eggs are often garnished with slices of chorizo, a spicy garlic sausage. Fried eggs are also liked in Spain, and are sometimes served with sliced sausage, rice and a tomato sauce.

Piperade, the Provençal dish of eggs and vegetables stewed gently until amalgamated into a creamy mass, is reflected in the Turkish *menemen*, a very similar dish, and the Spanish *pisto*, which is called *sanfaina* in Catalan. The Tunisian version, *chachouka*, differs slightly in that the eggs are usually cooked whole in hollows in the vegetables. All these dishes make light vegetarian meals, ideal for hot weather.

Hard-boiled eggs are often served in Spain, France and Italy, accompanied by one of the delicious Mediterranean sauces – mayonnaise, *aïoli* or *pesto*. In France, they are sometimes stuffed with *tapenade*, a purée of olives, capers and anchovies, or simply cut in half and laid, cut side down, in the purée. An unusual egg dish is the Egyptian *hamine* eggs; these are boiled for several hours, either with onion skins or with the dried *foul* beans which they so often accompany, or with *d'feena*, a beef stew. This lengthy cooking renders the whites a pale beige, and gives them a strange, slightly rubbery consistency not unlike the Chinese hundred-year-old eggs.

AUBERGINE OMELETTE   France

Fried aubergine strips make a delicious filling for a creamy omelette and, together with a lettuce salad, makes a perfect light meal for two people.

¼ lb/100 g aubergine	5–6 eggs
frying oil	sea salt and black pepper
1 small clove garlic	½ oz/15 g butter

Peel the aubergine and cut it in thin strips like matchsticks, about 1½ inches/3·5 cm long. Soak them in a bowl of salt water for 10 minutes, then drain and squeeze dry in a cloth.

Heat some oil in a sauté pan so that it comes about ½ inch/1 cm up the sides of the pan. When very hot, drop in the whole peeled clove of garlic and half the strips of aubergine. Cook for 3–4 minutes, till golden brown, stirring once or twice, then lift out and drain on soft paper. Transfer to a hot dish and keep warm while you fry the rest. When all are done, beat the eggs and add sea salt and black pepper. Melt the butter and make an omelette in the usual way. When it is almost ready scatter the aubergine strips – discarding the garlic clove – over it, then fold and turn onto a flat dish.

Serve with a green salad as a light main dish, or on its own as a first course. Serves 2.

GARLIC OMELETTE   **France**

1 slice stale white bread, ½
   inch/1 cm thick
1 oz/25 g butter
1 tablespoon oil
1 clove garlic, peeled

5 eggs
sea salt and black pepper
½ tablespoon finely chopped
   parsley

Remove the crusts and cut the bread in cubes. Heat half the butter and the oil in a frying pan with the whole clove of garlic. When it is sizzling hot, put in the bread cubes and cook, turning frequently, until they are golden brown all over. Discard the garlic and drain the croûtons on soft paper while you make the omelette.

Beat the eggs, add sea salt and black pepper. Put the remaining butter in a hot omelette pan, pour in the eggs and cook as usual. When almost ready, scatter in the croûtons and cook a moment longer, then fold over and turn onto a hot dish. Sprinkle with chopped parsley and serve. Serves 2, with a green salad.

PEPPER OMELETTE   **France**

Sweet peppers, grilled and cut in strips, make one of the most delicious fillings for a soft French omelette.

2 red, yellow or green peppers
5–6 eggs

sea salt and black pepper
½ oz/15 g butter

Grill the peppers, preferably over an open fire, or over a gas flame, or under the grill. Turn them constantly until the skin has blackened and blistered all over. Cool slightly, then pull away the skin, scraping off every little scrap with a small knife. Cut them in strips, discarding stalk and seeds.

Beat the eggs, add sea salt and black pepper, and make the omelette in the usual way. Just before it is ready, scatter the strips of pepper over it, cook a moment longer, then fold and turn out onto a hot dish. Serve immediately. Serves 2.

EGGS WITH PURSLANE OR PURSLANE OMELETTE   Greece

A Greek lady in a Cypriot shop in London told me how to make this dish; I find it totally delicious and make it often.

1 bunch purslane	5 eggs
1½ oz/40 g butter	sea salt and black pepper

Pinch the top 2 inches/5 cm off the purslane, wash and pat dry. Melt the butter in a frying pan and put in the purslane. Cook quite briskly for 3–4 minutes, until wilted. Beat the eggs as for an omelette, adding sea salt and black pepper, then pour over the purslane. Cook in the usual way, without attempting to fold it, but making a sort of flat omelette with the purslane enclosed within it. Turn onto a flat dish to serve. Serves 2.

RATATOUILLE OMELETTE   France

A stuffed omelette can be very delicious, and few things go better with creamy eggs than a well-seasoned ratatouille. The colours also look well together, and it is a good way of using up a small amount of ratatouille.

4–6 tablespoons ratatouille	sea salt and black pepper
5 eggs	½ oz/15 g butter

Warm the ratatouille in a small bowl standing over a pan of hot water. Beat the eggs, add sea salt and black pepper and melt the butter in an omelette pan. When hot, pour in the eggs and cook as usual, adding the ratatouille at the last moment, when the omelette is almost ready. Cook a moment longer, then fold and turn out onto a warm dish. Serves 2, with a green salad.

If you have slightly more ratatouille, say ⅓ pint/200 ml, you can spread it over the top of the finished omelette and serve without folding.

CHACHOUKA   **Tunisia**

This Tunisian version of *piperade* has a characteristic touch in the use
of one or two hot chilli peppers mixed with the sweet ones; it makes
an excellent light main course for lunch or dinner, accompanied by
bread and butter and a green salad.

½ lb/225 g mild onions
1 oz/25 g butter
1 tablespoon olive oil
¾ lb/350 g red and yellow
  peppers, mixed

1–2 hot chilli peppers
1½ lb/675 g tomatoes
sea salt and black pepper
½ teaspoon sugar, if needed
4 eggs

Cut the onions in half, then slice each half thinly. Heat the butter and
oil in a heavy-lidded pan and cook the onions until they start to colour.
Add the peppers, cut in strips, and cook for 8 minutes, together with
the finely minced chilli pepper(s), all seeds carefully removed. When
the peppers are nearly soft, add the skinned and quartered tomatoes.
Stir, and cook gently for another 8 minutes, or until all is soft and
blended without having turned into a mush. Season carefully with sea
salt and black pepper, adding a little sugar if the tomatoes are acid.
Make 4 depressions in the vegetables and break in the eggs. Cover and
cook gently until they have set, basting once or twice with the juices.
Serve immediately, with a green salad. Serves 4.

ÇILBIR   **Turkey**

This excellent dish is a combination of two Turkish dishes, and better
than either. It makes a splendid first course, or a light supper dish if
served with a green salad.

1½ lb/675 g mild onions
2½ oz/65 g butter
sea salt and black pepper
2 teaspoons sugar

⅓ pint/200 ml yogurt
1 clove garlic
¼ teaspoon paprika
4 eggs

Slice the onions and cook very gently in 2 oz/50 g butter in a lidded
sauté pan. After 10 minutes add sea salt, black pepper and sugar, and
2 tablespoons water; cover the pan, and stew gently for ½ hour stirring

occasionally to prevent sticking. Meanwhile beat the yogurt until smooth, stir in the crushed garlic, and stand at the back of the stove to warm slightly. Melt the remaining ½ oz/15 g butter in a cup and stir in the paprika. When the onions are cooked, poach the eggs and lay them on the onions. Cover with the yogurt, and dribble the paprika butter over all. Serve with crusty French bread or pitta. Serves 4.

HAMINE EGGS   Egypt

These eggs have a mysterious flavour that always reminds me of Chinese 'hundred-year-old' eggs. They are somewhat of an acquired taste, since the long cooking gives the egg a strange consistency as well as a curious flavour. They are the traditional accompaniment to *foul medames*, the Egyptian bean dish.

Put some eggs in a saucepan with the skins of 3–4 large onions. Cover generously with cold water and bring slowly to the boil, then cover the pan and cook steadily for 5–6 hours, or overnight. (Slow cookers are ideal for this dish.) Check now and then to see if more water is needed. The whites of the eggs are coloured a pale khaki by the onion skins. Serve, shelled, with *foul medames*. Sometimes the eggs are cooked with the beans instead of onion skins, or in the case of *d'feena*, an Egyptian meat stew, they are cooked in the stew. Allow 1 per person.

LEEK EGGAH   Egypt

This rather solid sort of omelette is typical of the Mediterranean, and makes a useful dish to serve for a luncheon or light supper, either alone, or with a dish of cold meat.

1½ lb/675 g leeks	a pinch of sugar
2½ oz/65 g butter	juice of ½ lemon
sea salt and black pepper	6 eggs

Cut the cleaned leeks in half lengthwise, then across in thin slices. Cook them gently in 2 oz/50 g of the butter in a sauté pan, uncovered, for 5–6 minutes, then add sea salt and black pepper, sugar and lemon juice. Cover the pan and stew gently for 10 minutes, or till soft. Beat the eggs, adding salt and pepper, then fold in the cooked leeks and their juices. Heat the remaining butter in a heavy frying pan and cook the leek-egg mixture over low heat, covered, for about 20 minutes, or till set through. Turn out on a flat dish to serve, and cut like a cake. Serves 3–4.

MENEMEN   Turkey

This is a Turkish egg and vegetable dish, similar to piperade, which I ate at a waterside restaurant in Izmir. It makes a good light luncheon dish, or a hot first course for a cold dinner.

1½ lb/675 g mixed red and yellow peppers	1 lb/450 g tomatoes
2 oz/50 g butter	sea salt and black pepper
	6 eggs

Have the peppers prepared beforehand, cut in thin strips with all seeds removed. Heat the butter in a lidded sauté pan and cook the peppers gently for 6 minutes. Skin the tomatoes, chop them and discard the seeds, then add to the peppers. Cook all together for 6–8 minutes, till soft but not mushy. Add plenty of sea salt and black pepper. Cool slightly, then stir in the beaten eggs, replace on a low heat, and cook gently until set, stirring constantly. Serve immediately, with a green salad if using as a main course, or simply some crusty bread. Serves 4.

PIPERADE   France

Everyone knows this Provençal dish of peppers cooked with onions and tomatoes, with beaten eggs blended into the juices. It makes a useful light main course served with a green salad and crusty bread, or a first course to precede a cold meat dish.

1 large mild onion	½ lb/225 g tomatoes
4 tablespoons olive oil	2 cloves garlic
1 lb/450 g mixed peppers – red, yellow and green	sea salt and black pepper
	5 eggs

Chop the onion and cook gently in the oil in a sauté pan. Cut the peppers in strips and add to the onion when it has started to colour. Cook gently for 10 minutes, then add the skinned and chopped tomatoes and the finely chopped garlic. Cook for another 10 minutes, adding sea salt and black pepper. Then cool for a few minutes, while you beat the eggs. Pour them into the pan, replace on a low heat and cook for 2–3 minutes, stirring constantly, until the eggs have set and blended with the juices. Serves 4–5.

TAGINE D'ÉPINARDS   **Tunisia**

This is a Tunisian *tagine*, as opposed to a Moroccan *tagine*, which is a sort of stew of lamb or chicken. The Tunisian *tagine* is a good dish, quite solid, composed of vegetables and meat enclosed in a setting of egg, rather like an Egyptian *eggah*, but more substantial. I find it useful as a main dish, eaten warm, or as a picnic dish.

¾ lb/350 g minced beef	*3 tablespoons olive oil*
sea salt and black pepper	*1½ tablespoons tomato purée*
½ teaspoon ground coriander	*6 tablespoons water*
½ teaspoon cinnamon	*3 hard-boiled eggs*
¼ teaspoon harissa (optional),	*5 raw eggs*
* or Tabasco*	*3 oz/75 g crumbled feta*
1½ lb/675 g spinach	*1 tablespoon butter*
1 medium onion	*2 tablespoons flour*

Put the minced meat in a large bowl. Mix in the sea salt, black pepper, coriander, cinnamon and *harissa* (available from Eastern shops). Beat well with a wooden spoon, till well mixed, then form into very small balls, no larger than marbles. Put aside.

Put the washed spinach in a large pot and pour boiling water over to cover. Cook till tender, 6–8 minutes. Drain well, rinse in cold water, and squeeze between the hands to get rid of the water. Chop with a long knife: it does not have to be too fine. Chop the onion and cook in the oil in a sauté pan till it starts to colour. Then add the tomato purée, the water and the meatballs. Cover the pan and turn the heat very low. Cook gently for 25 minutes, stirring now and then.

Chop the hard-boiled eggs coarsely. When the meatballs have finished cooking the sauce should be quite thick. Stir in the chopped spinach and mix with the sauce and the meatballs. Beat the raw eggs lightly and fold into the mixture. Add the grated cheese and the chopped hard-boiled eggs. Tip into a round ovenproof dish, well buttered and sprinkled with flour. (The dish should be about 2 inches/5 cm deep, so that it makes a fairly thick round cake.) Pat it down lightly in the dish and bake for 1 hour at 180°C/350°F/Gas Mark 4. Test by sticking a skewer into the centre; it should emerge dry. To serve, run a knife round the edges and invert on a flat dish.

I find this best about an hour after baking, but it can be eaten hot, warm or cold. Although not exactly an elegant dish, it can be kept warm successfully in a plate-warmer for eating after a theatre or late film. Serves 5–6.

OEUFS EN TAPENADE   France

These stuffed eggs have a very distinctive flavour of the Mediterranean, and make a perfect first course for a summer luncheon. They combine well with other dishes as part of a mixed hors d'oeuvre, and are also good served with drinks.

6 eggs	2 teaspoons olive oil
4 tablespoons tapenade (see	
Mezes and Tapas, page 65)	

Hard-boil the eggs, cool and shell them. Cut them in half lengthwise, scoop out the yolks and mash with a fork. Add the *tapenade* and mash till a smooth paste, moistening with a little extra oil. Fill the halved whites with this mixture, doming it slightly. Serves 4 as a first course, but they can easily be made in larger quantities, allowing roughly 1 heaped tablespoon of tapenade for every 2 eggs.

TORTILLA DI PATATES   Spain

The first time I ate a tortilla, on my first visit to Spain many years ago, I expected a French omelette and was disappointed. Now I think of it quite differently, as a fairly solid dish of eggs and potatoes, and find it rather delicious. I particularly like it served lukewarm, or even cold, for a picnic or luncheon out of doors.

½ large Spanish onion, about
  6 oz/175 g
1 lb/450 g waxy potatoes

frying oil
4 eggs
sea salt and black pepper

Cut the half onion in two pieces, then slice. Peel the potatoes and slice fairly thickly. Heat a layer of oil about ½ inch/1 cm deep in a sauté pan and cook the onion for a couple of minutes, then add the sliced potato. Cook gently for about 15 minutes, stirring often, without allowing them to brown. When they are soft, tip into a colander standing over a bowl and leave for a few minutes to allow the oil to drain off. Scrape out the pan and replace a thin film of oil, just enough to coat the bottom and sides. Beat the eggs, adding sea salt and black pepper, and stir in the onion and potato. Heat the pan and pour in the egg mixture; cook gently until set, about 8 minutes, without stirring. Invert the pan onto a large flat plate, and again scrape out the pan, replacing a thin layer of oil. Slide the tortilla back into the pan and cook another 4 minutes, till set underneath also. Slide onto a dish and leave to cool for an hour or so before serving. Cut in wedges like a cake (it should be about 1½ inches/3·5 cm thick) and serve with a green salad. Serves 3–4.

5 FISH

Despite pollution and over-fishing, I still consider Mediterranean fish among the best in the world. This may well be due to the simple fact that it is usually eaten far fresher than ever it is in England. Although Dover sole has a great reputation, I have eaten better sole from the Mediterranean, both in Spain and Italy. In most Mediterranean countries, fish are usually simply grilled and served with a sauce of oil (or melted butter) and lemon juice, sometimes with fresh herbs added. Since this is also my favourite way of eating fish, I would be the last to complain, but it does not lead to a fund of interesting recipes. In the past few years, the best fish I have eaten have been of this sort – a grilled sole at a fishermen's restaurant on the beach at Conil, near Cadiz; a small dentex eaten in a wooden shack overlooking the harbour at Boccadasse, originally a fishing village but now engulfed in the suburbs of Genoa; and a blue fish eaten in a village called Sariyer on the banks of the Bosphorus.

Many Mediterranean fish simply do not exist in English waters, therefore they have no English name, or at best a totally unfamiliar one. The excellent *chanquetes* of Malaga apparently also live in the river Thames (according to *Mediterranean Seafood* by Alan Davidson) under the name of 'transparent goby', but they are never eaten here to my knowledge. The large family of sea bream which includes the excellent *dentex*, *marmora* and all the *daurades*, are virtually unknown here also and tend to get confused with our fresh-water bream, a much less interesting fish. For some strange reason, however, some of the Mediterranean fish unknown to us are quite common on the other side of the Atlantic, off the north-eastern American coastline. Swordfish, for example, is much fished off the Massachusetts coast, as is the delicious blue fish, like an exquisite mackerel, much esteemed in

Turkey as the *lufer*. *Pompano*, another excellent solid-fleshed white fish found in the Mediterranean, is fished off the coast of Florida, while clams in varying sizes are also common to both American and Mediterranean shores.

An unusual habit peculiar to Spain is that of eating baby fish, of a size liable to embarrass any Anglo-Saxon fisherman. One of the specialities of southern Spain is the tiny *acedia*, baby soles no more than 4 inches/10 cm long, which are fried and served four or five at a time. Small hake called *pescadillos* are also widely popular, and can be found in all the excellent Spanish fish markets. Tiny eels, called *angulas* as opposed to the fully grown *anguilas*, are a speciality of the Catalan coast round Barcelona, but are also found in the south. These minute creatures, no fatter than vermicelli and no more than 2 inches/5 cm long, are cooked in boiling oil flavoured with hot chilli pepper and garlic, and served literally sizzling in the same oil in small brown earthenware dishes. They are eaten with a wooden fork, since the heat of the oil would render a metal fork unusable. The minute *chanquetes* of Malaga are simply immature versions of the larger goby, which is popular in Venice under the name of *go*. The *gianchetti* of Genoa, on the other hand, is a minute sardine. It is hard to distinguish one fish from another while in their larval state, and minute sardines, anchovies and sprats are commonly eaten in various ways in many of the Mediterranean countries, especially in Provence where they are called *poutine*, and made into omelettes, pickles and pastes.

An interesting anomaly in Mediterranean cooking is the widespread popularity of salt (and dried) cod. Although unknown in the Mediterranean Sea, cod has been one of the main ingredients of the winter diet of the poorer people ever since the first large-scale importation from Newfoundland, in the late fifteenth century. Owing to the rising cost of cod in recent years, it is no longer cheap but its popularity is such that it still figures widely. A hard taste for outsiders to appreciate, it seems bitter, coarse and leathery after our own smoked fish. The only ways I like it are when it has been pounded into a smooth mass and mixed with oil, or béchamel, or mashed potatoes. These dishes – the *brandade*, gratin of *bacalao* and croquettes – used to be labours of love since they require lengthy pounding in a mortar, but they can now be made relatively speedily in a food processor. *Bacalao* is salted and dried cod, much of it imported from Scotland; it can also be bought filleted, which is more expensive but worth the extra cost in terms of labour. It is particularly popular in Spain; a friend of mine has a Spanish cookery book called *1001 Dishes Made with Bacalao*. *Stoccafisso* is dried unsalted cod, usually imported from Norway; this is more expensive than *bacalao*, but in many places the two names seem to be used interchangeably. There are many Provençal and Niçois dishes made with salt cod, called *morue* in France. It is also a speciality of Genoa and Venice; I regret to say I have eaten it in good restaurants in both cities without being converted.

ACCIUGHE IN TORTIERA   Italy

This recipe from the Gulf of Naples calls for fresh anchovies, which are enormously popular all along the north shore of the Mediterranean, especially in Turkey. They can sometimes be bought in English fish shops, usually in July, but other fish such as small sardines or sprats can be used in their place, allowing 5–10 minutes longer in the oven.

1–1½ lb/450–675 g *fresh
    anchovies*
6 tablespoons *olive oil*
6 tablespoons *soft breadcrumbs*

3 cloves *garlic, minced*
4 tablespoons *chopped parsley*
sea salt and black pepper

Cut off the heads and tails and wash the anchovies. Pat them dry, then lay them like the spokes of a wheel in a shallow, lightly oiled, round dish. Pour 2 tablespoons of the olive oil over them. Mix the crumbs with the garlic, parsley, sea salt and black pepper. Stir in the remaining 4 tablespoons of oil and spread over the fish. Bake for 15 minutes at 200°C/400°F/Gas Mark 6. Serves 4, as a first course or a light main dish.

ACCIUGHE IN AGRODOLCE   Italy

Another dish of anchovies, this time in a sweet/sour sauce. Other small fish can be substituted when fresh anchovies are unobtainable.

1 lb/450 g *fresh anchovies*
seasoned flour
frying oil
2 tablespoons *finely chopped onion*
2 tablespoons *olive oil*

1 teaspoon *flour*
3 teaspoons *brown sugar*
¼ pint/150 ml *white wine
    vinegar*
1 tablespoon *chopped mint*

Cut the heads and tails off the anchovies, wash them and pat dry. Dip in the seasoned flour and fry in hot oil, allowing 2–2½ minutes altogether. Drain on soft paper while you fry the next batch, then transfer to a hot dish and keep warm.

When all are done, quickly make the sauce: brown the chopped onion in the olive oil, then stir in the flour and brown sugar. Cook for 1 minute, stirring, then pour on the vinegar and stir till smooth. Simmer for 3 minutes, then add the chopped mint and pour over the anchovies. Serves 4 as a first course.

ANGULAS
Spain

These baby eels, no longer than 1½ inches/3·5 cm and as thin as spaghettini, are called *angulas* as distinct from *anguilas*, which are the full-grown eels. They are cooked, for a minute or two only, in boiling olive oil in which a clove of garlic and a hot chilli pepper have already been cooking. They are served in the same brown earthenware dish, one for each person, literally sizzling hot, and eaten with a wooden fork since a metal one would be too hot to hold. I finally summoned up my courage and ate them in an excellent restaurant in Palma do Mallorca, but found them too oily for my taste.

BOURRIDE
France

I had a most delicious *bourride* in Michel's Brasserie des Catalans, one of the finest seafood restaurants in Marseilles. It consisted of a small bass and half a lobster, served with a plate of creamy fish broth enriched with *aïoli*, with slices of dried French bread spread with *aïoli* and *rouille*. Unlike bouillabaisse, a *bourride* can be made quite successfully outside Mediterranean France, since it does not use rock fish. It needs a firm white fish of quality, and several suitable ones are available in England; I have made it recently with halibut and with grey mullet, and both were excellent. Lobsters, crayfish, etc. are not necessary.

This is a fairly modest version; many recipes use as many as 8 extra egg yolks, or 1 per person. If preferred, the extra egg yolks can be omitted entirely, and the whole amount of *aïoli* used to thicken the sauce. In this case the soup is simply served with the fish in it, with dried bread if you choose.

2½–4 lb/1·25–1·75 kg whole fish: sea bass, sea bream, grey mullet or tail end of halibut or turbot, with extra fish bones
2 leeks
1 carrot
2 branches fennel
3 stalks parsley
1 bay leaf
a small glass white wine, or 2 tablespoons white wine vinegar

3–4 pints/1·75–2·25 litres water
5 tablespoons olive oil
2 cloves garlic
sea salt and black pepper
⅛ teaspoon cayenne pepper

aïoli:
2 egg yolks
4 cloves garlic
½ pint/300 ml olive oil
3–4 extra egg yolks
1 small French loaf, sliced and dried in a cool oven

If using a whole fish, cut off the head and tail and put them in a pan with the green part of the leeks, carrot, fennel, parsley, bay leaf, wine (or wine vinegar) and water. (If using the tail end of a large fish, put the extra fish bones in the pan with the vegetables.) Bring to the boil and simmer for 30 minutes; strain. Chop the white part of the leeks and cook in the oil until soft and golden, adding the minced garlic after a short time. Lay the fish on this, and pour over the hot stock, adding sea salt, black pepper and cayenne. Bring to the boil and simmer gently until the fish is cooked – probably about 20 minutes. Lift it onto a hot dish and keep warm.

Boil up the fish stock for about 5 minutes to reduce it; you will only need ⅓ pint/200 ml per person. Have the aïoli made beforehand (see page 244); put half of it in a deep bowl and beat in the extra egg yolks, one at a time. Pour the boiling fish stock through a conical sieve into a heat-proof jug, and add very gradually to the aïoli, beating all the time with a whisk. When all of the fish stock – or as much as you need – is amalgamated with the aïoli, stand the bowl over a large saucepan of simmering water and stir for 5–6 minutes, until it has very slightly thickened. Pour into a hot tureen.

Take 2 or 3 slices of the dry bread per person, spread with a dab of aïoli, and lay in deep soup plates. To serve – this is best done by the cook – fillet the fish and lay a piece in each plate, pouring the soup over it. Have extra bread and the remaining aïoli on the table. Serves 4–8, depending on the size of the fish.

BRANDADE DE MORUE   **France**

This popular dish, traditionally eaten on Fridays and other fast days, used to be very lengthy to make since it involved much pounding with mortar and pestle; for this reason it was often bought rather than made at home. Now, however, it can be quite quickly made in a food processor.

2 lb/900 g dried salt cod (bacalao), soaked for 24–48 hours
approx. 1½ pints/900 ml milk
1 clove garlic, crushed
¼ pint/150 ml olive oil
¼ pint/150 ml thin cream

sea salt (sometimes) and black pepper
2 slices white bread, crusts removed
1 oz/25 g butter
1 black olive (optional)

While the cod is soaking, change the water morning and evening. Wash the cod well, cut in large pieces and lay in a broad pan. Cover with the milk, and add water if necessary to cover it. (This method of cooking in milk rather than water makes it more bland and delicious.) Bring to the boil slowly, cover the pan and simmer for 8 minutes. Turn off the heat and leave for another 10 minutes, then lift out and carefully pick away all the bones and skin.

Put the roughly flaked fish in the food processor and process until reduced to a purée; this must be thoroughly done, scraping down the sides and starting again several times. Turn into a bowl and beat in the crushed garlic. Have the olive oil and cream in two small pans, heated to an equal degree of warmth, but not actually hot. Beat them in gradually and alternately, a spoonful at a time, until the whole is a fluffy mass. Add black pepper and sea salt if required.

This can be served immediately, piled onto a dish and surrounded with triangles of bread fried golden brown in butter, and garnished with a black olive, or it can be made several days in advance, stored in the refrigerator and warmed over hot water before serving, then garnished. It can be served as a first or a main course; if served as a main course it needs no vegetables, but may be followed by a green salad. Serves 5–6 as a first course, and 4 as a main course.

CREAMED SALT COD   Spain

This is one of the few salt cod recipes which I really like, since it is
converted into a smooth bland dish. It can be made in advance and
reheated in a low oven; add the croûtons just before serving.

1½ lb/675 g dried salt cod
  (bacalao)
1 pint/600 ml milk
½ onion
2 cloves
½ bay leaf
3 oz/75 g butter

4 tablespoons flour
sea salt and black pepper
2 slices dry white bread, crusts
  removed
2 tablespoons light oil
½ clove garlic (optional)

Soak the salt cod for 1–2 days, changing the water night and morning.
Cover with fresh cold water and bring to the boil. Simmer very gently,
covered, for 10 minutes, then turn off the heat and leave for another 10
minutes. Drain, and when it is cool enough to handle, remove all the
skin and bones and purée in a food processor.

Put the milk in a small pan with the onion, cloves and bay leaf.
Bring to the boil, turn off the heat, cover the pan and stand for 20
minutes, then pour through a strainer. Melt the butter, add the flour
and stir for 2 minutes. Pour on the flavoured milk and blend. Simmer
for 3 minutes, stirring, and add black pepper to taste; do not add salt
yet. Pour the sauce onto the fish in the food processor and blend till
smooth. Taste, and add salt if needed.

Spoon into a shallow dish and surround with croûtons, made by
cutting each slice of bread into 4 triangles and frying till golden on
both sides in oil. After frying, rub on both sides with a cut clove of
garlic, or not as preferred. Serves 4 as a first course, or a light main
dish with a green salad.

CROQUETTES OF BACALAO   Spain

These little croquettes are good served with a tomato sauce, or as a
snack with cocktails. They are also surprisingly good cold, for picnics.

1 lb/450 g dried salt cod
  (bacalao)
approx. ¾ lb/350 g potatoes
sea salt and black pepper

2 egg yolks
flour
frying oil and butter (optional)

Soak the salt cod for 1–2 days, changing the water night and morning. Cover with fresh cold water, bring to the boil, and simmer very gently for 10 minutes, covered. Then turn off the heat and leave for another 10 minutes. Drain. When cool, remove all skin and bones and purée in a food processor.

Weigh the resulting purée, and mix with an equal amount of freshly mashed potato, adding salt and pepper to taste. Beat in the egg yolks and form into small rolls, like the corks of wine bottles. Roll in flour and fry (in a frying pan) till golden on all sides. The Spaniards would use oil for this, but I like to use a mixture of butter and oil, roughly half and half. Makes about 16 croquettes; serves 4. Serve with a tomato or chilli sauce, or ketchup.

FRIED SQUID (CALAMAR)   Turkey, Greece, Italy

This is a popular hors d'oeuvre, especially in Turkey where it is often served cold. It is very much better when served hot, immediately after cooking, as is done in Italy.

1 lb/450 g small squid
seasoned flour

frying oil
2–3 lemons

Clean the squid as usual (see risotto alla pescara, page 189), and dry very thoroughly. Cut the bodies in rings ½ inch/1 cm wide, and divide the bunch of tentacles in half, or divide into singles if they are large. Dip them in seasoned flour and drop into deep hot oil. They will only take about 1 minute to become crisp and golden; drain on soft paper while you fry the rest. Transfer to a hot dish and serve with lemon wedges. Serves 3 as a first course, or 4 with one or two other dishes.

CALAMARI RIPIENE   Italy

This most delicious dish is made with small squid, stuffed and simmered in a sauce of tomatoes and white wine. This recipe comes from Genoa, but there are many similar versions from other parts of Italy, Provence and Spain.

8 small squid, about 4 inches/10 cm long in the body
3 medium onions
2 carrots
2 stalks celery
3 tablespoons olive oil
2 oz/50 g butter
1 clove garlic, minced
4 rashers back bacon, smoked (raw smoked ham in Italy, France or Spain)

2 tablespoons chopped parsley
1 tablespoon chopped basil
1 oz/25 g white bread, crusts removed
¼ pint/150 ml hot milk
sea salt and black pepper
1 egg yolk
½ lb/225 g tomatoes, skinned and chopped
6 fl. oz/175 ml white wine

Clean the squid as usual (see risotto alla pescara, page 189), and chop the tentacles. Chop 2 of the onions, the carrots and the celery to a fine hash – quickly done in a food processor – and brown in 2 tablespoons of the olive oil and 1½ oz/40 g of the butter in a sauté pan, adding the minced garlic. Chop the bacon quite finely and add to the pan with the chopped tentacles. Continue to cook gently for 4–5 minutes, stirring often, adding the chopped herbs at the end of the cooking.

Soak the bread for 10 minutes in the hot milk, then squeeze dry and add to the pan. Mix very well with the rest of the stuffing, pounding and mashing it with the back of a wooden spoon. Beat in the egg yolk. Stuff the bodies of the squid with the mixture, using a small teaspoon so as not to tear the opening. Do not fill them more than three-quarters full, then secure the opening with a wooden toothpick. Heat the remaining tablespoon of oil and ½ oz/15 g of butter in the clean sauté pan and cook the last onion, finely chopped, until it starts to brown. Add the stuffed squid, sprinkle with sea salt and black pepper, and cover with the chopped tomatoes and wine. Cover and simmer for 35 minutes. Serves 4, as a first course or a light main course. If serving as a main course, you can accompany it with steamed or boiled potatoes and a green salad.

CALAMAR SALAD Greece, Turkey

This dish of squid with garlic, olive oil and lemon juice might be found in a number of countries along the north shore of the Mediterranean.

1 lb/450 g small squid	black pepper
1 small onion	1 tablespoon lemon juice
4 tablespoons olive oil	1 tablespoon finely chopped
2 tablespoons water	parsley
2 cloves garlic, crushed	

Clean the squid as described for *risotto alla pescara*, page 189. Cut the sacs in rings about ¼ inch/5 mm wide, and divide the tentacles into pairs or singles, depending on size, cutting them in half if they are very long. Chop the onion finely and cook in 3 tablespoons of the olive oil until it starts to colour. Add the squid and fry gently for 5 minutes, stirring often. Then add the 2 tablespoons of water and the crushed garlic, cover the pan, and stew gently until the squid are tender, probably 5–10 minutes. Cool in the pan, then lift with a slotted spoon onto a dish and stir in the remaining tablespoon of oil, the black pepper, lemon juice and chopped parsley. Serves 3–4 with other dishes. Do not chill.

CHANQUETES, GIANCHETTI, BIANCHETTI Spain, Italy

The minute *chanquetes* are a speciality of Malaga, in southern Spain, but are also popular in Barcelona where I saw them in the fish market. There they made an unforgettable sight since they are totally transparent, except for their beady black eyes. From a distance they looked like a huge pile of caviare, or a vast grey jellyfish. I ate them in a small restaurant built over the sea outside Malaga and found them delicious. They are cooked exactly like whitebait, dipped whole in seasoned flour and fried in hot oil until golden, then served with lemons.

Although the name is so similar, the *gianchetti* or *bianchetti* of Genoa are larval sardines, as opposed to the Spanish *chanquetes* which are transparent gobies. In Genoa, they are often served boiled instead of fried, with lemons.

COUSCOUS AU POISSON   Tunisia

Fish with couscous is an unusual combination, but good once you become accustomed to the idea. It is a speciality of Tunisia, although there is one town on the Atlantic coast of Morocco which also makes it. The flavourings are slightly different from those of the meat couscous − saffron replaces the harissa, coriander and cumin. This recipe is a Jewish one, therefore slightly more complicated than others, since the Jews tend to add small balls of fish or meat to their couscous, according to the main ingredient. These can be omitted if preferred.

1 grey mullet, bream or bass
   weighing approx.
   3 lb/1·35 kg, with head cut off
   but included, and the body
   cut in 6 thick slices, or 1 per
   person
3 medium onions
⅓ pint/200 ml olive oil
2 stalks celery
½ lb/225 g small turnips
½ lb/225 g small carrots
sea salt and black pepper
2 bunches large spring onions,
   or ¼ lb/100 g pickling onions
½ lb/225 g small courgettes
2 packets saffron
½ lb/225 g tomatoes
1 lb/450 g peas (in pod)

couscous:
1 lb/450 g couscous
1 pint/600 ml water
2 teaspoons olive oil
1 oz/25 g butter
sea salt and black pepper
a little ground cinnamon

fishballs:
1 lb/450 g hake, whiting or
   other white fish
1 medium onion, chopped
2 stalks parsley, chopped
1 large clove garlic, minced
1½ oz/40 g white bread, crusts
   removed
1 egg
sea salt and black pepper

Make a stock with the fish heads and vegetable trimmings. Strain and measure. Cut the 3 medium onions into eighths and cook in the oil in the bottom of a couscousière, or any deep stock pot. After a little, add the celery cut in chunks, the quartered turnips and the carrots cut in quarters lengthwise. A few minutes later, add the fish stock made up to 3½ pints/2 litres with hot water, sea salt and black pepper. Bring to the boil and lower the heat so that it simmers.

Put the couscous in a bowl and pour over the 1 pint/600 ml cold water. Leave for 10 minutes, then pour off any water that has not been absorbed. Rub the couscous between the fingers, breaking up any lumps, and sprinkling with the oil, then tip about a third of it into the top part of the couscousière, or a strainer lined with muslin that fits nicely inside the stock pot without touching the liquid below. Lay over the vegetables cooking in their stock and increase the heat so that it boils steadily. Cover and leave for 10 minutes, until the steam has penetrated the couscous, then add half of the remaining couscous. Cook for another 10 minutes, then add the remainder.

At this point the spring onions (or whole peeled pickling onions), courgettes cut in thick chunks and the saffron are added to the pot. After another 15 minutes, add the skinned and quartered tomatoes and the shelled green peas. (The stock must boil steadily at all times or the couscous will be heavy; the level of the liquid must be watched, and extra boiling water added if necessary.) Now add the pieces of fish, lower the heat slightly, and simmer for about 12–14 minutes, until they are cooked.

(If fishballs are being served, they should be made in advance: scrape the fish away from the skin and chop. Put in a food processor with the chopped onion, chopped parsley, minced garlic, and the bread which has been soaked in water for 10 minutes and squeezed dry. Process to a smooth purée, then add the egg, sea salt and black pepper, and process again. Chill for an hour or two to firm, then form into small round balls, and poach for 5 minutes in simmering water, or fish stock.)

To serve: tip the couscous into a large bowl and break up any lumps with a wooden spoon; stir in the butter cut in small bits, and a little salt and pepper. Pile onto a large shallow dish and sprinkle with ground cinnamon. Lift out the pieces of fish and lay on a separate dish. Lift out the vegetables and lay on top of the couscous. Pour the sauce into a tureen and serve the fishballs on a separate dish. I am not sure whether it is correct to serve a hot sauce with a fish couscous, but I usually do anyway. See page 247 for the recipe. Serves 6. In Tunisia, at least double the amount of couscous would be cooked for 6 people, but I find English tastes are more moderate.

FRITTO MISTO   Italy

This dish exists, with slight variations, up and down both Italian coasts. Basically a mixture of fish fried in deep oil, it usually consists of small red mullet, prawns in their shells and squid cut in rings. Fresh sardines or anchovies are sometimes included, as also are strips of flat white fish like sole. The fish are sometimes dipped in well-seasoned flour and sometimes in batter and fried, each group separately, in deep hot oil. They must be served immediately, golden brown and very crisp, piled on a flat dish and accompanied by cut lemons.

4 small red mullet, or 1 per
  person
12 large prawns, unshelled
¾ lb/350 g small squid, cleaned
  and cut in rings
seasoned flour or frying batter
  (see scampi fritti)

frying oil
2–3 lemons

optional extras:
½ lb/225 g small sardines or
  anchovies
¾ lb/350 g sole, filleted and cut
  in strips

Leave the mullet whole, the prawns in their shells, and the squid cleaned as usual (see page 189) and cut in rings ½ inch/1 cm wide. The cluster of tentacles can be left whole, cut in half, or divided into singles according to size. Have the oil heated to about 180°C/360°F, and only dip the fish in the flour or batter just before frying. Cook the largest fish first, in this case the red mullet, allowing 3–5 minutes depending on size, then drain on soft paper and transfer to a hot dish. The prawns will take 2 minutes, and the squid only about 1½ if really small. The sardines and anchovies must be timed according to size, while the strips of sole will only take 2 minutes. Serves 4, or 6 with extras.

GAMBAS, SCAMPI   Spain, Italy

These large prawns are much prized all round the Mediterranean, but especially in Spain and Italy. In Spain they are usually served cold with mayonnaise, after boiling in their shells; they are also fried with garlic. In Italy they are usually fried, either in batter or simply in flour, or grilled on skewers, still in their shells. I have also eaten them in Venice simply boiled, after shelling, and served hot with lemons. The recipes which follow are for uncooked prawns, which can be bought frozen; prawns which are already cooked (i.e. pink) would only become tough and dry if submitted to a second cooking. They are best served cold, or gently reheated.

GAMBAS WITH MAYONNAISE   Spain

1–1½ lb/450–675 g large
   prawns, or scampi tails
salt

1 bay leaf
mayonnaise
2 lemons, quartered

Leave the prawns in their shells; wash and drain. Bring a pan of water to the boil with quite a lot of salt (use sea water whenever possible) and a bay leaf. Drop in the prawns and cook for 6 minutes; drain and cool. Serve after cooling – do not chill – with home-made mayonnaise and cut lemons. Serves 4 as a first course.

GAMBAS AL AJILLO   Spain

3 cloves garlic
4 tablespoons olive oil
1 lb/450 g shelled prawns,
   preferably uncooked

sea salt and black pepper
2 tablespoons finely chopped
   parsley

Chop the garlic very finely. Heat the oil in a heavy pan, add the garlic and cook very gently, watching like a hawk to see it doesn't burn. As soon as it starts to colour, after about 2 minutes, add the shelled prawns and cook gently for 5–6 minutes. Stir them frequently, still watching the garlic to prevent burning. As soon as the prawns are cooked, add sea salt and black pepper and stir in the chopped parsley. Serve immediately, either with bread and butter as a first course, or with boiled rice and a green salad as a light main dish. Serves 2–3. (If using cooked prawns, only cook them long enough to reheat, about 2 minutes.)

SCAMPI BOLLITI   Italy

1½–2 lb/675–900 g large
   prawns, uncooked
salt

1 bay leaf
2–3 lemons, cut in quarters

Shell the prawns and drop into a pan of boiling salted water (or sea water) with a bay leaf in it. Simmer for 3 minutes, then drain. Serve immediately, with cut lemons. Serves 4 as a first course or a light main dish. If serving as a main dish, accompany with a green salad.

SCAMPI FRITTI   Italy

1–1½ lb/450–675 g scampi
  (Dublin Bay prawns),
  uncooked
batter:
3 oz/40 g flour
a pinch of salt

1 tablespoon light oil
¼ pint/150 ml water
1 egg white
frying oil
2–3 lemons

Wash the scampi and pat dry. Carefully remove the heads (if any) and shells, leaving the tail still attached to the body. Make the batter an hour in advance. Put flour, salt and oil in a food processor and add the water through the lid while processing. Leave for 1 hour, then process again, tip into a bowl, and fold in the beaten egg white. Dip each prawn in this, shaking off any excess, and drop into a pan of hot oil. Fry for 4 minutes, then drain on paper, transfer to a hot dish, and keep warm while you fry the rest. Serve immediately with lots of cut lemons. Serves 4 as a first course.

SCAMPI ALLA GRIGLIA   Italy

1–1½ lb/450–675 g giant
  prawns, heads removed, or
  scampi tails, uncooked
5 tablespoons olive oil
2–4 tablespoons lemon juice

sea salt and black pepper
2 tablespoons chopped herbs:
  fennel, dill, chervil, parsley
2–3 lemons, cut in quarters

Wash the prawns, still in their shells, and pat dry. Thread onto skewers, one for each person, and lay on a flat dish. Mix the oil and lemon juice, beating well, add sea salt and black pepper to taste, and pour over them. Leave for 1 hour to marinate, turning once or twice. Grill gently, allowing 3–4 minutes on each side, basting frequently with the marinade. Lay the skewers on a flat dish, discard the basting juices and sprinkle with the chopped herbs. Serve with cut lemons. Serves 4–5 as a first course, or 3–4 as a main course. If serving as a main course, accompany with a lettuce and tomato salad.

GRILLED MEDITERRANEAN FISH

This to me sums up everything I most love about Mediterranean cooking. It is utterly delicious, healthy and simple, and appeals to the senses of smell and sight as well as that of taste. It encompasses the whole range of fish, from the costly lobster to the common mackerel. It is served, sometimes with pretension, in the grandest restaurants, but I like it best of all in the small fish restaurants one so often finds built out over the water near the fishing harbour in Mediterranean towns. Since it needs no other accompaniment than bread and salad, and sometimes a mayonnaise to eat with the cold shellfish, it is ideally suited to these unpretentious and sympathetic places. In one such restaurant on the outskirts of Malaga I ate fried *chanquetes*, a local speciality, followed by cold *gambas* with mayonnaise, and a most excellent salad of lettuce and tomato. In a small wooden shack in a fishing village on the outskirts of Genoa I had a grilled sole and a *dentex*, and on a second visit, some *moscardini fritti*. These are a speciality of Genoa, tiny octopi no bigger than large spiders, the body exactly the same size as my thumb nail. In a similar restaurant on the Bosphorus, I ate my first blue fish, grilled as usual, and with a mixed Turkish salad.

Some of the finest fish for grilling are the bass and breams; these include the *loup* and *daurade* of France, and the *denté*, *sar*, *pagre*, *pageot* and *marbre*, for the bream is a large family of fish. Another fish that is ideal for grilling, although I have never quite understood its very high reputation, is the red mullet. When very fresh indeed, mackerel and sardines are surprisingly good too. The treatment of the various fish is similar, with slight variations. With the exception of the red mullet, which is never cleaned but simply scaled, they are cleaned as usual, sprinkled with salt and pepper and rubbed with oil, or with the oil and lemon sauce on page 248. They are sometimes stuffed with herbs: branches of fennel, sprigs of thyme, rosemary, parsley, chervil or tarragon, and two or three diagonal cuts are made in each side, except in the case of the red mullet. They are then laid on a grill over burning wood or charcoal and basted while cooking with more oil, or oil and lemon sauce; sometimes a branch of thyme is used as a brush. After cooking, they are laid on a dish and garnished with cut lemons, or the oil and lemon sauce mentioned above. Some fish, in particular the bass and the *daurade*, are flambéd with fennel just before serving. This is done by laying dried branches of fennel on the fire when they are almost ready to eat so that they finish their cooking in the perfumed flames and smoke of the fennel. When ready to serve, the skin should be slightly charred and blackened, with the tender white flesh just ready to come away from the bone. There is a current fashion in France for serving fish undercooked, with the flesh still tinged with pink around the bone, but this I find abhorrent.

FISH PLAKI   Greece

Apart from grilling, this is the most usual way of cooking fish in Greece. It can be served hot or cold, as a first course or as a main dish. It needs no accompaniment, although if serving as a main course, you can have some plain boiled potatoes and a green salad with it.

2 medium onions, halved and
    sliced
3 tablespoons olive oil
1 carrot, halved and sliced
1 stalk celery, sliced
2 cloves garlic, crushed
¼ pint/150 ml water
sea salt and black pepper

2 tomatoes, skinned and
    chopped
¼ pint/150 ml dry white wine
2 lb/900 g bass, halibut, or
    other firm white fish, cut in
    steaks
2 tablespoons chopped parsley

Cook the sliced onions in the oil until they start to colour, then add the carrot and celery. Cook gently for 6–8 minutes, then add the crushed garlic and ¼ pint/150 ml water. Add sea salt and black pepper and cover the pan; simmer for 10 minutes, then add the chopped tomatoes and cook gently for another 4 minutes. Pour in the wine and leave to cool.

Lay the fish steaks in a buttered ovenproof dish. Spoon the sauce over them, cover with foil, and bake for 30–35 minutes at 180°C/350°F/Gas Mark 4, or until the fish flakes easily from the bone. If serving hot, allow to cool slightly (for about 15 minutes), before sprinkling with chopped parsley and serving. Alternatively, allow to cool completely, sprinkle with parsley and serve at room temperature; never chill. Serves 4–6.

INSALATA DI MARE   Italy

This is a popular seafood dish up and down both Italian coasts; the ingredients vary according to what is in season at the time.

½ lb/225 g small clams or 6 large clams	4 tablespoons olive oil
½ lb/225 g small mussels	1 clove garlic, minced
½ lb/225 g prawns or shrimps, unshelled	¾ lb/350 g small squid
4 scallops	sea salt and black pepper
1 small onion	2 tablespoons very finely chopped parsley
	2 lemons, cut in quarters

Steam the clams in a heavy pan, covered, with 2 tablespoons water until they open. Remove the clams and strain the juice. Do the same with the mussels. Shell the prawns or shrimps and make a small amount of stock by simmering the shells for 20 minutes in lightly salted water; strain. Put the prawn stock in a pan with the clam and mussel juice and bring to the boil. Drop in the cleaned scallops and poach gently for 8 minutes. Drain and cool.

Chop the onion finely and cook in half the oil in a sauté pan until it starts to colour; add the minced garlic, and the squid which have been cut in ¼-inch/5-mm rings, and the tentacles in 1-inch/2·5-cm lengths. Fry gently, stirring now and then, for 5 minutes, then add 2 tablespoons water, cover the pan, and cook for another 5–10 minutes, until the squid are tender. Tip into a serving dish and cool. If the clams are very small, leave them in their shells, otherwise take them out and chop them. Do the same with the mussels; if both are tiny, shell half and leave half of each still in their shells. Mix with the squid. Slice or chop the scallops and add also, including the coral tongues or not as you wish. Stir into the salad, adding sea salt and black pepper, 2 more tablespoons olive oil, and some very finely chopped parsley. Serve with lemon quarters; serves 4 as a first course.

TURKISH STUFFED MACKEREL   **Turkey**

This curious dish is a speciality of Istanbul, and I found a recipe for it in an old Turkish cookery book. It is not easy to do, since it involves taking the flesh and bones out of a mackerel without splitting the skin. I made it once for the sake of interest, and found the stuffing so delicious that I have made it several times since as a dish in its own right. I give both versions here.

2 mackerel weighing about
  ½ lb/225 g each
1 medium onion
1½ tablespoons olive oil
1 oz/25 g coarsely chopped
  almonds
½ tablespoon currants
sea salt and black pepper
a pinch of allspice
2 tablespoons chopped parsley

for version I:
seasoned flour
1 egg, beaten
fine breadcrumbs
frying oil
2 lemons

for version II:
juice of ½ lemon

version I:
Ask the fishmonger to cut off the heads of the mackerel quite low down and to clean them through the neck, without splitting the skin. Have the tails cut off also. When you get home, bang them down hard several times on the table, turning them round as you do so. This helps to loosen the bones from the skin. Then, using a small knife – a grapefruit knife is ideal since it curves inward – separate the flesh from the skin all around and gently slip out the interior of the fish through the neck. Use the knife to clean out the skin, which can be turned inside out. Remove any bones still clinging to it, and wash it well inside and out. Cut the flesh off the bones and chop it quite finely. Chop the onion and cook gently in the oil until pale golden. Add the chopped fish, the nuts and currants, adding sea salt, black pepper and allspice. Stir round for 5 minutes, cooking gently. At the end of the cooking, stir in the chopped parsley and stuff the mixture back into the fish skins, using the handle of a wooden spoon to push it well down into the tail. Dip each fish in seasoned flour, then in beaten egg and in dry breadcrumbs. Fry until golden on each side in shallow oil. Serve hot as an hors d'oeuvre, cut in thick slices. Garnish with quartered lemons. Serves 4.

version II:
The same ingredients as above, except for those involved in the final frying. Ask the fishmonger to fillet the fish, then skin them yourself and chop the flesh. Cook the chopped onion in the oil till golden, then add the fish, nuts, currants, sea salt, black pepper and allspice. Cook gently for 5 minutes stirring almost constantly, then stir in the chopped parsley and turn into a shallow serving dish. Leave to cool and sprinkle with lemon juice before serving. Serve at room temperature, as an hors d'oeuvre. Serves 3–4 alone, or 5–6 with other dishes.

MARINATED FISH   Italy

This recipe comes from the Gulf of Naples, and provides a useful way of using up left-over fried fish, or preparing fresh fish a day in advance. In Italy it is normally made with small whole fish or squid, but in England I often make it with fillets of plaice or lemon sole, cut in strips about 1 by 2 inches/2 by 5 cm.

fish:
*small whole fish, either small
    red mullet, small sardines,
    sprats, anchovies or
    whitebait or
squid cut in rings or
fillets of larger fish, skinned
    and cut in strips*

*seasoned flour
frying oil
white wine vinegar, enough to
    cover fish
chopped mint, roughly 3
    tablespoons per
    ½ pint/300 ml vinegar*

Dip the fish in well-seasoned flour and drop, one sort at a time, into deep hot oil. Fry until golden brown and cooked through. (Small whole fish will take from 2–5 minutes depending on size, rings of small squid 1½ minutes, and strips of filleted white fish about 2 minutes.) Take out each batch as it is done and drain on soft paper, then transfer to a china dish with straight sides, such as a soufflé dish. When all are cooked, pour over enough vinegar to just cover, and stir in the chopped mint. Leave in a cool place, or the bottom of the refrigerator, for 24 hours. Serve at room temperature, as an hors d'oeuvre, alone or with other dishes.

FRIED MUSSELS   Turkey

The Mediterranean countries do not observe seasons for mussels as we do in England, and continue to eat them all year round. The most usual way of eating them in Turkey is taken out of their shells, dipped in batter and deep fried. The Turks are very skilled at opening the raw mussel shells, which I find impossible, so I steam them briefly first.

2 lb/900 g large mussels	*1 tablespoon olive oil*
batter:	*¼ pint/150 ml water*
3 oz/75 g flour	*1 egg white*
a pinch of salt	*2–3 lemons*

After cleaning, steam the mussels with 3 tablespoons of water in a heavy pan only until they start to open, about 3 minutes. When cool enough to handle, take them out of their shells. Make the batter an hour in advance. Put the flour, salt and oil in a food processor and add the water through the lid while processing. Just before using, beat the egg white and fold into the batter. Dip the mussels in this, shaking off any excess, then drop into a large pan of hot oil. Cook 3–4 minutes only, turning once. Lift out and drain while you cook the next batch; do not crowd them. Keep hot, and serve on a flat dish with lots of cut lemons. Serves 4.

STUFFED MUSSELS   Turkey

This spectacular and delicious dish is very lengthy to prepare, since I find myself unable to open raw mussels, as the Turks do habitually. This failing on my part involves me in first steaming the mussels; once opened, the shells refuse to close unless I bind them shut with a twist of aluminium foil. I give the recipe for those with time on their hands.

24 large mussels	*sea salt and black pepper*
1 small onion	*a pinch of allspice*
2 tablespoons olive oil	*¼ teaspoon sugar*
1 oz/25 g rice	*¼ pint/150 ml boiling water*
1 tablespoon currants	*2 lemons, quartered*
1 tablespoon pine nuts	

Clean the mussels well. Open by steaming for 2 minutes only with ¼ pint/150 ml water in a heavy lidded pan. Chop the onion and fry in the oil until golden. Add the rice and stir around for a moment, then add the currants and pine nuts. Cook for a couple of moments, then add the seasonings and ¼ pint/150 ml boiling water. Cook for 15 minutes covered, till the liquid is absorbed. Leave to cool.

Open the mussels without separating the shells. Spoon some of the stuffing over the mussel in its half shell, then close the shell and bind with a twisted piece of foil. Lay the stuffed mussels in layers in a broad heavy pan. Measure the mussel stock and make up to ½ pint/300 ml with water; pour over the mussels. Cover the pot and steam for 45 minutes. Leave to cool.

To serve, pile the mussels on a dish and surround with lemon quarters. Do not chill. Serves 4 as a first course, alone or with other dishes.

PICKLED FISH   Turkey

This recipe comes from an old Turkish cookery book, written a hundred years ago, and was intended for pickling swordfish. Salmon or mackerel are suggested as alternatives; I made it with halibut steaks and it was excellent.

4–6 halibut steaks, 2–2½ lb/900 g–1·15 kg	1 tablespoon sugar 4 cloves garlic
sea salt	6 bay leaves
2 tablespoons olive oil	½ teaspoon mixed spice, or
1 pint/600 ml white wine vinegar	allspice 2 teaspoons black peppercorns

1 packet saffron, soaked in 3
  tablespoons water
	1 oz/25 g shelled pistachios
	  (2½ oz/65 g unshelled)

Wash and pat dry the fish steaks, which should be about ¾ inch/2 cm thick. Sprinkle them with sea salt. Heat the oil in a frying pan and cook the steaks quickly, until lightly browned without being cooked through. Remove the fish and leave to cool. Put the vinegar in a pan with the saffron water and the sugar. Bring to the boil, stirring, and cook for 3 minutes, or till the sugar has melted. Peel the garlic and chop coarsely. Lay half the bay leaves in the bottom of a stoneware jar, or porcelain dish with a lid. Lay some of the fish on them and sprinkle with half the garlic, spice, peppercorns and shelled halved pistachios. Add more bay leaves, another layer of fish and the remaining spices. Pour over the vinegar: there should be just enough to cover the fish. Press down – not too much – with a weight on a small plate. Cover the jar and leave in a cool place for 3 days before eating. Eat within the week; it will keep longer, but the flavour deteriorates. Serves 4–6 as a first course, or more with other dishes. (The steaks can be divided in pieces.)

SARDE EN SAOR   Italy

This is a popular Venetian dish which makes a good first course for lunch or dinner. It must be made a day in advance.

2 lb/900 g fresh sardines	4 tablespoons olive oil
seasoned flour	sea salt and black pepper
frying oil	½ pint/300 ml white wine
1¼–1½ lb/600 g onions	vinegar

Cut the heads and tails off the sardines and dip them in the seasoned flour. Have a pan of deep oil heated to about 180°C/360°F, or till a small cube of bread starts to sizzle instantly on being dropped in. Lower in the sardines, a few at a time, so that they can float freely, and cook for about 4–6 minutes, depending on size. Turn them over once during the cooking, and test one if in doubt to see if they are cooked. Drain them on soft paper, then lay them in a shallow dish, preferably a round one in brown earthenware, arranging them in a circle like the spokes of a wheel. Slice the onions and cook very slowly in the olive oil in a sauté pan, allowing at least 30 minutes for them to soften, without allowing them to brown. Lift them out with a slotted spoon, draining off any remaining oil, and spread over the sardines. Sprinkle with sea salt and black pepper, pour the vinegar over all, and leave for 24 hours in a cool place. Serve as a first course, with French bread. If there are any left, add some more vinegar and leave till the next day. Serves 5–6.

SAYADIEH

This Middle Eastern dish consists of rice cooked in fish broth flavoured with onions, with fillets of white fish laid on it, garnished with pine kernels.

2 lb/900 g firm white fish fillets:
  halibut, bass, haddock or cod
salt
¾ lb/350 g onions
4 tablespoons olive oil
1¾ pints/1 litre water

½ teaspoon ground cumin
¾ lb/350 g long grain rice
2 tablespoons pine kernels
1 tablespoon sunflower seed oil
juice of ½ lemon

Sprinkle the fish with salt and chill for 1 hour in the refrigerator. Rinse under cold water, skin the fillets and cut in large pieces. Chop the onions and cook in the olive oil in a large pan until golden. Add 1¾ pints/1 litre water, salt and ground cumin. Bring to the boil and simmer for 15 minutes. Add the fish and bring back to the boil. Simmer 8–10 minutes, or until the fish is cooked. Lift out the fish and keep warm. Take 1¼ pints/750 ml of the onion/fish stock and pour into a clean pan. Bring to the boil, add the rice and cook till tender, covered. When the rice is soft and the stock absorbed, spoon it into a shallow dish and lay the fish over it. Toss the pine kernels in the sunflower seed oil till pale golden and scatter over the fish. Heat the remaining stock – there will probably be about ½ pint/300 ml; if more, reduce by fast boiling – and add lemon juice to taste. Serve in a small jug with the fish. Serves 6.

6

POULTRY AND GAME

Poultry and game play an important part in the diet of the Mediterranean countries, especially the poorer ones, for they are one of the few available sources of animal food. The general shortage of meat, due to the aridity and lack of pasture lands, gives game of all sorts a special importance. Not only chicken, but pigeons and other small birds are popular, particularly in Italy, Greece, Egypt and Morocco, where one of the national dishes is a sort of pie filled with pigeons, called *pastella*. Mediterranean chickens also have more flavour than the pallid English birds; in Tuscany and other parts of northern Italy they are corn-fed, and almost as bright yellow as the polenta that so often accompanies them. In Greece they may look stringy and unimpressive but they are full of flavour, while in the Middle Eastern countries they also belie their appearance. Throughout the countries of the Mahgreb they are eaten with *couscous*, either alone or mixed with lamb.

Rabbits are widely eaten, especially in Spain, France, Italy and Greece. These are often bred at home and kept in small hutches until they are killed for the pot, much to the distress of the children in the family. Mediterranean ways with rabbit succeeded in converting me to what I had previously considered a boring food. In the south of France particularly I grew to love the dishes of rabbit cooked in a pale creamy sauce with mustard and wild herbs. In Italy it is also well cooked, while a Greek dish called *stifado* is one of my favourites. Somewhat like a chicken marengo, the rabbit is cooked in a mixture of white wine, stock and tomato purée, and garnished with lots of tiny onions and fried bread croûtons.

Few Anglo-Saxons would consider game as typical of the Mediterranean, but this is because we connect these lands mainly with summer holidays. No sooner have the summer visitors left, and the first signs of autumn approach, than game starts to make its appearance in the markets. By late autumn the game stalls are among the most colourful and interesting. In Tuscany, game is highly valued: wild boar is prized, hare is eaten in many forms including a sauce for tagliatelle, and pheasants and pigeons abound. Further north, as we approach Piedmont, the chamois and the roe deer are highly esteemed. In Trieste, which was long part of the Austro-Hungarian empire, and in Yugoslavia, whose cooking is closer to the central European traditions than the Mediterranean, roe deer, venison and wild boar are widely popular. In Venice I have seen smoked leg of wild boar for sale, still with trotter and bristles, but at a price I could ill afford, even in the interests of gastronomy.

Small birds have for centuries been one of the favourite foods of the Egyptians, and they cook them to perfection, subtly flavoured with herbs and spices. These small birds are somehow typical of the austere Mediterranean landscape, just as the fat ducks and goese, with their over-extended livers, represent the rich lands of the north: France, Germany and Belgium.

ARROZ CON POLLO I   Spain

There are two different ways of making this well-known Spanish dish, and both are good. In the first, the chicken is poached and the rice cooked in its stock. In the second, the chicken is fried and cooked with the rice in water, like a paella.

2½ lb/1·15 kg chicken, jointed	seasoned flour
1 large onion, halved	3 tablespoons olive oil
1 carrot	1 green pepper, cut in strips
1 stalk celery	2 tomatoes, skinned and
2 stalks parsley	chopped
sea salt and black pepper	½ lb/225 g risotto rice, Spanish
1 packet saffron	or Italian, washed
1¼ pints/750 ml hot water	2 oz/50 g shelled peas

Poach the jointed chicken with half the onion, the carrot, celery, parsley, sea salt, black pepper and saffron in the 1¼ pints/750 ml of hot water. Bring to the boil, lower the heat and simmer for 30 minutes, taking out the white meat 5 minutes before the time is up. Strain the stock; you will need about 1 pint/600 ml, so make up with water if necessary.

Pat the chicken joints dry and dip in the seasoned flour. Heat the oil and fry the chicken until golden; put aside and keep warm. Fry the remaining half onion, chopped, in the same oil till pale golden, then the pepper, cut in strips. Cook for 5 minutes, then add the chopped tomatoes. After 2 minutes add the rice and cook for 3 minutes, stirring often. Add the reheated stock with the peas, bring to the boil, reduce the heat and simmer gently for 10 minutes. Lay the chicken pieces on top of the rice and continue to cook slowly for another 20 minutes; do not stir again. Serves 4.

ARROZ CON POLLO II   Spain

4 tablespoons olive oil
2½ lb/1·15 kg chicken, jointed
½ large onion, chopped
1 clove garlic, finely chopped
1 red pepper, cut in small
  strips
½ lb/225 g tomatoes, skinned
  and chopped

sea salt and black pepper
1 teaspoon paprika
½ lb/225 g risotto rice, Spanish
  or Italian, washed
1 pint/600 ml boiling water
1 packet saffron
¼ lb/100 g shelled peas

Heat the oil in a sauté pan with a lid and brown the chicken joints. Remove and keep warm. Chop the onion and cook in the same oil, adding the chopped garlic, red pepper and tomatoes, allowing 5 minutes for each before adding the rest. Add sea salt, black pepper and paprika, then stir in the rice and cook for 2 minutes, stirring. Pour on the boiling water, add the saffron and bring to the boil. Add the chicken and shelled peas (unless using frozen peas) and simmer for 30 minutes, covered, until the chicken and rice are cooked and the water all absorbed. If using frozen peas, add 5 minutes before the end. Serves 4.

CIRCASSIAN CHICKEN   Turkey

This recipe for a well-known Turkish dish was given to me by the Turkish Ambassadress in Tunis. Its bland flavour and smooth consistency may seem strange at first to European palates, but it is much loved in the Middle East.

1 roasting chicken
1 medium onion, halved
3 stalks parsley
sea salt
4 slices dry white bread, crusts removed

½ lb/225 g shelled walnuts
1 clove garlic, crushed (optional)
½ teaspoon paprika
5 tablespoons light oil (sunflower seed or peanut)

Put the chicken in a pan with the halved onion and the parsley. Barely cover with water, adding sea salt. Bring to the boil and simmer for 1 hour, or until tender. Lift out and strain the broth. Carve the chicken, discarding all skin and bone, and cut in neat pieces. Lay in a shallow dish. Tear the bread in small pieces and put in the food processor or blender. Reduce to crumbs, then add the shelled nuts and the garlic, if used. (This was not in the original recipe but I find it makes the sauce more appealing to Europeans; it is sometimes included in Turkey.) Process again, then add enough of the strained stock to make a sauce like thin cream, adding a little more salt if necessary. Pour over the chicken. Mix the paprika with the oil and dribble over the surface of the dish. This is usually served warm, as an hors d'oeuvre. Serves 6 as a first course, or 4 as a main dish with a green salad.

CHICKEN COUSCOUS   Tunisia

This couscous was made for me by a Tunisian chef but, apart from the choice of spices, it did not seem to me to differ much from a Moroccan couscous. It would be interesting to know how much influence the French had on the cooking of both these countries during their years there; certainly the French grew to love couscous, as can be seen by its presence in so many Parisian restaurants – there is even one on the left bank that serves nothing else.

The choice of vegetables varies according to the season, and personal choice. The Tunisian chef added potatoes, but I prefer to omit these, and three artichokes trimmed down to their fronds. I usually leave these out also since the big ones that are all we can get in England are both expensive and lengthy to trim. I have added tomatoes, which were not in the original.

1 medium roasting chicken,
  jointed
1 teaspoon ground coriander
1½ teaspoons ground cumin
1 teaspoon powdered coeurs de
  roses, when available
½ teaspoon harissa, or chilli
  powder
sea salt and black pepper
1 small tin tomato purée
  (approx. 2 tablespoons)
3 medium onions, cut in
  eighths
⅓ pint/200 ml olive oil, + 2
  teaspoons
¼ pint/150 ml water
1 lb/450 g couscous
1 pint/600 ml water

½ lb/225 g small carrots, cut in
  quarters lengthwise
½ lb/225 g small turnips, cut in
  quarters
½ lb/225 g kohlrabi, when
  available, cut in chunks
½ lh/225 g courgettes, cut in
  chunks
¼ lb/100 g large spring onions,
  or pickling onions
½ lb/225 g tomatoes, skinned
  and cut in quarters
1 lb/450 g peas (in their pods)
1½ oz/40 g butter
ground cinnamon
extra harissa, to taste (optional)

Rub the chicken joints all over with a paste made by mixing the coriander, cumin, coeurs de roses (available from the Herbier de Provence shops), harissa or chilli powder, sea salt and black pepper into the tomato purée. Put the chicken in the bottom of a couscousière or a deep stock pot, with the onions. Mix the ⅓ pint/200 ml olive oil with ¼ pint/150 ml water and pour over them. Bring to the boil and simmer, covered, for 10 minutes.

Meanwhile put the couscous in a bowl and cover with 1 pint/600 ml cold water. Leave for 10 minutes, then stir with a wooden spoon, breaking up any lumps, and sprinkle the 2 teaspoons of olive oil over it, squeezing between the fingers. Tip a third of it into the top part of the couscousière, or into a strainer lined with muslin that will fit inside the stock pot without touching the chicken below. Add the carrots, turnips and kohlrabi to the chicken, with enough boiling water to come level. Bring back to the boil and cover with the couscous, covering with a lid. After about 8 minutes, when the steam has penetrated the couscous, put half the remaining couscous on top of the first lot, and continue cooking. (The contents of the pan must boil quite hard, faster than one would normally cook a chicken, otherwise the couscous will be heavy. For this reason it is important to keep checking that the pot is not boiling dry, and to add more boiling water as needed.) After another 6–8 minutes add the remaining couscous, and put the courgettes, whole spring onions (bulbs only) or pickling onions into the pot below. After another 15 minutes add the tomatoes and the shelled peas; cook for a further 15 minutes.

By now the chicken will have been cooking for about 1 hour, and the grain for some 30–45 minutes, and both should be tender. Tip the *couscous* into a large bowl and break up any lumps, then stir in the butter, sea salt and black pepper. Pile onto a large shallow dish and sprinkle with cinnamon. Lift out the chicken joints and lay on the *couscous* with the vegetables, forming a huge mound. Alternatively, the chicken can be served on a separate dish. The sauce is usually divided into two parts, and some extra *harissa* stirred into one for those who like it. Otherwise it can be served in one bowl, with a little dish of hot sauce (see Sauces, page 247) on the table. Serves 6.

I have modified the amount of *harissa* used; with practice, one learns how much is acceptable to English palates. I have also cut the amount of *couscous* by half, since the Tunisians consume this in huge quantities. For some reason, chick peas were not included in this *couscous*; if you wish to add them, soak them overnight, and add to the chicken and onions at the start of the cooking.

GRILLED CHICKEN WITH AÏOLI   Mallorca

This is the nearest I can get to a most excellent dish of grilled rabbit with *aïoli* which I ate one Sunday in a small restaurant in the hills outside Palma. Try as I may, I cannot grill any rabbit successfully, whether English or imported. Crisp grilled chicken, however, makes a most delicious combination with the velvety *aïoli*.

3–3½ lb/1·5 kg roasting chicken, jointed	*2 tablespoons coarsely chopped flat parsley*
6 tablespoons olive oil	*aïoli (see page 244)*
3 tablespoons lemon juice	*2 lemons, cut in quarters*
sea salt and black pepper	
2 tablespoons chopped spring onions	

Lay the chicken joints in a shallow dish and pour over the oil and lemon juice. Sprinkle with sea salt and black pepper and leave for 1 hour before grilling. Grill gently, allowing about 8–10 minutes on each side, and basting with the marinade. When crisp outside and tender within, lay the joints on a flat dish and sprinkle the chopped onions and parsley over all. Serve with a bowl of *aïoli*, cut lemons, boiled new potatoes, and a lettuce and tomato salad. Serves 4.

MEDITERRANEAN CHICKEN   Greece

This simple chicken dish with a tart sauce is reminiscent of many Greek dishes. Accompanied by braised chicory, it makes a good main dish for a light meal.

1 small chicken,
  3–3¼ lb/1·35 kg
¼ pint/150 ml olive oil
⅛ pint/75 ml lemon juice

sea salt and black pepper
¼ pint/150 ml red wine,
  preferably a Burgundy

Brown the chicken in the oil in a heavy casserole, turning from side to side. Add the lemon juice, cover the pan, and cook gently for 45 minutes, till almost cooked, basting from time to time. Then add sea salt and black pepper and the red wine. Cook quite fast, uncovered, until the gravy has reduced by half and the bird is tender. Serve with braised chicory (see Cooked Vegetable Dishes, page 200). Serves 3–4.

CHICKEN WITH POLENTA   Italy

This chicken dish has a particularly light fresh-tasting sauce, unthickened by flour or any other starch. If preferred, the polenta can be replaced by rice or noodles.

2 lb/900 g tomatoes
2 oz/50 g butter
2 sprigs marjoram, thyme or
  basil
1 teaspoon sugar
1 medium onion
1 tablespoon olive oil
4 lb/1·75 kg roasting chicken,
  jointed

1 medium carrot, halved
1 stalk celery, halved
1 small bay leaf
3 stalks parsley
sea salt and black pepper
½ lb/225 g polenta (coarse
  cornmeal)
2½ pints/1·5 litres water
2 teaspoons salt

Skin the tomatoes and chop roughly, either in the food processor or by hand. Melt half the butter in a broad heavy pan and add the chopped tomatoes and the herbs. Add the sugar and cook gently, uncovered, for about 45 minutes till reduced to a jammy consistency, stirring occasionally. You should have about 10–12 fl. oz/300–350 ml thick purée. Put aside.

Chop the onion and cook in the remaining 1 oz/25 g of butter and the oil until it starts to colour. Add the chicken joints and cook until golden on all sides. Add the halved carrot and celery, the bay leaf and parsley, and some sea salt and black pepper. Pour on enough very hot water to come level with the contents of the pan and simmer gently, covered, for 35 minutes. Lift out the white joints and keep warm; cook the dark meat for a further 10 minutes or until tender. Remove the flavouring vegetables and herbs from the stock and discard them.

Pour the stock into a bowl and allow to cool for a few moments; do not strain. Skim the fat from the surface, and measure ⅓ pint/200 ml. Mix it with the tomato purée in a clean saucepan and stir over gentle heat. Bring to the boil and simmer for 4–5 minutes. Have the polenta already cooked (see Pastry, Rice and Pasta Dishes, page 185), and spooned into a shallow dish. Lay the chicken joints on this, and pour the thick tomato sauce over all. Serves 5–6 with a green salad; no other vegetables are necessary.

CHICKEN SMOUTINA

Greece

This Greek recipe makes a good dish for a summer meal; it is light and fresh in taste.

medium chickens, jointed
–3 lemons
oz/50 g butter
pprox. 2 pints/1·2 litres
  chicken stock

sea salt and black pepper
2 tablespoons flour
¼ pint/150 ml sour cream

Remove the skin from the chicken joints, and rub them with a cut lemon. Either sauté them briefly in the butter, until lightly browned all over, or grill them for 4–5 minutes on each side, basting with the melted butter. Lay the joints in a broad pan and add enough hot stock barely to cover them. Add sea salt and black pepper, bring to the boil, cover the pan and simmer for 35 minutes, or until the joints are tender.

Take them out and cut the flesh off the bones; leave it in quite large pieces, and lay in a shallow dish in a warm place.

Strain the stock and measure 1 pint/600 ml. Stir the flour into the sour cream in a bowl, and add 4 tablespoons of lemon juice, beating until smooth with a wire whisk or electric beater. Add a few spoons of the strained stock, beat till smooth, then return the contents of the bowl to the rest of the measured stock. Stir over moderate heat until slightly thickened and smooth; simmer for 2–3 minutes, stirring often, then pour some of it over the chicken and serve the rest separately. Accompany with rice or noodles, a green vegetable or a green salad. If serving noodles, the remaining sauce may be mixed with them. Serves 6.

CHICKEN STUFFED WITH FRUIT   Morocco

Dried fruit is often combined with chicken or lamb in Morocco, and the results can be very delicious.

1 medium onion	1 oz/25 g almonds, chopped
3 oz/75 g butter	sea salt and black pepper
½ lb/225 g mixed dried fruit –	3½ lb/1·5 kg roasting chicken
apricots, prunes, raisins,	
apples, pears – soaked,	
stoned and chopped	

Chop the onion and cook in a third of the butter until pale golden. Add the chopped dried fruit and stir around for 3 minutes. Remove from the heat, stir in the chopped nuts and add sea salt and black pepper to taste. Leave to cool.

Stuff the chicken and tie it up; if there is too much stuffing leave the remainder in the pan. Melt the remaining 2 oz/50 g of butter in a casserole and brown the chicken on all sides. Sprinkle with sea salt and black pepper, lay the bird on its side and cover the pan. Cook for 1½ hours at 150°C/300°F/Gas Mark 2, turning from side to side once or twice. Reheat the remaining stuffing and lay around the chicken on its serving dish. Serve with boiled rice or steamed couscous. Serves 4–5

DUCK (OR PHEASANT) WITH SAUERKRAUT   Yugoslavia

In Yugoslavia, sauerkraut is often made with a duck cooked in it, but I find this too rich. I prefer either to cook the sauerkraut alone and serve it with a roast duck, or use it with reheated joints of cold roast duck. On the other hand, less fatty birds like pheasant or guinea fowl can be cooked in it with excellent results.

¼ lb/100 g lard or duck fat
3 medium onions, finely
   chopped
2 lb/900 g tinned sauerkraut
1½ pints/900 ml stock (game,
   chicken or beef)

½ teaspoon paprika
2 chilli peppers (optional)
3 oz/75 g rice
1 pheasant, guinea fowl, or a
   few joints of cold roast duck

Melt the lard in a heavy casserole and brown the finely chopped onion. Rinse the sauerkraut under cold running water, squeeze dry and add to the onions. Stir well and let it stew gently in the fat until it becomes slightly dark and soft. Add the stock gradually, then the paprika, the whole chillies (if used) and the rice. Cover closely and cook for 2 hours in the oven at 180°C/350°F/Gas Mark 4, stirring once or twice and adding more stock if it becomes too dry. Discard the chillies and serve with roast duck, roast game, grilled pork chops or frankfurters.

If cooking a pheasant or guinea fowl with it, first brown the bird all over in a little butter and oil mixed, then add to the sauerkraut after half an hour's cooking; continue cooking all together for another 1–1½ hours. (An old bird will take longer.) To reheat joints of cold roast duck or game, simply add them to the pan and bury in the sauerkraut for the last 20 minutes' cooking. Serves 4–5.

GUINEA FOWL WITH FIGS   Italy

This dish comes from Calabria, in the very south of Italy. It is a delicious combination and worth making whenever figs are in the shops. I accompany this with a dish of new potatoes in their skins, cooked in butter, and a green salad. If cooking for three, use 1 bird only and decrease the oil to 4 tablespoons and the stock to ¼ pint/150 ml. Use the same amount of vegetables, but only 2 oranges and 3 figs.

2 guinea fowl
6 tablespoons olive oil
1 large onion, thinly sliced
1 large carrot, thinly sliced
2 stalks celery, thinly sliced

⅓ pint/200 ml chicken stock
sea salt and black pepper
3 medium oranges
1 oz/25 g butter, melted
6 figs

Brown the birds all over in the oil in a heavy casserole. Remove them, and put the thinly sliced vegetables into the pan and brown them slightly, stirring round for 4–5 minutes. Replace the birds on their sides, heat the stock and pour over, sprinkle with sea salt and black pepper and cover the pan. Cook in the oven for 1¼ hours at 160°C/325°F/Gas Mark 3.

Just before the time is up, peel the oranges and cut them across in four thick slices. Grill them gently, basting with the melted butter, for 2–3 minutes on each side. Put aside. Cut the figs in half and lay under the grill for a couple of minutes only, just long enough to warm them without actually cooking. Keep warm with the oranges.

When the birds are cooked, carve them in neat joints. Using a slotted spoon, lay the braised vegetables in a shallow dish and arrange the carved birds on them. Pour the cooking juices over all, and lay the figs and oranges over the top. Serves 6.

PHEASANT WITH POLENTA   Italy

Polenta goes particularly well with game, and in this dish the birds are served lying on a bed of soft light polenta, covered with an excellent sauce. Other game birds, guinea fowl or even chickens can be used instead of pheasant if preferred.

2 pheasants
5 tablespoons olive oil
1 large onion, chopped
1–2 cloves garlic, chopped
2 medium tins (14 oz/400 g
  each) tomatoes
1 small tin tomato purée
sea salt and black pepper

1 sprig thyme
1 small bay leaf
1 sprig rosemary
¼ pint/150 ml dry white wine
2½ pints/1·5 litres water
½ tablespoon salt
½ lb/225 g polenta
2 tablespoons grated parmesan

Brown the birds in the oil in a heavy casserole. Remove them and add the chopped onion to the pan. When it starts to colour, add the chopped garlic, the roughly chopped tomatoes with their juice, the purée, seasonings, herbs and wine. When well blended, cover the pan and cook in a low oven (160°C/325°F/Gas Mark 3) till tender. (I use roasting birds which take 1½ hours; casserole birds would need 2½–3 hours.)

Three-quarters of an hour before they are ready, heat 2½ pints/1·5 litres water with the salt in a large pan. When it starts to boil, shake in the polenta and stir over moderate heat for 10 minutes. Then cook over very low heat – either in a double boiler or standing on an asbestos mat – for 30 minutes, stirring now and then. It should be quite thick, like porridge. Spoon into a shallow dish and keep warm. Carve the birds and lay them on the polenta. Skim the fat from the sauce and discard the herbs. Spoon some of the sauce over them. Boil up the rest a little to reduce, and serve separately in a sauceboat. Sprinkle the grated parmesan over the birds before serving. Accompany with a green salad. Serves 6.

An excellent soup can be made from the carcasses, while any remaining sauce is good with pasta.

PIGEONS WITH PEAS   France

This Provençal dish is not unlike an Italian one; the combination of smoked ham with game and the fresh taste of green peas is particularly good.

1 medium onion
2 tablespoons olive oil
2 oz/50 g butter
4 pigeons
1 clove garlic, crushed
sea salt and black pepper
¾ pint/450 ml chicken stock
1 bunch of mixed herbs:
  rosemary, sage, thyme,
  marjoram

4 small pieces toast
1 teaspoon flour
3 oz/75 g smoked ham,
  preferably uncooked (i.e.
  prosciutto, serrano, etc.)
¼ lb/100 g shelled green peas
  (fresh, not frozen), cooked

Chop the onion; heat the oil with half the butter in a casserole and fry the onion gently until pale golden. Add the pigeons and brown on all sides. Add the crushed garlic, sea salt and black pepper, then pour on the heated stock. Add the herbs, cover the pan, and simmer until the birds are tender. (English wild pigeons take about 3 hours; alternatively they can be cooked for 1 hour in a pressure cooker.) When the birds are cooked, lay each one on a piece of toast in a shallow serving dish and keep warm.

Strain the sauce into a clean pan. Mix ½ oz/15 g of the butter with the flour to make a paste, and drop by degrees into the simmering sauce to thicken it slightly. If it becomes lumpy, rub it through a food mill. Simmer for 3 minutes. Chop the ham and toss in the remaining ½ oz/15 g of butter until golden. Add the cooked peas, stir till mixed and well heated, then spoon around the birds on the dish, and pour the sauce over all. Serve with a green salad; serves 4.

RABBIT WITH POLENTA   Italy

Rabbit and polenta go particularly well together.

1 domestic rabbit, jointed	sea salt and black pepper
3 tablespoons olive oil	½ teaspoon sugar
1 medium onion, chopped	2–3 sprigs thyme or marjoram
1 clove garlic, crushed	¼ lb/100 g boiled polenta (see
1 medium tin (14 oz/400 g)	Pastry, Rice and Pasta
tomatoes	Dishes, page 185)
1 tablespoon tomato purée	½ oz/15 g butter
¼ pint/150 ml white wine	½ tablespoon olive oil

Brown the rabbit joints in the oil in a casserole. Remove them and cook the chopped onion in the same oil, adding the crushed garlic halfway through. When the onion starts to soften, add the tinned tomatoes, drained of their juice and roughly chopped with the edge of a palette knife. Stir in the tomato purée, wine, sea salt, black pepper, sugar and herbs, and replace the rabbit pieces. Cover the pan and simmer gently for 1½ hours, stirring occasionally.

While it is cooking, fry the polenta (which should have been cooked the day before) in butter and olive oil. When the rabbit is tender, lift out the pieces and keep warm in their dish. Boil up the sauce a little to reduce, and discard the herbs. Adjust the seasoning and spoon over the rabbit. Serve the fried polenta separately, with a green salad. Serves 3–4, or can be made in double quantities.

KOUNELI (RABBIT) STIFADO

This is a truly excellent dish, both in flavour and appearance.

2 rabbits, jointed (use the best parts only)
seasoned flour
2½ oz/65 g butter
4½ tablespoons olive oil
2 lb/900 g pickling onions, peeled
1 clove garlic, minced

1 tablespoon tomato purée
½ pint/300 ml dry white wine
½ pint/300 ml chicken stock
sea salt and black pepper
2–3 sprigs thyme
2 slices dry bread, crusts removed
2 tablespoons chopped parsley

Dip the rabbit pieces in the seasoned flour. Heat 2 oz/50 g of the butter and 4 tablespoons of the oil in a casserole. Fry the rabbit pieces until they are golden, then remove them and add the onions to the pan. Fry until they start to colour, then add the garlic and the tomato purée. Stir and simmer gently for 2 minutes, then add the wine and stock which have been heated together, and replace the rabbit. Sprinkle with sea salt and black pepper, add thyme, cover and cook for 2 hours, either on top of the stove or in a low oven (160°C/325°F/Gas Mark 3).

When it is almost ready, cut the bread in triangles and fry till golden in the remaining ½ oz/15 g of butter and ½ tablespoon of oil. To serve, lift out the rabbit and lay on a shallow dish. Surround with the onions, pour the sauce over, and garnish with the croûtons. Serve with a green salad, and boiled potatoes if you like; serves 6.

LAPIN PROVENÇAL

Domestic rabbit is a popular dish in France, and combines well with the herbs of Provence.

1 rabbit, jointed
seasoned flour
2 oz/50 g butter
2 tablespoons olive oil
¼ lb/100 g shallots
¼ pint/150 ml white wine
½ pint/300 ml chicken stock
sea salt and black pepper

1 teaspoon Dijon mustard
3 sprigs thyme
3 sprigs savory (sarriette), or marjoram
¼ lb/100 g small button mushrooms
⅛ pint/75 ml thick cream
2 tablespoons chopped basil

Dip the rabbit joints in seasoned flour. Heat half the butter and the oil and cook the chopped shallots until pale golden. Add the rabbit, and fry till lightly coloured on all sides. Heat the wine and stock together and pour onto the rabbit. Add sea salt and black pepper, mustard, thyme and savory (or marjoram), and cover the pan. Simmer gently for 1½ hours, stirring now and then. Shortly before the end of the time, toss the whole mushrooms in the remaining 1 oz/25 g of butter. Lift the rabbit pieces onto a warm serving dish, strain the sauce and reheat, adding the cream. Adjust the seasoning, pour over the rabbit and scatter the mushrooms over the dish. Sprinkle chopped basil over all and serve with noodles, rice or boiled potatoes, and a green salad. Serves 4.

7

MEAT

Lamb is the most prevalent meat in the lands bordering the Mediterranean, followed by veal. As we have seen, this is clearly a result of the climate, since it is almost impossible to feed mature animals throughout the long dry summers. Even when dishes specify beef it is rarely beef as we know it, but closer to veal. The only areas where true beef is found are Provence and the Côte d'Azur, and in northern Italy. In Tuscany particularly the beef is of marvellous quality, coming as it does from the huge white cattle of the Chiana Valley. Even these are killed much younger than our Scottish beef, but since they mature quickly, the steaks from Tuscan cattle are first-rate. In Spain the beef is more like mature veal, while further east beef hardly exists. In Greece and Turkey the many dishes of meatballs, meat loaf and stuffed vegetables are usually made from lamb, while in Syria and Lebanon this is inevitably the case. In North Africa, again, beef is little known, except in hotels and restaurants catering for foreigners, and lamb figures almost exclusively in the dishes of couscous, and the Moroccan tagine.

Offal is eaten frequently in Mediterranean countries, as in most poor lands. Tripe is popular throughout Italy, with specialities particular to Genoa, Venice and Tuscany. *Zuppa di trippa* is especially delicious, far removed from English tripe dishes, and tripe is also very popular in Nice and Marseilles. Innards of various sorts are much loved in Greece, where the traditional Easter soup is made from the liver, spleen, lungs, heart and entrails of a baby lamb, or sometimes a baby kid. This habit of cooking baby animals is impossible to duplicate here, since we are unable to obtain them at this early age. In Spain I have eaten a leg of lamb no more than 8 inches/20 cm long; at this age the meat has a totally different character, like the sucking pig which is so popular in Spain. Calves' brains are boiled and served in a vinaigrette as an hors d'oeuvre in western Turkey, while calves' liver is a speciality of Venice.

Pork figures in Italian cookery, but usually in salted or cured forms. Most peasant families keep a pig, or even two, which are killed off in November or early December. Whole families gather together to help with the processing: hams are cured and smoked, and a wide range of sausages prepared to last through the winter. Some of the pig is cooked fresh, but the larger part of the animal will be preserved in some way to last through the lean months between Christmas and spring.

ARNI FRIKASE   Greece

This is an example of Greek cooking at its best, as it once was, and still is in some homes. Like a more interesting version of a French *blanquette de veau*, it consists of cubes of lamb in a sauce enriched with egg yolks and lemon juice, containing spring onions, artichoke hearts and cos lettuce, and flavoured with fresh dill.

1 shoulder of lamb, boned	1 tin artichoke hearts
1 medium onion, thinly sliced	1½ oz/40 g butter
1 carrot, thinly sliced	2 tablespoons flour
1 stalk celery, thinly sliced	sea salt and black pepper
approx. 1¼ pints/750 ml light veal or chicken stock	2 egg yolks
	juice of 1 lemon
2 bunches large spring onions	2 tablespoons chopped dill
heart of a cos lettuce	

Cut the lamb in neat pieces, discarding all fat, and put in a heavy pot with the thinly sliced onion, carrot and celery. Add enough light stock (or water) to just cover the meat, about 1¼ pints/750 ml. Bring to the boil, and skim until the surface is clear. Cover and simmer for 1 hour, or until the meat is just tender. Add the whole spring onions, trimmed at the ends and cut in 1-inch/2·5 cm pieces, bring back to the boil and simmer for 5 minutes. Then add the lettuce heart, cut across in 2-inch/5-cm lengths. Bring back to the boil, then add the drained artichoke hearts. (Fresh ones, boiled till just tender, can of course be used with advantage.) Simmer for 2 minutes, then transfer the contents of the pan to a deep serving dish, using a slotted spoon so that the liquid is left in the pan. Keep the dish warm while you make the sauce.

Strain the stock, skim the fat from the surface and measure ¾ pint/450 ml of it. Melt the butter, add the flour and stir for 2 minutes. Pour on the measured stock, stir till smooth, and simmer for 3 minutes, adding sea salt and black pepper as required. Beat the egg yolks in a bowl with a wire whisk, add the lemon juice and beat again. Stir in the chopped dill. Pour a ladleful of the boiling sauce into the egg and lemon mixture and whisk till smooth. Pour the contents of the bowl into the simmering stock and whisk over very low heat for 3 minutes, keeping it just below boiling point. Pour over the meat and mix lightly but thoroughly. Serves 5. Serve with boiled rice and a green salad, or some boiled carrots.

STUFFED AUBERGINES WITH TAMARIND   Syria

This unusual dish should be made with a syrup of bitter pomegranates called *dibis ruman*. I have failed totally to find this in London, so suggest using as an alternative the tamarind syrup given in Pickles, Preserves and Spice Mixtures, page 268.

6 small aubergines	2 tablespoons dibis ruman, or
butter and oil	tamarind syrup
2 medium onions	⅛ pint/75 ml chicken stock
½ oz/15 g butter	2 pitta (flat bread)
1 lb/450 g minced lamb	1 large carton (¾ pint/450 ml)
2 oz/50 g pine kernels	yogurt
sea salt and black pepper	2 cloves garlic, crushed
1 tablespoon tomato purée	

Cut the unpeeled aubergines in half and scoop out the insides. Soak the shells in cold salt water for 10 minutes, then drain and pat dry. Fry them in a mixture of butter and oil on both sides, quite briefly, just until they start to become limp; set aside. Chop the onions and fry in ½ oz/15 g of butter until pale golden, then add the meat. Stir till browned all over, then add the pine kernels and continue to cook till they have coloured also, adding sea salt and black pepper to taste. Tip into a colander and stand for 5 minutes over a plate, to allow the fat to drain away.

Fill the aubergine halves with this mixture, which should be quite highly seasoned. Put them carefully in a broad heavy casserole, in one layer if possible. Mix the tomato purée and *dibis ruman*, or tamarind syrup, with the chicken stock and pour between the aubergines. Cover and cook over low heat for 30 minutes, or until they are soft. Cut the pitta in triangles and toast lightly in a low oven; lay the pieces in the bottom of a large shallow dish. Lift the aubergines carefully out of the cooking pot and lay on a flat surface. Pour the juices over the toasted bread, then lay the aubergines on top of it. Have the yogurt slightly warmed by standing it on the back of the stove. Crush the garlic and mix with the yogurt. Pour over the aubergines and serve. Serves 6. Serve with a green salad.

This dish can be prepared in advance, if preferred, but do not pour over the yogurt until just before serving. The stuffed aubergines lying on the bread soaked in the juices can be reheated for 40 minutes at 180°C/350°F/Gas Mark 4, then served with the yogurt poured over them.

BOEUF BRAISÉ AUX OLIVES NOIRES   France

I like this Provençal or Niçois dish even better than the usual *daube*, where the meat is cut up before cooking.

4 tablespoons olive oil
1 large onion, coarsely
  chopped
2 oz/50 g unsmoked bacon,
  chopped
2 cloves garlic, minced
2 stalks celery, sliced
2½ lb/1·15 kg rolled topside of
  beef
3 tablespoons brandy
¼ lb/100 g young carrots,
  thickly sliced

½ lb/225 g tomatoes, skinned
  and coarsely chopped
⅓ pint/200 ml stock
⅓ pint/200 ml red wine
sea salt and black pepper
1 bay leaf
3 stalks parsley
3 sprigs thyme
1 strip dried orange peel
16 black olives

Heat 3 tablespoons of the olive oil in a heavy casserole just large enough to hold the meat. Cook the chopped onion in it for 2–3 minutes, then add the bacon. After another 2 minutes add the garlic and celery. Cook all together for 5 minutes, then remove from the pan with a slotted spoon. Put the remaining tablespoon of oil in the pan and brown the meat, turning on all sides. Warm the brandy in a soup ladle, set light to it and pour over the beef. When the flames have died down, put the half-cooked vegetables back in the pan and add the carrots and tomatoes. Heat the stock and wine and pour over the meat, adding sea salt and black pepper, bay leaf, parsley, thyme and orange peel. Cover and cook for 3½ hours at 150°C/310°F/Gas Mark 2, then add the olives and cook for another half hour. To serve, cut the meat in thick slices and lay in a shallow dish. Lift off as much fat as possible from the surface of the sauce, spoon the vegetables and olives over the meat and pour the sauce over all. Serves 6.

KASAPSI JUVETCH (BUTCHERS' STEW)   Yugoslavia

A dish of mixed meat, more usual in central European cooking than in our own, this should be made with equal parts of boneless mutton and pork, but it is very good made with middle neck of lamb, left on the bone.

1 lb/450 g boned shoulder of lamb, cubed and
1 lb/450 g fore end of pork, cubed
or 2½ lb/1·15 kg middle neck of lamb
2 lb/900 g onions, sliced
sea salt and black pepper
½ teaspoon paprika
½ lb/225 g string beans, cut in short lengths

½ lb/225 g okra, trimmed
4 large tomatoes, skinned and cut in quarters
2 red peppers, cut in chunks
2 chilli peppers, minced
1 aubergine, peeled and cut in cubes
3 tablespoons rice
½ oz/15 g lard or dripping
¼ pint/150 ml hot water

Put the meat in a deep bowl and cover with the sliced onions, sea salt, black pepper and paprika. Leave for 30 minutes. Meanwhile prepare the vegetables and mix with the meat when the time is up. Add the rice and the fat cut in small pieces. Tip into a casserole and add the water. Cover closely and bake for 3 hours at 160°C/325°F/Gas Mark 3, by which time there will be practically no liquid left. Serves 4–6.

DAUBE DE BOEUF   France

A *daube* is a Provençal beef stew and can be made either with one large piece of beef or cubes. It can be served hot, usually accompanied by noodles rather than potatoes, or cold when the rich sauce sets to a firm jelly. If serving hot, I like to have the beef in quite large pieces, but if to be served cold, it is better to cut it in small cubes.

2½–3 lb/1·15–1·35 kg chuck
  steak
2 large onions, sliced
2 large carrots, sliced
2 cloves garlic, chopped
1 bay leaf
2 sprigs thyme
2 stalks parsley
1 stalk celery
sea salt and black pepper

3 tablespoons olive oil
½ bottle red wine
6 oz/175 g unsmoked streaky
  bacon, in thick slices
½ lb/225 g tomatoes
1 small piece knuckle of veal, if
  to be served cold
¼ pint/150 ml good stock
8 black olives, stoned

Cut the beef in rectangular pieces, quite large if to be served hot, but smaller if to be eaten cold. Put them in a deep bowl. Cover with the sliced onions and carrots, the chopped garlic, the herbs tied in the celery stalk, and sea salt and black pepper. Pour over the olive oil and wine and leave to marinate for 24 hours.

Next day, cut the bacon in strips and lay in the bottom of a heavy casserole. Put the sliced vegetables on top of the bacon, then the cubed beef with the bouquet of herbs buried among it. Skin the tomatoes, cut in quarters, and lay over the beef. If serving cold, put the veal in the centre; this ensures a firm jelly. Pour the marinade over all, and add the stock. Bring slowly to the boil on top of the stove, then cover the pot and put in the oven for 4 hours at 150°C/310°F/Gas Mark 2.

To serve hot, discard the veal and the herbs and lay the meat and vegetables in a serving dish. Keep warm for a few minutes while the sauce cools slightly. Skim off as much fat as possible and spoon over the meat. Garnish with the halved stoned olives. Serves 6, with noodles and a green salad.

To serve cold, prepare several hours in advance and skim off the fat from the surface of the sauce before serving. Garnish with olives at the last moment only. Serve with French bread and a green salad, or a cold dish of haricot beans in a vinaigrette sauce, or new potatoes dressed with oil and a little vinegar.

CARNE ALLA GENOVESE

If you can persuade your butcher to let you have the eye of the blade steak this will give you an extremely good and relatively inexpensive dish. Otherwise use a compact piece of chuck steak, or rolled topside.

2 lb/900 g eye of blade steak, in
  one piece
2 tablespoons olive oil
2 onions, quartered
2 carrots, halved
sea salt and black pepper

1 large glass (6 fl. oz/175 ml)
  dry white wine
½ bay leaf
2 sprigs oregano
¼ pint/150 ml thick cream

Heat the oil in a casserole and brown the meat all over. Add the cut-up onions and carrots and brown these lightly also. Add sea salt and black pepper and pour over the white wine, adding the herbs. Cover and cook gently on top of the stove for 1½ hours, basting and turning over from time to time. Pour the cream into the pan and mix with the wine. Baste and cook for another 30 minutes. Lift out the meat and carve in fairly thick slices. Lay them in a serving dish. Discard the herbs, stir round the sauce and reheat if necessary, then pour over the meat. Serve with new potatoes or a potato purée, and a green salad. Serves 4.

CARNE ALLA PIZZAIOLA

This dish from Naples is usually made with rump steak; this is a cheaper version devised by a cook from Positano, but it does involve persuading your butcher to let you have the eye, or best part, of the blade steak. Failing this, use topside, chuck steak or any good braising steak.

3–3½ lb/1·35–1·5 kg eye of
  blade steak, or good braising
  steak
2 tablespoons olive oil
2 cloves garlic
3 tablespoons chopped parsley

1½ tablespoons chopped
  oregano
sea salt and black pepper
2 medium tins (14 oz/400 g
  each) tomatoes

Cut the meat in neat slices, as thinly as possible, using a very sharp knife. Put the oil in the bottom of a heavy, very broad casserole, and lay the slices overlapping in it. Chop the garlic, parsley and oregano and scatter over the meat. Add sea salt and black pepper. Open the tins and add to the pan, squeezing the tomatoes between the hands to pulp them. Add a quarter tin of water, cover the pan and cook slowly for 1½ hours, or till the meat is tender. To serve, transfer the meat to a shallow serving dish and spoon the sauce over. Serve with boiled pasta or a purée of potatoes, and a green salad. Serves 6.

CIMA ALLA GENOVESE   Italy

This stuffed breast of veal is a speciality of Genoa; one sees it everywhere in the city, in food shops and restaurants. Served cold, in very thin slices, it is beautiful to look at: the thin casing of veal encloses a mosaic of pink, green and yellow. When made at home, I cannot hope to emulate the visual perfection of the professionals' results, but the taste is just as good. Unfortunately brains and sweetbreads are hard to buy now in this country; it can be made without, but will not have the same smooth unctuous quality.

2½ lb/1·15 kg boned breast of
  veal, with bones
sea salt and black pepper
½ calf's brain,
  3½–4 oz/85–100 g
1½ tablespoons wine vinegar
¼ lb/100 g veal sweetbread
2 oz/50 g bread, crusts removed
a little milk
¼ lb/100 g shelled peas
½ oz/15 g butter
½ tablespoon olive oil
½ small onion, finely chopped

1 clove garlic, minced
¼ lb/100 g minced veal
1 oz/25 g pine kernels
1 oz/25 g pistachios, shelled
½ tablespoon chopped
  marjoram
1 tablespoon chopped basil
2 tablespoons grated parmesan
4 eggs
1 onion, sliced
1 carrot, sliced
1 bay leaf

You will need the co-operation of your butcher in order to make this dish successfully. If you explain to him that you are going to sew the veal into a pouch and stuff it, not roll it in the English fashion, he will cut you a thin square piece and possibly even slit it in half horizontally. When you get it home, sprinkle it inside with sea salt and black pepper, and sew up three sides to form a sort of bag, using a strong needle and coarse thread. Keep the bones.

Wash the brain carefully under running water, and pull off the pinkish-red membrane which covers it. Leave to soak for 30 minutes in a bowl of cold water with a dash of vinegar. Bring some lightly salted water to the boil in a small pan, add 1 tablespoon of vinegar, drop in the brain and poach for 5 minutes. Drain, and chop when cool. Wash the sweetbread also, cover with cold water and bring to the boil; simmer 5 minutes, drain, cool and chop. Tear the bread in pieces and soak in milk for 10 minutes, then squeeze dry. Drop the peas into boiling water and boil for 2 minutes; drain. Heat the butter and oil and cook the finely chopped onion, adding the minced or crushed garlic. When they start to colour, add the minced veal and stir round until lightly browned all over. Remove from the heat and stir in the chopped brain and sweetbread and the soaked bread. Turn into a food processor and process until smooth and blended. Spoon into a large bowl and stir in the green peas, nuts, chopped herbs, grated parmesan, salt and pepper. Beat the eggs lightly and stir in also. Spoon the soft semi-liquid stuffing into the veal bag and sew up the remaining side; it must not be more than about half full as it will swell during cooking. Lay the veal bones in a casserole and put the stuffed veal on them. Cover with sliced onion and carrot, add the bay leaf, sea salt and black peppercorns. Cover with cold water, bring to the boil and simmer for 2 hours. Turn off the heat and leave to cool in its liquid.

Next day, lift out the veal and wrap in foil. Chill in the refrigerator until needed; it will keep for a week, so can be prepared several days in advance. To serve, cut in thin slices and serve with a green salad. Serves 8. It makes a useful joint for a summer dinner party or cold buffet. (In the professional version, the different ingredients are not blended together, as here, but are set in a sort of yellow egg custard. It is too difficult to attempt this on a small scale, and without a lot of practice, since the egg yolks would escape through the stitches before they have had time to set.)

D'FEENA   Egypt

This Jewish dish, very similar to the Moroccan *sefrina*, is a popular luncheon dish for the Sabbath since it can be prepared the evening before and left cooking overnight, thus leaving the Sabbath free from work. It usually contains potatoes and 1 egg per person; I prefer to omit the potatoes and only cook 2 eggs, chopping them coarsely before serving.

½ lb/225 g chick peas, soaked overnight
2 lb/900 g brisket of beef
1 medium onion, chopped
1 clove garlic, finely chopped

sea salt and black pepper
½ teaspoon ground cumin
½ teaspoon ground coriander
2 eggs in their shells, or 1 per person

Soak the peas overnight, then drain them. Cut the beef in neat pieces and put in a casserole with the chick peas. Add the coarsely chopped onion, the finely chopped garlic, sea salt, black pepper and spices. Wash the eggs and lay them in the stew. Barely cover with cold water and put a lid on the pan. Bring to the boil on top of the stove and simmer for 1 hour, then transfer to the oven at the lowest possible setting, or to a slow cooker, and cook for 6–8 hours, or overnight. Shell the eggs before serving, chop them coarsely, and scatter over and among the stew. (If preparing in the traditional manner, leave the eggs whole.) Serves 5–6.

DOLMAS IN LEMON SAUCE   Turkey

This Turkish dish of stuffed vine leaves is very similar to many Greek dishes, and is like a larger version of the tiny *dolmades* so common in Greece.

24 vine leaves, fresh or preserved in brine
½ lb/225 g minced lamb
1 medium onion, finely chopped
4 tablespoons rice
sea salt and black pepper
1 tablespoon water

approx. 1 pint/600 ml veal or chicken stock

lemon sauce:
2 eggs
4 tablespoons lemon juice
stock from cooking dolmas

If using fresh vine leaves, blanch them for 10 minutes in boiling water, then drain. Preserved leaves must first be soaked for 30 minutes in a basin of cold water, then blanched for 5 minutes in boiling water. Mix the finely minced meat with the finely chopped onion; this is easily done in a food processor. Then add the rice, mix well, and add sea salt and black pepper plus 1 tablespoon water to form a sort of thick paste. Take a large teaspoonful of the mixture and form into a roll between the palms of the hands. Lay on a vine leaf and roll up, folding in the ends and squeezing lightly. Continue until all the stuffing is used up, then make a layer of unused leaves in the bottom of a sauté pan. Lay the stuffed leaves on this, and pour over enough hot stock barely to cover them. Lay a small plate on top to weight them down and prevent them coming unrolled, cover the pan and simmer for 50 minutes, checking once or twice to make sure they are not boiling dry. There should be about ½ pint/300 ml liquid left at the end of the cooking. Add extra stock, or water, if necessary. When cooked, lift them onto a hot serving dish and keep warm while you make the sauce.

Beat the eggs in a small bowl, add the lemon juice and beat again. Strain the stock into a clean pan and reheat; when boiling, pour some of it onto the eggs and beat well with a small whisk. Tip back into the pan and stir gently over low heat, without allowing it to boil, until slightly thickened. Pour over the *dolmas* and serve. Serves 4.

FEGATO ALLA VENEZIANA   Italy

This delicious dish is a speciality of Venice, where the liver is especially good. It must be sliced as thinly as possible. It is traditionally served with fried polenta (see page 186).

1 lb/450 g onions, sliced	1 lb/450 g calves' liver, very
6 fl. oz/175 ml olive oil	thinly sliced indeed
4 tablespoons water	sea salt and black pepper

Cook the sliced onions very slowly in ¼ pint/150 ml of the olive oil in a sauté pan. After 10 minutes add the 4 tablespoons of water, cover the pan and continue to stew very gently. Allow 45 minutes for the onions to become really soft and easy to digest. Cut the thin slices of liver into little squares, about 1½ inches/3·5 cm across. Heat the remaining oil – I sometimes add a small piece of butter, although this is not strictly correct – in a clean frying pan and when it is hot, add the liver and cook very quickly, just until it changes colour. Turn the little pieces once and cook briefly on the other side. Lift them out with a slotted spoon and add to the onions. Stir all together for a moment, adding sea salt and black pepper. Serve immediately; serves 4.

FOIE DE VEAU PERSILLÉ   France

This quickly made and tasty dish is the speciality of a small restaurant in the old town at Nice, where I first ate it.

4 thin slices calves' liver
seasoned flour
1 oz/25 g butter
2 tablespoons olive oil
2 cloves garlic, chopped

2 tablespoons white wine
  vinegar
4 tablespoons dry white wine
2 tablespoons chopped parsley

Lay the slices of liver in the seasoned flour, coating both sides and shaking off any excess. Heat the butter and oil in a frying pan and cook the liver briefly, about 2 minutes on each side; it should still be pink in the centre. Lift out and keep warm, and put the chopped cloves of garlic in the frying pan. Cook gently, stirring often to prevent burning, until pale golden; add a little more butter or oil if required. When the garlic starts to turn colour, pour in the vinegar and wine, swirl round the pan for a moment or two, then add the chopped parsley, mix briefly, and pour over the liver. Serve immediately, with boiled potatoes and broccoli. Serves 4.

GAMMON WITH ORANGES   Italy

This dish comes from southern Italy, and is an excellent way of cooking a large joint of gammon.

4½ lb/2 kg gammon
½ bottle dry white wine
4 oranges
10 cloves
1 onion, halved

1 carrot, halved
1 stalk celery
10 black peppercorns
3 oz/75 g soft brown sugar
2 teaspoons Dijon mustard

Soak the gammon for 12 hours. Reserve 6 tablespoons of the wine, and pour the rest into a pan large enough to hold the gammon. Add 1 orange stuck with the cloves, and the halved onion and carrot, celery and peppercorns. Squeeze the juice of the remaining 3 oranges, reserve 4 tablespoons, and add the rest to the pan. Add enough cold water to cover the gammon easily, but don't put it (the gammon) in yet. Bring slowly to the boil, cover the pan and simmer for 1 hour, then leave to cool. Later, put in the gammon and bring slowly to the boil. Skim, then simmer very gently for 1¾ hours. (Allow 20 minutes per 1 lb/450 g if cooking a larger piece.) Lift out the gammon, remove the skin and lay on a rack in a roasting tin. Mix the brown sugar and mustard to a paste with some of the reserved wine and orange juice. Spread over the ham and bake for 45 minutes at 180°C/350°F/Gas Mark 4, using the extra wine and fruit juice to baste with. Serves 6–8.

HAN KEBAB   Turkey

This dish is a speciality of the Han Restaurant in Bodrum, in south-west Turkey. The crisp fried potatoes make a change from the bread in the better-known *yogurtlu* kebab.

1½ lb/675 g fillet, or leg, of veal
1 lb/450 g potatoes
frying oil
3 tablespoons olive oil
1 large carton (¾ pint/350 ml)
  yogurt

2 tablespoons finely chopped
  green pepper
2 cloves garlic, crushed
sea salt and black pepper

Cut the veal in thin strips about 1½ inches/3·5 cm long, like match-sticks. Peel the potatoes and grate finely, making very fine strips like shoestring potatoes. Fry them in deep oil until golden; drain and keep hot. They should be very crisp. Fry the strips of veal in the olive oil until they are just cooked; keep hot. Have the yogurt draining for 1–2 hours beforehand, until it is the consistency of sour cream. Warm it gently – do not attempt to make it hot – and add the meat juices, chopped green pepper, crushed garlic, sea salt and black pepper. Mix some of it with the meat, and pour over the potatoes on a flat dish. Pour the remaining yogurt over all. Serve immediately. Serves 4–5.

YOGURTLU KEBAB   Turkey

I have eaten this dish on successive visits to Istanbul, in the Greek restaurant called Pandeli's, above the spice market. It is typical of the sort of Middle Eastern dish which most appeals to me, with its combination of lamb, flat bread and yogurt, and its garnish of lightly toasted pine nuts. In Lebanon, it is called *yogurtliya*.

1½ lb/675 g boned leg of lamb
2 flat bread
¾ lb/350 g tomatoes
½ pint/300 ml yogurt
1 oz/25 g pine kernels

1½ oz/40 g butter
3 tablespoons olive oil
sea salt and black pepper
2 cloves garlic

Cut the meat in thin strips about 1½ inches/3·5 cm long, removing all fat. Cut the bread in small triangles and toast lightly, in the oven or under the grill, until pale golden. Skin and chop the tomatoes, not too finely. Drain the yogurt for 1–2 hours, until it is the consistency of thick cream. Stand on the back of the stove to warm slightly. Toss the pine kernels in ½ oz/15 g of the butter until pale golden; put aside.

Shortly before serving, start the actual cooking. Fry the strips of meat quickly in olive oil, until just cooked but slightly pink in the centre. Keep warm in their juices. Toss the tomatoes briefly in 1 oz/25 g butter, until just softened. Lay the toasted bread pieces on a warm flat dish, keeping back about a third as a garnish. Spoon the tomatoes and their juices over the bread, adding sea salt and black pepper. Drain the meat and lay over the tomatoes. Crush the garlic and stir into the yogurt, then mix with the meat juices and pour over all. Scatter the pine nuts over the yogurt, and surround with the remaining bread pieces. Serve immediately. Serves 5–6. This dish needs no accompaniment, although a green salad may be served at the same time, or to follow.

KEFTEDES

Greece

This recipe comes from a Greek cook who uses crumbled rusks instead of breadcrumbs, claiming that it gives a lighter result.

1 lb/450 g minced beef or lamb
3 medium rusks, soaked for 10
    minutes in hot water and
    squeezed dry
2 tablespoons chopped dill or
    parsley or ½ teaspoon
    ground cumin

sea salt and black pepper
1 egg, lightly beaten
4 tablespoons olive oil
1 teaspoon ouzo or cognac
flour

Put the meat in a large bowl with the squeezed rusks. Mix together, breaking up the meat. Add the herbs and seasonings and the whole egg, lightly beaten. Stir in 1 tablespoon oil and ouzo or cognac. Work all together hard, using the bare hands, until it is blended into a smooth homogenous mass. At this point, old Greek cooks would make the sign of the cross in the mixture, and leave it to rest for a while. Later, heat 3 tablespoons of oil in a frying pan. Form the meat into balls and flatten slightly, to make small round patties about 1½ inches/3·5 cm across. Dip in flour and fry till well browned on both sides and cooked through. Makes 16–18 *keftedes*; serves 4.

KIBBEH   Lebanon, Syria

Kibbeh is a Middle Eastern speciality which exists in various forms. Basically a filling of fried lamb, onions and pine kernels enclosed within a shell of minced and pounded raw lamb mixed to a paste with burghul (cracked wheat), it can be made either in the form of round or torpedo-shaped meatballs, or baked in layers in a tray. Formerly, and still in rural areas, making *kibbeh* involved pounding the meat for many hours in a huge mortar. In the cities, however, butchers now sell meat specially prepared for *kibbeh*, while food processors can be used which make mortars unnecessary. In much of Lebanon and Syria, *kibbeh* is made without spices, except for a little cinnamon in the filling, but this recipe comes from the south of Lebanon where both shell and filling are seasoned with a blend of spices including dried rose buds and dried savoury (*mardakoush*). The filled balls are tricky to make, rather like making small clay pinch pots, but can be fun if you have plenty of time to spare. The finished *kibbeh* are usually deep fried, although they can be baked in the oven, and served with a yogurt sauce. Small *kibbeh* make cocktail snacks, or are served in soups, or in a yogurt sauce. The baking tin version is much simpler, but less immediately appealing to those who are unaccustomed to the *kibbeh* mixture, since it lacks the crisp browned surfaces of the balls.

shell mixture:
¼ lb/100 g fine burghul
1 lb/450 g finely minced lamb
1 medium onion, chopped
1½ teaspoons sea salt

freshly ground black pepper
1 teaspoon pounded coeurs de
  roses (dried rose buds) (optional)
1 teaspoon dried savory
  (optional)

filling:
1 large onion, not too finely
  chopped
1 tablespoon oil
½ lb/225 g minced lamb
2 oz/50 g pine kernels
1 teaspoon sea salt
black pepper

½ teaspoon pounded coeurs de
  roses (optional)
½ teaspoon dried savory
  (optional)
½ teaspoon ground cinnamon
½ teaspoon ground allspice
  (optional)

To make the shell mixture, put the burghul in a large bowl and cover with cold water. Wash well, then take out a handful at a time, squeeze out all the water, and transfer to a clean dry bowl. Put a quarter of the washed burghul in a food processor with roughly a quarter of the lamb, onion, sea salt, black pepper and spices. Process thoroughly, until very fine and well blended; put aside while you make the filling.

The filling should be much coarser, and crumbly, in contrast to the fine smooth exterior, so it is best not to use a food processor. Fry the onion in the oil until it starts to colour, then add the lamb and brown that also. English lamb is much more fatty than Lebanese lamb, so I usually brown the pine kernels separately, in a little extra oil in a frying pan, then add them to the drained meat together with the sea salt, black pepper and spices. In the Middle East, one simply adds the pine kernels to the meat and browns them all together. Leave to cool.

To make kibbeh balls:
Take a piece of the shell mixture weighing about 2 oz/50 g. Have a bowl of iced water nearby; dip the hands in this while working. Holding the meat mixture in the palm of the left hand, form it into a round ball, then make a hole in the centre with the right thumb. Gradually thin the walls by pinching between the finger and thumb of the right hand, forming a hollow shell. Put a teaspoon of the filling inside, then slowly mould the shell round it so that the filling is totally enclosed. The finished ball may be round or torpedo shaped (the latter is more difficult to achieve). The finished kibbeh are usually fried in deep oil until well browned and crisp, but they can be baked on an oiled baking sheet for about 40 minutes at 190°C/375°F/Gas Mark 5. Serve with a bowl of yogurt, or a yogurt sauce (see Sauces, page 256), or tzatziki (see page 78). Makes about 8 kibbeh. Serves 4, with a green salad.

To make small kibbeh for serving in soup, or with drinks:
Experienced Lebanese cooks can make small filled kibbeh no larger than walnuts, but for foreigners I would suggest leaving these unfilled, as it is very tricky to do on a small scale. Simply make small round balls of the shell mixture and cook. For serving with drinks, fry in deep oil, shallow fry, or bake in the oven for 20 minutes at 190°C/375°F/Gas Mark 5.

To make kibbeh in a tray:
Divide the shell mixture in half and smooth one part into an oiled tin. In Lebanon this would be a round tin about 1½ inches/4 cm deep; English flan tins are too shallow, so I use a square tin of the right depth. When you have a smooth layer, cover with the filling, then the remainder of the first mixture. Smooth very evenly, then use a small sharp knife to cut through the top layer in diagonal lines about 1 inch/2·5 cm apart to form a diamond pattern. Pour 8 tablespoons melted butter or oil over the top surface, then bake at 190°C/375°F/Gas Mark 5 until very brown and crisp, about 40 minutes. Serve with a yogurt sauce (see Sauces, page 256), or a bowl of yogurt, and a green salad. Serves 6.

KIBBEH IN YOGURT SAUCE   Lebanon

2 pints/1·2 litres yogurt
1 tablespoon cornflour
2 tablespoons cold water
2 cloves garlic, minced
½ tablespoon butter

1 tablespoon dried mint
½ teaspoon sea salt
8 filled kibbeh
2 oz/50 g rice, parboiled
  (optional)

Put the yogurt in a pan and beat it with a whisk. Stir in the cornflour mixed with 2 tablespoons cold water, and bring slowly to the boil, stirring all the time in the same direction. When it reaches boiling point, lower the heat as much as possible and leave to simmer, uncovered, for 10 minutes, stirring now and then. Meanwhile fry the minced garlic gently in the butter without allowing it to burn; add the crushed mint and fry for a moment or two longer, then stir into the yogurt when the 10 minutes are up. Add the sea salt and the kibbeh and simmer until they are cooked, about 30 minutes. If adding rice, this should have been boiled for 10 minutes in lightly salted water, then well rinsed and drained. Stir into the yogurt sauce 4–5 minutes before the end of the cooking. Alternatively, serve with a dish of boiled rice. Serves 4.

A simpler version of this dish can be made using unfilled *kibbeh*; using the shell mixture alone, make round balls about the size of table tennis balls and simmer 20 minutes in the yogurt sauce. Serves 6. Alternatively, they can be fried until almost cooked, then just finished off for a few minutes in the sauce. They can also be made in half quantities to serve 3–4 people.

LAMB LAGOTO   Greece

A Greek casserole of lamb, good for a summer luncheon.

2 lb/900 g loin of lamb	*2 cloves garlic, finely chopped*
4 tablespoons olive oil	*⅛ pint/75 ml white wine*
sea salt and black pepper	*½ lb/225 g tinned tomatoes*
4 tablespoons lemon juice	*2 tablespoons chopped parsley*

Cut the lamb in pieces, rub with 2 tablespoons of the olive oil and sprinkle with sea salt and black pepper. Grill briefly, until the meat changes colour, but stop before it is cooked. Sprinkle with 2 tablespoons of the lemon juice. Heat the remaining 2 tablespoons of olive oil in a pan and cook the finely chopped garlic. As soon as it starts to colour, add a few drops of water and put in the meat. Stir constantly for 2–3 moments over low heat, being careful not to let the garlic burn. Add the wine and the remaining 2 tablespoons of lemon juice. Chop the tinned tomatoes and add to the pan, also the finely chopped parsley. Cook gently for 10 minutes, then add 2 tablespoons water and simmer for another 30 minutes. Accompany with boiled rice and a green salad. Serves 5.

LAMB WITH OKRA   Turkey

A light meat and vegetable dish with a delicious thin sauce. It needs some plain boiled potatoes or crusty bread to mop up the juice.

½ boned shoulder of lamb,
    about 2 lb/900 g meat
3 oz/75 g butter
1 teaspoon sea salt
6 tablespoons water
6 oz/175 g small pickling onions

6 oz/175 g small carrots
½ lb/225 g small okra
approx. 1 pint/600 ml veal or
    chicken stock
juice of 1½ lemons
ground cinnamon

Cut the meat in neat pieces the size of a walnut. Put them in a pan with
1 oz/25 g of the butter, 1 teaspoon of sea salt and 6 tablespoons of
water. Bring to the boil, stirring, and boil gently for 10 minutes until
it forms a thick whitish gravy. Lift out the meat and put in a buttered
round baking tin or straight-sided china dish. Peel the onions and
brown gently in the remaining butter, then lift out and lay over the
meat. Cut the carrots in quarters lengthwise and cook briefly in the
butter, then lay over the onions. Trim the okra and cook for a few
minutes in the butter until starting to colour. Lay over the carrots. Pour
over the gravy from the first cooking, the juice of the lemons, and
enough stock to come almost level with the okra. Cook, uncovered, for
1½ hours at 180°C/350°F/Gas Mark 4. Turn the okra over now and then
so that they brown evenly all over. To serve, tip into a serving dish and
sprinkle with ground cinnamon. Serves 4.

LAMB WITH QUINCE   Greece

This unusual stew, combining the somewhat fatty lamb with the sharp
taste of quince, comes from the island of Corfu.

2 lb/900 g middle end of neck
    of lamb
½ lb/225 g onions
3 tablespoons olive oil
sea salt and black pepper

1 lb/450 g quinces, peeled and
    cored
1 teaspoon sugar
a pinch of nutmeg

Divide the meat into neat pieces, leaving on the fat. Chop the onions
and cook slowly in the oil till pale golden. Add the lamb and brown
that also. Add just enough water to come level with the meat, and
season with sea salt and black pepper. Bring to the boil and lower the
heat, cover the pan and simmer slowly for 1 hour. Add the thickly
sliced quinces, the sugar and nutmeg, and cook for another 30 minutes,
or until both fruit and meat are tender. Serves 4.

LAMB TAGINE   **Morocco**

This dish of lamb cooked with dried apricots is typical of many Moroccan dishes which combine meat with fresh or dried fruit, and similar to the lamb stewed with quince, from Corfu. I sometimes like to serve it with steamed couscous, but this would not be done in Morocco.

1½ lb/675 g boneless lamb (½ a
   small boned leg or shoulder)
2 medium onions
2 green peppers
1 head fennel
seasoned flour
3 tablespoons olive oil

½ teaspoon ground ginger
1 pint/600 ml veal or chicken
   stock
1 packet saffron
sea salt and black pepper
¼ lb/100 g dried apricots
1–2 tablespoons lemon juice

Cut the lamb in cubes. Slice the onions, cut the peppers in strips and slice the fennel. Toss the lamb in seasoned flour and brown in the oil, stirring often. Remove from the pan and add the vegetables. Cook gently for 4–5 minutes, stirring often, until lightly coloured, adding the ginger towards the end. Replace the meat, pour on the heated stock, and add the saffron, sea salt and black pepper. Cover and simmer for 1 hour, then add the chopped dried apricots. (These do not need soaking unless they are very hard.) Cook for a further 15 minutes, until all is tender, then add a little lemon juice, to taste. Serves 4, with boiled rice and a green salad.

LEBANESE MEAT LOAF   **Lebanon**

This Lebanese meat loaf is usually baked in a shallow rectangular tray, and covered with a sauce.

1½ lb/675 g minced lamb
1 large onion
a large handful parsley, tops
   only

sea salt and black pepper
6 oz/175 g tinned tomatoes
a pinch of sugar

Put the minced meat in a bowl and break up the lumps with two wooden spoons. Cut the onion in chunks and put in a food processor with the parsley. Process until finely chopped, then stir into the meat so it is well mixed, adding plenty of sea salt and black pepper. Try out a small ball in a frying pan to test the seasoning. Oil a shallow square tin and tip the meat loaf mixture into it, spreading it evenly with a palette knife. Tip the tinned tomatoes into a bowl and chop roughly with the edge of a palette knife. Add sea salt and black pepper, and a pinch of sugar. Pour over the meat, spreading evenly. Bake for 1 hour at 180°C/350°F/Gas Mark 4. By the end of the cooking the meat will have shrunk from the sides of the tin, and the cavity will have filled up with juice. Suck this out with a bulb-type baster and serve separately, in a small jug, accompanied by a lettuce salad, and boiled potatoes if you like. Serves 4–5.

A Lebanese variation is to spread 4–6 tablespoons of *tahini* over the meat instead of the tomato sauce. Sprinkle generously with salt before baking.

TURKISH MEAT LOAF   Turkey

Dishes of minced meat, whether meatballs or meat loaves, are very common throughout all the Mediterranean countries. The meat may be beef, lamb or veal, and the herbs and spices vary according to the country. The use of allspice is typical of Turkish meat cookery.

1½ lb/675 g minced beef or veal	2 cloves garlic, crushed
2 slices white bread, crusts	1 tablespoon oil
removed	1 teaspoon allspice
a little milk	sea salt and black pepper
1 onion, grated	2 tablespoons chopped dill

Put the minced meat in a large bowl and break up. Soak the torn-up bread in milk for 10 minutes, then squeeze dry and add to the meat. Mix well. Add the grated onion and the crushed garlic and mix again. Stir in the oil, allspice, sea salt, black pepper and chopped dill. Knead hard between the hands for several minutes. Try out a small ball in a frying pan to test the seasoning. When ready to cook, form into a rectangular shape and tip into a buttered bread tin. Cover with foil and bake, standing in a tin half full of water, for 50 minutes at 180°C/350°F/Gas Mark 4. Serve hot, with pickles, relishes, or a yogurt sauce. Serves 4, with a mixed salad and some boiled potatoes.

POACHED MEATBALLS IN AVGOLEMONO   Greece

Until I started to work on this book I just didn't realize how many
different sorts of meatballs there are in Greece. Unfortunately the
tavernas have chosen to make, ad nauseam, the least interesting one,
or so it seems to me. These poached meatballs in an avgolemono sauce
are far superior.

¾ lb/350 g minced lamb or veal
1½ oz/40 g soft breadcrumbs
1½ tablespoons grated onion
1½ tablespoons chopped
    parsley
sea salt and black pepper

1 egg, beaten
2 tablespoons chopped parsley

avgolemono sauce:
1½ pints/900 ml chicken stock
2 egg yolks
4 tablespoons lemon juice

Mix the minced meat with the breadcrumbs, grated onion, chopped
parsley, sea salt, black pepper and the beaten egg. Form into oval
meatballs, using a large teaspoon. The mixture should make about 16.
Bring the stock to the boil and drop in the meatballs. Bring back to the
boil, lower the heat, and simmer for 20 minutes. Lift the meatballs out
with a slotted spoon and put in a warm dish. Beat the egg yolks with
the lemon juice in a bowl. Strain the stock and reheat. When it boils,
pour a little of it onto the eggs, beating with a fork, and then return to
the pan. Stir over very low heat for 3 minutes. Pour over the meatballs
and sprinkle with chopped parsley. Serves 4. Accompany with a dish
of boiled rice.

MEATBALLS IN TOMATO SAUCE   Spain

These Spanish meatballs are quite different from the Greek ones, and
are usually served in a spicy tomato and pepper sauce.

½ Spanish onion
1 clove garlic
3 tablespoons chopped parsley
1 lb/450 g minced chuck steak

sea salt and black pepper
a little flour
2 tablespoons olive oil
2 tablespoons chopped parsley

tomato and pepper sauce:
½ Spanish onion
3 tablespoons olive oil
1 clove garlic, crushed
1 small tin (6½ oz/184 g)
  tomatoes
1 small tin (6½ oz/184 g) red
  peppers

1 small green pepper
sea salt and black pepper
a pinch sugar
½ chilli pepper, or a dash
  Tabasco
1 bay leaf
1 stalk celery

First make the meatballs: chop the onion finely with the garlic and parsley and mix with the minced steak. (This is quickly done in a food processor, including the mincing of the meat.) Add plenty of sea salt and black pepper. Try a small ball of the mixture out in a frying pan to test the seasoning. Then form into small balls and roll in flour. Set aside while you make the sauce.

Chop the onion and fry gently in the oil till pale golden. Add the crushed garlic and tinned tomatoes, drained of their juice and roughly chopped. Cook for 2–3 minutes, then add the tinned peppers, drained and roughly chopped, the green pepper which has been chopped quite finely and sea salt, black pepper and sugar. Add the half chilli, if used, free from all seeds and very finely minced, or the Tabasco, also the bay leaf and celery, left whole. Simmer for 5 minutes.

Meanwhile fry the meatballs quite briefly in a little oil, just long enough to brown them all over, then add to the sauce, cover the pan and simmer gently for 1 hour, stirring now and then. Remove the bay leaf and celery and sprinkle with chopped parsley before serving. Serves 4, with rice or noodles, and a green salad.

AUBERGINE MOUSSAKA   Greece

There are many different recipes for moussaka; this is a fairly classic one made with aubergines and minced lamb, topped with a thick béchamel sauce enriched with beaten eggs. It is quite lengthy to prepare but makes a meal in itself with a green salad. It can be prepared in advance up to a certain point, and also reheats well.

2 lb/900 g aubergines
salt
2–3 medium onions
1 oz/25 g butter
2 lb/900 g minced lamb, from
   the shoulder or leg
1 tablespoon tomato purée
¼ pint/150 ml white wine
¼ pint/150 ml water
sea salt and black pepper

frying oil
2 thick slices toast
butter .

béchamel sauce:
2 oz/50 g butter
3 tablespoons flour
1 pint/600 ml milk
sea salt and black pepper
2 eggs, beaten
1 oz/25 g grated parmesan

Cut the aubergines in diagonal slices ¼ inch/5 mm thick. Sprinkle them with salt and leave to drain for 1 hour. Chop the onions and cook in the butter; when they start to change colour, add the minced meat, breaking it up with two wooden spoons. Stir round until browned all over, then add the tomato purée, the wine and water. Add sea salt and black pepper, cover the pan and simmer gently for 30 minutes. Then remove the lid, increase the heat, and cook more briskly until the liquid has all boiled away, stirring often.

Meanwhile, pat dry the aubergines. Heat enough oil in the broadest pan you have to come ½ inch/1 cm up the side of the pan. When it is very hot drop in the aubergines, a few at a time, and fry until golden on both sides, turning once. Drain on soft paper while you fry the next batch. (This frying in very hot deep oil causes them to absorb much less oil than shallow frying.)

When the meat is cooked, tip into a colander and leave for a few minutes to allow the fat to drain away. Cut the crusts off the toast and make into coarse crumbs in the food processor or blender. Rub a fireproof dish with butter and spread 2 tablespoons of the toast crumbs over the bottom. Make a layer of a third of the aubergine slices over this, then stir the remaining crumbs into the meat mixture and spoon half of it over the aubergines. Cover with another layer of aubergines, then the remaining meat. Make a top layer of aubergines, then cover with the béchamel sauce which you have made as usual, stirring in the two beaten eggs off the fire at the very end. Sprinkle with the grated parmesan and bake for 35 minutes at 180°C/350°F/Gas Mark 4, or till a golden brown. Serves 6 with a green salad.

If using a very broad shallow dish or a square baking tin, you may need more sauce to cover it completely; in this case, make a sauce with 3 oz/75 g butter, 5 tablespoons flour, 1½ pints/900 ml milk and 3 beaten eggs. Increase the parmesan to 1½ oz/40 g also. If preparing in advance, do not make the sauce, or at least do not add the beaten eggs, until ready to cook.

MOUSSAKA WITH THREE VEGETABLES   **Greece**

Although *moussaka* is only ever made nowadays with aubergines, it used to be made with other vegetables too, or even with a mixture. Courgettes can be substituted for the aubergines, or a mixture of aubergines, courgettes and tomatoes. For the latter, buy ¾ lb/350 g each aubergines, courgettes and tomatoes. Cook the aubergines as described for aubergine *moussaka*, and shallow fry the sliced courgettes and tomatoes separately in a little oil and butter mixed. Make a layer of each of the vegetables separately, and proceed as for aubergine *moussaka*.

SAMOS MOUSSAKA   **Greece**

On Samos they make a sort of moussaka with semolina, which I grew to love; in fact, it is more like a shepherd's pie, but with semolina instead of potatoes.

1 oz/25 g butter	sea salt and black pepper
1 medium onion, chopped	1 pint/600 ml milk
1 clove garlic, crushed	3 oz/75 g semolina
1 lb/450 g minced lamb	1 thick slice of toast
½ lb/225 g tomatoes, peeled	2 tablespoons chopped parsley
and chopped	

Heat half the butter in a sauté pan and cook the chopped onion until pale golden. Add the crushed garlic and cook for another minute. Put the minced meat in the pan and stir round, breaking it up with two wooden spoons. When brown all over, add the peeled and chopped tomatoes, sea salt and black pepper. Cover and cook gently for 25 minutes, stirring occasionally. Meanwhile put the milk in a saucepan and bring towards boiling point. Shake in the semolina and stir constantly until thickened and smooth. Add salt and pepper and simmer gently for 10 minutes, stirring often. Cut the crusts off the toast and put in the food processor or blender to reduce to coarse crumbs. When the meat is cooked, pour off any excess fat and stir in 2 tablespoons of the toast crumbs and the chopped parsley. Spoon into a shallow dish and spread the semolina over the top so that it completely covers the meat. Smooth it with a wet palette knife. Sprinkle 2 more tablespoons of toast crumbs over the top and dot with the remaining butter. Bake for 40 minutes at 190°C/375°F/Gas Mark 5 till slightly puffed up and golden brown. Serve immediately, with a green salad. Serves 4.

SERBIAN SAUERKRAUT   Yugoslavia

This typically Yugoslavian dish is a hearty one, composed of a mixture of smoked and fresh meat cooked in sauerkraut. It makes a good meal for a cold winter's day, possibly more suitable for lunch than dinner since it is quite heavy, and is even better reheated. In Yugoslavia, where it often includes two pigs' feet and a pig's ear in addition to the other meats, it is accompanied by proya, a dish of baked polenta, but I don't find it needs any accompaniment.

oil
3–3½ lb/approx. 1·5 kg
  sauerkraut
black pepper
3 medium onions, chopped
3 red peppers, cut in small
  squares
4 tablespoons chopped parsley
a handful celery leaves,
  chopped

2 lb/900 g boned brisket of beef,
  cut in cubes
½ lb/225 g smoked spare ribs of
  pork, cut up into ribs
6 oz/175 g smoked pork
  sausage, sliced thickly
¼ lb/100 g bacon, chopped
sea salt

Rub a casserole, earthenware if possible, with oil and lay half the sauerkraut in it. (I use it straight from the tin, but if you want a milder flavour, turn it into a colander and rinse it under cold running water, then squeeze dry.) Sprinkle with ground black pepper, then lay the chopped onions, red peppers, parsley and celery leaves over it. Lay the meats on top of this, sprinkle with sea salt and black pepper, and cover with the remaining sauerkraut. Add enough cold water to come almost level with the sauerkraut and bring to boiling point slowly, on top of the stove. Then cover the pot, transfer to a low oven 150°C/310°F/Gas Mark 2, and cook for 4 hours. To serve, lay the sauerkraut in a broad earthenware dish, cover with the meats, and scatter the red pepper over all. Serves 6.

SERBIAN STEW   Yugoslavia

A really excellent dish, a meat stew with a slightly sour flavour, it is a meal in itself, with a green salad.

2–2½ lb/1 kg boned brisket of
  beef
sea salt and black pepper
1 lb/450 g onions, sliced
½ oz/15 g lard
½ teaspoon paprika
a few celery leaves, roughly
  chopped

3 stalks parsley, chopped
1 bay leaf
7 large cloves garlic, peeled
4 medium potatoes, peeled
6 fl. oz/175 ml wine vinegar

Cut the beef in neat pieces and sprinkle generously with sea salt and black pepper. Leave for 30 minutes. Cook the sliced onions in the lard (butter can be substituted if you have no lard), adding paprika and ground pepper. When it starts to colour, add the roughly chopped celery leaves, parsley, bay leaf and the whole cloves of garlic. Cut the peeled potatoes in thick slices lengthwise and add to the pan. Remove from the heat after a minute or two, add the meat and mix well. Add enough warm water just to cover, pour on the vinegar and cover closely with foil and the lid. (Ideally, this should be cooked in an earthenware pot, its lid sealed with a flour and water paste.) Cook for 4 hours at 150°C/300°F/Gas Mark 2. Serves 4–5.

SOUTZOUKAKIA   Greece

These little pork meatballs are traditionally cooked with strips of white cabbage.

Make as for youvarlakia (see page 159), but substituting pork for veal and omitting the parsley. You need 2 or 3 leaves of white cabbage, blanched for 4 minutes in boiling water and cut in strips about 1 inch/2·5 cm wide. Lay the meatballs in a sauté pan in concentric circles, weaving the cabbage strips in and around them, and also round the edges of the pan. Lay more cabbage strips between each layer of meatballs. Cook as for *youvarlakia*, and make the sauce in the same way. The strips of cabbage are usually discarded, as they have given most of their flavour to the sauce, but they can be served with the meatballs if preferred. Serves 4–5.

SOUVLAKIA   Greece

I ate these every day for two weeks one summer in Crete, accompanied by bread, *tzatziki* and a Greek salad, and never grew tired of them. They are nicest when made on a small scale, as they are in the Greek tavernas, with small cubes of lamb threaded 4 or 5 at a time on small skewers, preferably of wood. Each person has 2 or 3 skewers according to his appetite.

½ *leg of lamb, boned*
sea salt and black pepper
4 tablespoons olive oil
2 tablespoons lemon juice
dried oregano

1 Spanish onion, cut in
  quarters and thinly sliced
a few lettuce leaves, shredded
2–3 lemons, cut in quarters

Cut the lamb in small neat cubes, about 1 inch/2·5 cm across. Thread them, 5 at a time, onto small skewers and lay on a flat dish. Sprinkle with sea salt and black pepper and pour the oil and lemon juice over them. Leave for 1 hour, then grill over a quick flame, turning frequently, until they are well browned outside and just cooked within. Sprinkle them with dried oregano and garnish with the sliced raw onion, shredded lettuce and lemon quarters. Serve with *tzatziki*, hot flat bread and a Greek salad. Serves 4–5. For a more substantial dish, they can be accompanied by a rice pilav, or *dolmades*, made slightly larger than usual.

TRIPPE ALLA GENOVESE   Italy

A Genoese speciality, this dish of tripe with pounded pine kernels is a favourite among lovers of tripe.

2 lb/900 g tripe
6 tablespoons olive oil
1 oz/25 g dripping or butter
1 large onion, chopped
1 large carrot, chopped
2 stalks celery, chopped
½ oz/15 g dried mushrooms,
  soaked for 10 minutes and
  chopped
1 bay leaf

3 tablespoons pine kernels,
  chopped and pounded in a
  mortar
3 tablespoons chopped parsley
sea salt and black pepper
6 fl. oz/175 ml dry white wine
8 fl. oz/250 ml veal or chicken
  stock
sea salt and black pepper

Wash the tripe, pat dry and cut in strips about ½ inch by 1½ inches/1 cm by 3·5 cm. Heat the oil with the fat and cook the chopped onion, carrot and celery gently for 5 minutes, adding the chopped soaked mushrooms and the bay leaf. Then add the tripe, the pounded pine nuts, chopped parsley, sea salt and black pepper. Cook gently for another 5 minutes, stirring now and then, then add the wine and stock. (There should be not quite enough liquid to come level with the meat; adjust the amount of stock accordingly.) Cover and cook gently for 1½ hours, then test to see if the tripe is tender; it may need another 10–15 minutes. When ready, the liquid should be more or less absorbed. Serve with rice, or crusty bread, and a green salad. Serves 5–6.

TRIPES À LA NIÇOISE   France

This is a good and simple way of cooking tripe, which provides an excellent soup at the same time.

2 lb/900 g tripe
sea salt and black pepper
2 large onions, sliced
½ lb/225 g piece knuckle of
  veal
2 stalks celery, sliced
5 carrots, sliced
4 tomatoes, skinned and
  roughly chopped

3 cloves garlic, finely chopped
1 bay leaf
2 stalks parsley
2 sprigs thyme
2 sprigs oregano
6 tablespoons marc or cognac
1 oz/25 g grated parmesan

Wash the tripe well, pat it dry and cut in strips roughly 1 inch by 2½ inches/2 cm by 5 cm. Season well with sea salt and black pepper and mix with the sliced onions. Put in the bottom of a heavy casserole and lay the knuckle of veal on it. Cover with the other vegetables, add the herbs, and pour over the marc (or cognac). Add enough warm water to come almost level with the contents of the pan, cover closely and simmer for 1½ hours. Lift out the tripe and vegetables with a slotted spoon and lay in a shallow fireproof dish, moistening with a little of the stock. Cut the veal off the bone and mix with the tripe. Cover with the grated parmesan and brown quickly under the grill. Serve with rice or pasta, and a green salad. Serves 4.

The remaining stock can be used for soup for another meal.

ESCALOPE DE VEAU AU BASILIC   France

I ate this in a restaurant overlooking the port in Marseilles; it is a light creamy dish, perfect for a summer meal.

1 oz/25 g butter
4 veal escalopes
2 teaspoons flour
¼ pint/150 ml white wine
¼ pint/150 ml veal or chicken
  stock

½ pint/300 ml thin cream
sea salt and black pepper
3 tablespoons basil leaves cut
  in strips

Heat the butter in a large frying pan and cook 2 of the escalopes, turning once. Lift onto a hot dish and keep warm while you cook the remaining 2. When all are cooked, stir the flour into the juices and cook for 1 minute, stirring. Heat the wine and stock together and pour on gradually, stirring till smoothly blended. Boil quite rapidly for several minutes, until reduced by half, then lower the heat and add the cream. Stir till blended, add sea salt and black pepper, and allow to simmer for 2–3 minutes. Then stir in 2 tablespoons of the basil leaves cut in strips and pour over the escalopes in the dish. Sprinkle the remaining basil over the top and serve. Serves 4, with new potatoes and a green vegetable, or a green salad.

YOUVARLAKIA **Greece**

These excellent meatballs are best made with veal, and part of their charm is the raw rice mixed with them. They are served in their cooking stock, enriched by the addition of egg yolk and lemon juice to make a tart *avgolemono* sauce.

1 lb/450 g minced veal
1 large onion, very finely
   chopped
2 tablespoons rice
sea salt and black pepper

2–4 tablespoons chopped
   parsley
1 egg, separated
juice of ½ lemon

Put the minced veal in a large bowl and add the very finely chopped onion, the rice, sea salt and black pepper, chopped parsley and the lightly beaten egg white. (Keep the yolk for the sauce.) Work the mixture very well between the hands, almost kneading it like bread. Divide into oval shapes, like damsons, and lay in a buttered sauté pan. Arrange them evenly in layers and add enough boiling water barely to cover them. Bring to boiling point, cover the pan and simmer for 40 minutes. Lift out the youvarlakia with a slotted spoon and lay in a serving dish in a warm place, while you make the sauce. Strain the cooking stock into a clean saucepan and reheat. Beat the egg yolk with the lemon juice in a bowl, pour a ladleful of boiling stock onto it, mix well, then return to the saucepan over very gentle heat. Cook for a few moments, stirring constantly, without allowing it to boil. Taste for seasoning, then pour over the meatballs. Serve with a green salad. Serves 4–5.

8   PASTRY, RICE AND
PASTA DISHES

As we have seen in the introduction, wheat is the main crop of the Mediterranean, and farinaceous dishes play a large part in the diet, especially in winter time. These include the pasta that is eaten not only in Italy, but also in France and Spain, the bread dough and yeast pastry that are used almost interchangeably around Nice and the west coast of Italy, Italian gnocchi, the flaky pastry dishes of Greece, Turkey, Tunisia and the Middle East, the dumplings and pancakes of Yugoslavia and the *couscous* of North Africa.

In Greece, Turkey, Tunisia, and to a lesser extent in Syria and Lebanon, the most popular pastry is the paper-thin strudel-type pastry, called *filo* in Greece, *yufka* in Turkey, *warka* in Morocco and *malsouqua* in Tunisia. This is rarely made any more at home, since it demands a high degree of skill and a lot of time, but it is manufactured and widely available in shops. The thin sheets of pastry are used four or five at a time, each one brushed with oil or melted butter, and in baking they merge together to form a light flaky pastry. The fillings vary in detail, but can be limited to three basic sorts: feta cheese mixed with eggs; chopped spinach and herbs mixed with cheese and eggs; and minced meat mixed with herbs and sometimes pine nuts. In Greece, shallow round tins are used for baking pittas almost as big as cart wheels; in country areas these are usually sent to the local baker's for cooking, since few houses have ovens, or on a large enough scale. The resulting pies are usually eaten hot one day and cold the next. Small pastries are also made, with similar fillings, in shapes that vary according to local tradition. Some of the most common are triangular, semi-circular or square. In Turkey, the *boreks* are usually made in individual sizes, in fat rolls, small squares or half-moons, or cigarette shapes. They are filled with similar mixtures, including one I have not seen before – an excellent mixture of puréed potato mixed with chopped herbs. In Tunisia, the *malsouqua* (pastry sheets) are round, as opposed to the rectangular sheets of Greece and Turkey, and the resulting pastries are known as *briks*. One which is special to Tunisia, and has become almost a national dish, is the *brik à l'oeuf*; this consists of a raw egg with minced onion and herbs, enclosed within a folded sheet of pastry, and fried so briefly that the egg remains soft. In Morocco, a similar thin pastry is used to make an immense pie filled with pigeons, combined with nuts, raisins, herbs and spices.

In some parts of the Mediterranean rice has replaced wheat as the dominant crop – in Valencia, for instance, the home of the paella, and in the Camargue, the swampy rice-growing area west of Marseilles. It is also the predominant cereal crop in parts of northern Italy, particularly around Milan, where the best risottos are made with the excellent short-grained rice that grows in the Po valley, and in Venice, where *risi e bisi* is one of the favourite spring dishes. Turkish pilavs rival Italian risottos in their excellence, while Egypt also has some excellent rice dishes. Another cereal food that is very popular in north-eastern Italy is polenta, made from the corn (or maize) grown in the Friuli area.

Diagrams for folding tiropitakia, boreks, briks, etc.

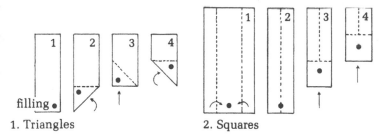

1. Triangles   2. Squares

3. Cigarettes: fold as for squares, but roll instead of folding in steps 3 and 4.

BRIK À L'OEUF   **Tunisia**

Anyone who has visited Tunis must have eaten at least one *brik à l'oeuf* for they are served everywhere, from private houses, hotels and restaurants down to barrows in the street. They are extremely delicious, a soft egg wrapped in paper-thin crisp pastry, served with a squeeze of lemon. Sometimes chopped onion and parsley are added, sometimes a little tunny fish. They are impossible to duplicate here since we cannot buy the authentic pastry, the Tunisian *malsouqua* or the Moroccan *warka*; we can, however, make a reasonable substitute using Greek *filo* pastry, although this is slightly different in consistency and rectangular instead of round. It is quite tricky to make them without losing a few eggs, especially the first time.

1–2 sheets filo *pastry*	*sea salt and black pepper*
1 oz/25 g melted butter	*4–5 small eggs*
2 tablespoons grated onion	*frying oil*
2 tablespoons finely chopped parsley	*2 lemons, cut in quarters*

Cut the *filo* in rectangles roughly 10 × 5 inches/25 × 13 cm and brush the edges with melted butter. Put ½ teaspoon each grated onion and finely chopped parsley in the centre of each, with the pastry lying over a saucer. Add a pinch of sea salt and black pepper, and break an egg carefully into the centre, folding over the pastry and sealing the edges by pressing them together. Slide into a pan of hot oil and fry for 30 seconds on each side. Serve immediately they are made, on hot plates with lemon quarters. Serves 4–5 as a first course, or as a snack.

BRIKS AUX POMMES DE TERRE   Tunisia

These little pastries are extremely good, similar to the Turkish potato *boreks*, but smaller and creamier. They are usually deep fried, but can be brushed with melted butter and baked if necessary.

¾ lb/350 g potatoes	*sea salt and black pepper*
1 small onion, chopped	*1 egg yolk, beaten*
2 tablespoons olive oil	*3–4 sheets* filo *pastry*
1 clove garlic, minced	*2 oz/50 g melted butter*
2 tablespoons chopped parsley	*frying oil*

Boil the potatoes and mash them. Chop the onion and fry in the olive oil, adding the minced garlic after a little. When both are golden, stir in the chopped parsley and remove from the heat. Beat into the potato purée, adding sea salt and black pepper. Stir in the beaten egg yolk.

Lay out 1 sheet of *filo* pastry at a time, leaving the others covered with a damp cloth. Cut it in strips measuring 2 × 10 inches/5 × 25 cm. Brush each strip with melted butter and lay a teaspoon of the filling on one end. Fold into triangles (see diagram at start of chapter). When all are filled, drop them a few at a time into hot oil and fry for 1 minute on each side, until brown and crisp. Alternatively, brush the rolled triangles all over with melted butter, lay them on a greased baking sheet, and bake for 15 minutes at 180°C/350°F/Gas Mark 4. Serves 5–6 as part of a mixed meze, or with drinks.

MEAT BOREKS   Turkey

For those who have the patience, these little pastries can be made in thin rolls like cigarettes, excellent for serving with drinks. Alternatively they can be made in larger squares or triangles, which is less fiddly, and served either with drinks or as a first course.

1 small onion	1 teaspoon ground coriander
1 tablespoon olive oil	¼ teaspoon ground cinnamon
½ oz/15 g butter	1 raw egg
½ lb/225 g minced beef	4–5 sheets filo pastry
sea salt and black pepper	2 oz/50 g butter, melted
1 egg, hard-boiled and chopped	
3 tablespoons chopped parsley, or 2 tablespoons chopped mint	

Chop the onion finely and cook in the olive oil and ½ oz/15 g butter till it starts to colour. Add the minced beef, stirring well with two wooden spoons, until lightly browned all over. Lower the heat and cook gently for 15 minutes, stirring now and then, adding sea salt and black pepper to taste. When cooked, stir in the chopped egg, herbs and spices, and remove from the heat. After cooling slightly, stir in the beaten egg and leave to cool completely.

Cut the sheets of *filo* pastry in strips roughly 4 × 10 inches/ 10 × 25 cm. Brush the strips with the melted butter and lay a very thin strip of filling along the short edge of each strip, leaving ½ inch/

1 cm free along each long edge. Fold over the two long edges to enclose the filling, and roll up. Brush again with melted butter and press down the end. Lay on a greased baking sheet and bake for about 12 minutes at 180°C/350°F/Gas Mark 4, till golden brown and crisp. Alternatively fold up the pastry strips to make a square shape, and brush with melted butter. Bake for 15 minutes at 180°C/350°F/Gas Mark 4. Makes about 16 square boreks, or 20 cigarette-shaped boreks. Serve immediately.

POTATO BOREKS   Turkey

I had these delicious rolls of thin pastry filled with a potato purée mixed with herbs in a pretty restaurant built round a courtyard in Bodrum, a small town on the south-west coast of Turkey. They were served as part of a large selection of hors d'oeuvre, but I also like them as an accompaniment to meat dishes.

1 lb/450 g potatoes
4 tablespoons milk
1 ½ oz/40 g butter
2 tablespoons chopped parsley
2 tablespoons chopped dill or
   chives

sea salt and black pepper
2 sheets filo *pastry*
2 oz/50 g melted butter

Boil the potatoes and push through a food mill to make a dry purée. Heat the milk and butter, stir in the chopped herbs, sea salt and black pepper, and beat into the purée; leave to cool.

Cut each sheet of *filo* in 4, making 8 rectangles roughly 10 × 5 inches/25 × 13 cm, and brush all over with melted butter. Divide the purée into 8 parts and form each into a roll like a fat cork. Lay on the pastry rectangles, fold over the long edges and roll up, sealing the ends and brushing all over with melted butter. Lay on a buttered baking sheet and bake for 20–25 minutes at 180°C/350°F/Gas Mark 4, until golden brown. Serve as soon as possible. Serves 4.

TIROPITAKIA I   Greece

These little hot cheese pastries are also found in Turkey and in the Middle East. They are extremely good, either with drinks, or as a first course.

6 oz/175 g feta cheese	*black pepper*
1½ oz/40 g grated parmesan	*about 4–5 sheets* filo *pastry*
1 small egg, beaten	*approx. 1½ oz/40 g butter,*
1 level tablespoon chopped mint	*melted*

Mash the feta with a fork and beat in the grated parmesan; it does not need to be absolutely smooth. Beat the egg and stir in, also the chopped mint and some black pepper. (No salt, as feta cheese is very salty already.)

Take a sheet of *filo* at a time, covering the others with a damp cloth to prevent them drying out and becoming brittle, and cut it in strips about 2 × 10 inches/5 × 25 cm. Brush each strip with melted butter and lay a small teaspoon of cheese filling at one end. Fold up in triangular shapes, as shown in the diagram, brushing the finished triangle all over with melted butter which will seal down the edge. Lay on a buttered baking tray and bake for 15 minutes at 180°C/350°F/Gas Mark 4, till golden brown and crisp. Serve as soon as possible. They can also be reheated, but are never quite so good. This makes about 24 *tiropitakia*.

TIROPITAKIA II   Greece

An alternative filling – equally delicious – for the little hot cheese pastries which are so good.

¼ lb/100 g feta cheese	*black pepper*
2 oz/50 g cream cheese	*4–5 leaves* filo *pastry*
1 medium egg	*approx. 1½ oz/40 g butter,*
1 level tablespoon chopped	*melted*
mint	

Grate the feta onto a plate and mash the cream cheese into it; it does not matter if it is slightly lumpy. Beat the egg and stir in, also the chopped mint and black pepper. Cut the leaves of *filo* into strips as described above, and brush with melted butter. Fill, roll up, and bake as for *tiropitakia* I. Makes about 22–24 *tiropitakia*. Serve very hot.

SPANAKOPITTA   Greece

This large spinach pie is a handsome and useful dish. I make it often, for vegetarian meals, picnics or as part of a buffet supper. I particularly like it cold.

2 lb/900 g spinach
2 bunches spring onions
1–2 oz/25–50 g parsley, heads
  only
4 sprigs dill
1 tablespoon salt
5 oz/150 g butter

2 onions, finely chopped
2 large eggs
¼ lb/100 g feta cheese,
  crumbled
(sea salt and) black pepper
8–10 leaves filo pastry

Wash the spinach, spring onions, parsley and dill. Chop them all quite finely – this is quickly done in a food processor. Put them in layers in a large bowl, sprinkling the salt over the layers. Leave for 15–20 minutes.

Meanwhile heat 3 oz/75 g of the butter and cook the chopped onions gently until they turn pale golden. Squeeze the chopped greens between the hands to get rid of all the moisture, and return to the bowl after rinsing and drying it. When the onions are ready, tip them over the greens with their juices, and mix well. Beat the eggs, stir in the crumbled feta, and stir into the spinach mixture. Add plenty of black pepper, and a little sea salt if required (probably not necessary, due to the initial salting and the saltiness of the cheese).

Have a broad shallow baking tin ready, either a round one about 11 inches/28 cm across, or a square one 10 inches/25 cm across and about 1½ inches/3–4 cm deep. Melt the remaining 2 oz/50 g butter and brush the tin with some of it. Line it with a sheet of *filo*, trimming it with scissors so that it overlaps the tin by 1–2 inches/3–5 cm, and brush it with melted butter. Lay another sheet over it, and brush again with melted butter. Continue until you have 4 or 5 layers of pastry, then cover the remaining sheets with a damp cloth. Brush the top layer with melted butter and cover with the spinach mixture, smoothing it down to fill the tin nicely. Cover with another 4 or 5 sheets of pastry, brushing each one with melted butter and trimming them to fit the tin exactly. When complete, fold the corners and edges of the bottom sheets over the top, brushing them with melted butter to make them stick. Brush the whole top layer with more butter, and if you have a pastry wheel, make perforated lines across the top surface to form strips about 3 inches/8 cm wide (or cut with the point of a sharp knife). Bake for 40 minutes at 180°C/350°F/Gas Mark 4. Serve either warm, or after cooling completely; do not chill. Serves 6–8.

BIGUOLI EN SALSA   Italy

This is a speciality of Venice which is traditionally eaten on Good Friday, when meat and fresh fish are forbidden. It consists of wholemeal spaghetti, called *biguoi* or *biguoli* in Venice, in a sauce made from salted or tinned anchovies. It is a simple dish, quite austere but good on occasions; it is also useful in that the ingredients are all in the store cupboard, as it were. Wholemeal spaghetti similar to the Venetian *biguoli* can be bought in health food shops.

2 medium onions
1 oz/25 g butter
1½ tablespoons olive oil
1–2 cloves garlic
¼ lb/100 g flat anchovy fillets
a little milk

2 tablespoons water
black pepper
1 lb/450 g wholemeal spaghetti
extra butter or olive oil
   (optional)

Chop the onion and cook slowly in the butter and olive oil in a sauté pan. When it starts to soften, add the minced or crushed garlic, then the chopped anchovy fillets which have been soaked in milk for 10–15 minutes. Cook gently for 5 minutes, then add 2 tablespoons of water, cover the pan, and continue to cook very gently until the sauce is soft and creamy, stirring from time to time and adding a little black pepper.

In the meantime cook the spaghetti; it takes rather longer than ordinary spaghetti, about 18–20 minutes. When ready, drain it and turn into a heated bowl. Spoon the finished sauce over it – if it seems a little dry, add extra butter or oil. Toss well and serve, with no accompaniment. Serves 4.

CANNELONI AUX POISSONS   **France**

In Nice, canneloni is sometimes made with a fish filling, under a béchamel sauce sprinkled with grated parmesan. I feel this dish is only worth considering if you have a food processor and a pasta machine.

dough:
1 egg
2 teaspoons olive oil
1 teaspoon water
a pinch of salt
¼ lb/100 g flour

filling:
2 lb/900 g filleted hake, pike or
  other white fish
approx. ½ pint/300 ml milk
  mixed with enough water to
  cover fish

¾ lb/350 g mushrooms
1½ oz/40 g butter
sea salt and black pepper
2 eggs, beaten

béchamel sauce:
2½ oz/65 g butter
4 tablespoons flour
¾ pint/350 ml milk, heated
¼ pint/150 ml thin cream
sea salt and black pepper
ground mace or grated nutmeg
1½ oz/40 g grated parmesan

First make the dough. Put the egg, oil, water and salt in a food processor and process for 30 seconds. Add the sifted flour and process for another 30 seconds. Turn out onto a floured piece of cling-film, wrap and rest for 5 minutes. Then flatten the dough and feed it through the widest roller of the pasta machine 5 times, folding it in 3 after each time. Then reduce the rollers gradually till one away from the thinnest setting, rolling it through once each time, and folding it again in 3. For the last turn, it may be easier to cut it in 2 pieces. Once rolled to a long thin sheet, let it rest for 3–4 minutes, then cut it in rectangles roughly 2½ × 3½ inches/6 × 8·5 cm. (It will stretch 1 inch/2·5 cm in each direction on cooking.)

Drop the rectangles, about 8 at a time, into a large pan of boiling water, stirring now and then to prevent them sticking together, and cook steadily for 5 minutes. Lift out and drop into a bowl of cold water with a drop of oil in it. Then drain on a cloth while you cook the next batch. When all are done, they can be left draining until needed.

To make the filling, poach the fish in a mixture of milk and water, lightly salted, until tender. Cool slightly, then break into flakes, discarding all skin and any odd bones. Chop the mushrooms coarsely and stew in the butter until softened. Put the flaked fish and mushrooms into the food processor in two batches. Process until thoroughly blended, adding sea salt and black pepper. Turn into a bowl and stir in the beaten eggs.

Take 1 tablespoon of filling at a time, form into a roll and wrap in a sheet of canneloni. Continue until all the filling is used up, laying the rolled canneloni into a buttered gratin dish. If it is necessary to make more than one layer, stop at this stage and make the sauce. Melt the butter, stir in the flour and cook for 1 minute. Pour on the heated milk and stir till blended; simmer for 3 minutes, adding the cream, sea salt and black pepper, and a little ground mace or grated nutmeg. When smooth and creamy, pour over the canneloni in their dish; if making in two layers, pour a thin layer of sauce over the first layer and sprinkle with some of the grated cheese before making the second layer. Then cover with the remaining sauce and sprinkle with the rest of the grated parmesan. Bake for 30 minutes at 190°C/375°F/Gas Mark 5 or until golden brown and bubbling. This can be made in advance and reheated, in which case it will need an extra 5 minutes or so. Serves 5–6 with a green salad.

LASAGNE AL PESCARA   Italy

Like all lasagne dishes this Venetian version is lengthy to make, taking about 2 hours, but it is unusual, and useful in that it can be prepared in advance and reheated, or kept hot for a couple of hours, or frozen. It can be made with bought lasagne, but is of course not so good; I would not attempt making the lasagne myself unless I had a food processor and a pasta machine, however. If making with bought lasagne, the green sort looks pretty, but is tricky to make at home.

fish filling:
1 pint/350 g unshelled prawns
2½ lb/1·15 kg firm white fish:
  bream, bass, snapper, monkfish
1 onion, halved
1 carrot, halved
1 stalk celery, halved
1 bay leaf
⅓ pint/200 ml dry white wine
2½ pints/1·5 litres water
sea salt and black pepper

lasagne:
1 egg
2 teaspoons olive oil
1 teaspoon water
a pinch of salt
¼ lb/100 g flour, sifted

mushroom filling:
1½ lb/675 g mushrooms,
   coarsely chopped
1½ oz/40 g butter
juice of ¼ lemon
2 teaspoons flour
¼ pint/150 ml thin cream
sea salt and black pepper

béchamel sauce:
2 oz/50 g butter
2 tablespoons flour
1 pint/600 ml fish stock
sea salt and black pepper
¼ pint/150 ml thin cream
1 oz/25 g grated parmesan

First make some fish stock: shell the prawns and put the shells in a fish kettle with the fish heads, the flavouring vegetables, bay leaf, wine and water. Add sea salt and black pepper and bring slowly to the boil. Simmer for 30 minutes, then lift out the shells, fish heads and vegetables.

Next make the lasagne: put the egg in the food processor with the oil, water and salt. Process for 30 seconds, then add the flour and process for another 30 seconds. Turn out onto a square of cling-film, wrap and rest for 5 minutes. Assemble the pasta machine set to its widest gauge (no. 1). Flatten the dough and feed it through the roller 5 times, folding it into 3 each time. Then set the rollers progressively closer and roll it once through nos 2, 3 and 4. Then cut the ribbon of dough in half, and fold each piece once through no. 5. (I find this thin enough for easy handling; you can go one stage further if you wish.)

Bring a large pan of water to the boil and cut the dough into rectangles roughly 4½ × 5 inches/11 × 13 cm. Drop them 4 at a time into the pan and cook steadily for 5 minutes. (If you have rolled it to the thinnest possible stage the timing will be shorter.) Lift them out of the water and drop them into a bowl of cold water with a spoonful of oil in it. Then drain them on a cloth while you cook the rest.

Next cook the fish: lower them into the stock, bring back to the boil, and poach for 10–12 minutes, until they are just cooked. Lift out and flake the flesh, dropping the bones back into the stock. Boil up until reduced by about half. Strain and measure 1 pint/600 ml.

Make the mushroom filling by cooking the chopped mushrooms in the butter, adding a squeeze of lemon juice. When they are softened, stir in the flour, and finally the cream. Stir till smooth and blended, adding sea salt and black pepper.

Next make the béchamel sauce: melt the butter, stir in the flour and cook for 2 minutes. Reheat the strained fish stock and add, stirring till blended. Add sea salt and black pepper and 2 tablespoons of the cream.

Have the flaked fish mixed with the shelled prawns in a large bowl; pour on enough of the sauce to moisten well – probably just under half – and mix lightly, adding more salt and pepper if needed.

Assemble the dish by making a layer of lasagne in a well-buttered rectangular dish, cutting the sheets of dough to fit, overlapping each other slightly. Cover with half the fish, then more lasagne, then half the mushrooms. Make 4 layers of pasta in all, with 2 layers of fish and 2 of mushrooms. Reheat the remaining sauce, stir in the rest of the cream and pour over the whole dish. Sprinkle with grated parmesan and bake for 35 minutes at 190°C/375°F/Gas Mark 5. Serves 5–6 with a green salad.

PASTA E FAGIOLI   Italy

This comforting dish is like a cross between a thick soup and a bean stew. I serve it as a first course, in soup plates with fork and spoon. It is delicious in cold weather, or any time when one is tired and hungry. Like all bean dishes, it is particularly delicious when made with fresh haricots, in late summer.

½ lb/225 g dried cannelini
   beans or 2½ lb/1·25 kg fresh
   haricots
1 small onion
3 tablespoons olive oil
2 oz/50 g chopped bacon
1 clove garlic, minced
1 carrot, chopped
1 stalk celery, chopped

sea salt and black pepper
¼ lb/100 g fatty pork, in one
   piece
2 pints/1·2 litres light stock or
   water
3 oz/75 g soup pasta, or
   spaghetti broken in short
   lengths

Soak the dried beans for 4–5 hours, then drain. Chop the onion and cook in the oil until it starts to colour, then add the chopped bacon. When that is also turning golden, add the minced garlic, chopped carrot and celery. Cook all together for 5 minutes, then add the drained beans, sea salt and black pepper, and the piece of pork. Heat the stock or water and add to the pan, cover, and simmer until the beans are soft, about 45 minutes.

Lift out about a third of the beans and purée in a food processor, blender or food mill. Return the purée to the pan and stir till blended with the rest. Bring back to the boil and add the pasta; cook, stirring frequently, for about 15 minutes, until the pasta is tender. (If the liquid is absorbed before the pasta is quite soft, simply turn off the heat and leave covered for 5–8 minutes; the pasta will continue cooking.) Discard the pork, pour into a bowl and serve hot. Serves 4–5.

In Italy, this is served with grated parmesan, but I prefer it without.

If making with fresh beans, simply shell them and add to the sautéed vegetables. They will probably be tender after 20–25 minutes' cooking.

PASTICCIO ALLA PESCARA   Italy

This unusual combination of pasta and fish is sometimes found in Venice. I had it made with a sort of fettucine called *trenette*; it is sometimes made with lasagne. It is quite complicated to make, since it has 2 sauces: the layering sauce is made with flaked white fish in a béchamel, while the covering sauce is made with pounded prawns and tomato purée.

1½ –2 lb/675–900 g mixed firm
   white fish with heads, tails,
   etc. – bass, bream, monkfish
2 pints/1·2 litres water
⅓ pint/200 ml dry white wine
1 onion, halved
1 carrot, halved
1 stalk celery, halved
1 bay leaf
sea salt and black pepper

prawn sauce:
½ lb/225 g unshelled prawns
3½ oz/90 g butter
2 tablespoons flour

½ pint/300 ml prawn stock
sea salt and black pepper
½ tablespoon tomato purée
4 tablespoons cream

béchamel sauce:
1½ oz/40 g butter
2 tablespoons flour
¾ pint/350 ml fish stock
sea salt and black pepper
2 tablespoons cream

¾ lb/350 g fettucine, or flat
   noodles

Put the fish heads, tails, etc. in a fish kettle with the water and wine. Add the halved flavouring vegetables, bay leaf, sea salt and black pepper. Bring to the boil and cook for 30 minutes, then add the whole fish and simmer gently for 10–20 minutes, depending on size. Lift them out as they are cooked, and remove the skin and bones as soon as they are cool enough to handle. Drop these back into the kettle and continue to boil until reduced by about half. Flake the fish and keep warm. Taste the stock while reducing to make sure it does not become too strong, then strain and measure ¾ pint/350 ml.

While this is under way, prepare the prawn stock. If using cooked prawns, shell them and put the shells in a pan with 1 pint/600 ml water. Bring to the boil and simmer for 30 minutes, then strain and measure ½ pint/300 ml. (If using uncooked prawns, make a stock by dropping them into ½ pint/300 ml of slightly salted water and simmering for 2 minutes. Drain the prawns, reserving the stock for the sauce, and shell them as soon as they are cool enough to handle.) Chop the prawns roughly and put in a food processor with 2 oz/50 g of the butter, cut in bits. Process until reduced to a paste.

Next make the béchamel sauce: heat 1½ oz/40 g butter and stir in 2 tablespoons flour. Cook for 1 minute, then add the ¾ pint/350 ml hot fish stock. Stir till blended, and simmer for 3–4 minutes, adding sea salt and black pepper and 2 tablespoons cream. Stir about half this sauce into the flaked fish, using just enough to make it moist without being soupy. Cook the fettucine as usual and drain well; mix with the remaining fish sauce and divide in three parts. Put a third into a buttered baking dish and cover with half the flaked fish. Put a second layer of fettucine over the fish, then top with the remaining fish, then the rest of the noodles.

Finally make the prawn sauce: melt 1½ oz/40 g butter and stir in 2 tablespoons flour. Simmer 1 minute, then add the ½ pint/300 ml prawn stock. Stir till smooth, then add the prawn paste by degrees, stirring until each addition is smoothly blended. Add sea salt and black pepper, tomato purée and cream; continue to stir and simmer until all is amalgamated. Pour over the fettucine and bake for 15 minutes at 190°C/375°F/Gas Mark 5. Serves 5–6 as a main dish, with a green salad.

POTATO GNOCCHI   Italy

This, my favourite form of gnocchi, is at its most delicious served with *pesto* melting over it, as is the practice in Genoa. It is also good served with a sauce bolognese, or a simple *coulis de tomates*, or as the accompaniment to a dish of braised beef, as is done in Yugoslavia. The consistency of the dough varies greatly according to the texture of the potatoes; it is best made in winter with old potatoes, but then of course there is no fresh basil for the *pesto*.

1½ lb/675 g floury potatoes
¼ lb/100 g flour
1 oz/25 g butter

1 egg yolk
sea salt and black pepper

Boil the potatoes in their skins and drain; as soon as they are cool enough to handle, skin them and push through a medium food mill. Dry out the purée over gentle heat for a few minutes, then turn them into a warm bowl. Stir in the flour, and the butter cut in small bits. When this is amalgamated, beat in the egg yolk. Add salt and black pepper to taste.

If the dough is firm enough to handle easily, form it into several long rolls about 1 inch/2·5 cm thick, and cut in ½-inch/1-cm slices. Flatten each one slightly between the prongs of a fork and the palm of the hand, then drop into lightly salted simmering water. Poach for 4–5 minutes, when they will float to the surface; do not do too many at one time as they must be able to float freely. If the dough is too soft to roll in this way, simply form into ovals like a small bird's egg, using two floured teaspoons, and drop into the simmering water. Drain, then transfer to a hot dish.

Serve as soon as made, either with *pesto*, *ragú bolognese*, *salsa pizzaiola*, a *coulis de tomates* or simply dotted with melted butter and grated cheese as the accompaniment to a stewed beef dish. When serving with *pesto*, have extra butter and grated parmesan on the table. Serves 4.

SPAGHETTI PORDENONE   Italy

I ate this in a small restaurant in Venice and recreated it to the best of my ability when I got home. The shiny purple skin of the aubergines looks very pretty shining through the pale spaghetti.

1 lb/450 g aubergines
salt
frying oil
6 oz/175 g red pepper
6 oz/175 g green pepper
3 tablespoons olive oil

1–2 cloves garlic, crushed
6 black olives, stoned
1 tablespoon capers, drained
sea salt and black pepper
1 lb/450 g spaghetti

Cut the unpeeled aubergines lengthways in ½-inch/1-cm slices. Salt them on both sides and leave to sweat for 30 minutes. Pat dry. Heat 2 inches/5 cm oil in a broad pan and when it is very hot, put in some of the aubergine slices, being careful not to crowd them. Cook until golden on each side, turning once; drain on soft paper. Cut the peppers in strips about 1½ × ½ inch/4 × 1 cm. Heat the olive oil in a sauté pan and cook the peppers slowly for about 20 minutes, adding the crushed garlic halfway through. Cover the pan and stir occasionally. After 20 minutes add the halved olives and the capers. Cook for 5 minutes more, then stir in the aubergines, cut across in ½-inch/1-cm strips. Add sea salt and black pepper and cook gently for a final 5 minutes. Cook the spaghetti as usual, drain well, and mix lightly with the sauce. Serve immediately, without grated cheese. Serves 4.

SPAGHETTINI ALLE VONGOLE   Italy

One of the best versions of this dish is *spaghettini alle tartufi di mare*, a Venetian speciality. Any small clams, such as the Italian *telline* or the French *clovisse*, are particularly suitable for this dish, but these are seldom seen in England. This is how it is cooked in a small Venetian restaurant that specializes in fish dishes.

4 tablespoons olive oil	*6 fl. oz/175 ml white wine*
1 lb 2 oz/500 g tartufi di mare or	*3 tablespoons very finely*
other small shellfish	*chopped parsley*
1–2 cloves garlic, chopped	*1 lb/450 g spaghettini*

Put 2 tablespoons of the olive oil in a heavy pan and add the cleaned clams or shellfish. Cover the pan and steam just until they open. Take them out of their shells and put aside in a warm, but not hot, place. (If the clams are not very small indeed, they should be chopped.) Strain the juice. Heat another 2 tablespoons of olive oil and cook the chopped garlic for 1½–2 minutes, very gently, stirring to make sure that it does not burn. Add the wine, then the clam juice, and boil gently until reduced by half. Stir in the parsley and remove from the heat. Have the spaghettini cooked *al dente* and in a warm bowl. Pour the sauce over, adding the little clams, and toss well. Stand, covered, in a warm place for 4 minutes to allow the flavour to develop. Serves 4 as a first course.

In France, dishes of spaghetti with mixed shellfish are common, while in Italy, at least in Venice, it seems more usual to cook them with one variety alone. Staying with a friend near Toulon, we had a delicious dish of spaghetti cooked with a mixture of clams and small mussels, whatever we happened to find in Toulon market that morning. The mussels were left in their shells, gleaming blue-black through the creamy white strands of spaghetti.

CRÊPES AUX FRUITS DE MER   France

Although this is not a typically Mediterranean dish, it is one that is often found in restaurants in the south of France.

batter:
6 oz/175 g flour
¼ teaspoon salt
1½ eggs
6 fl. oz/175 ml milk
6 fl. oz/175 ml water

filling:
¾ lb/350 g firm white fish: bass, halibut, turbot, etc.
6 scallops
1 lb/450 g prawns, unshelled

sauce:
2 oz/50 g butter
3 tablespoons flour
¾ pint/350 ml fish stock
sea salt and black pepper
1 tablespoon tomato purée
1–2 dashes Tabasco
⅛ pint/75 ml thick cream
2 tablespoons grated parmesan

Make the batter as usual and stand for 1 hour, if possible.

Poach the white fish in lightly salted water until tender, remove it and add the scallops. Poach them for 6 minutes, then remove. Shell the prawns and add the shells to the fish stock; boil for 15–20 minutes, until well flavoured, adding more water if necessary. Strain and measure ¾ pint/350 ml.

Make a sauce with the butter, flour and the fish stock. Add sea salt and black pepper to taste, then divide the sauce in 2 equal parts. Stir the tomato purée into one half, then mix with the flaked white fish, sliced scallops and prawns, each cut in 3 pieces. Add a dash of Tabasco, and extra salt and pepper if needed. Beat the batter once more and make 8 large thin pancakes. Fill each one with some of the filling, then roll up and lay in a buttered gratin dish. Reheat the remaining sauce, stir in the cream and the grated parmesan, and pour

over the pancakes. Bake for 20 minutes at 190°C/375°F/Gas Mark 5.
Serves 4 as a light main course, with a green salad.

MEGADARRA

Lebanon

This is supposedly the original 'potage of lentils' for which Esau sold
his birthright. Whether this is so or not, it is certainly a most excellent
dish, comforting and sustaining, and a useful standby to make on a
Friday, before a long weekend.

¾ lb/350 g brown lentils,
  washed
2½ pints/1·5 litres water
2 large onions, sliced

6 tablespoons olive oil
¼ lb/100 g long grain rice
sea salt and black pepper

Pick over the washed lentils and put in a large pan with the cold
water. Bring to the boil and cook for 30 minutes, until the lentils are
almost tender. Meanwhile fry the sliced onions in the oil until golden,
then lift out half of them, with most of the oil, into a small dish.
Continue to fry the remainder until very brown, then lay them on soft
paper to drain, and pour any remaining oil onto the first lot of onions.
When the lentils have finished cooking, stir in the rice and the first lot
of fried onions with their oil. Add sea salt and black pepper, and cook
for another 14 minutes. (The rice will continue to cook for a bit after
the heat has been turned off.) Leave for 5–10 minutes covered, then tip
into a bowl and scatter the brown fried onion rings over the top.

In the Lebanon, this dish is usually served warm, or cold with spring
onions and a salad. I like it best about 1 hour after cooking, and often
serve it with hard-boiled eggs. Serves 5–6.

SEAFOOD PAELLA   Spain

This is my favourite paella, although less well known than the *paella Valenciana*.

¾ lb/350 g *firm white fish: monkfish, conger eel, bass, etc.*
1 lb/450 g *small squid*
1 pint/350 g *prawns, unshelled*
1½ pints/900 ml *water*
salt
12 *mussels*
4 tablespoons *water*
12 *small clams, when available*
1 *medium onion*
6 tablespoons *olive oil*
2 *cloves garlic, minced*

½ *green pepper, chopped*
½ lb/225 g *tomatoes, skinned and chopped*
1 lb/450 g *peas, in their pods*
1 lb/450 g *Spanish Valencia rice, or Italian risotto rice, washed*
1½ pints/900 ml *fish stock*
sea salt and black pepper
2 packets *saffron*
5 *large prawns*
½ *red pepper*

Cut the white fish off the bone, if there is one. Clean the squid (see *risotto alla pescara*, page 189) and cut the bodies in rings ¼ inch/5 mm wide, and the tentacles in half, or in short lengths. Shell the small prawns. Make a fish stock with the prawn shells and the fish bones, if there are any: cover with 1½ pints/900 ml water, add salt, and simmer for 30 minutes, covered. Strain and cool. Put the mussels in a pan with 4 tablespoons water; steam until they open, then remove from the pan and put in the clams. Steam them also just long enough to open, then strain the liquid and add to the fish stock. Measure and make up to 1½ pints/900 ml.

Chop the onion and brown in the oil in a heavy saucepan. Add the minced garlic, then the sliced squid. Simmer gently for 10 minutes, then add the white fish cut in smallish pieces. After a few minutes, add the chopped green pepper, and 5 minutes later stir in the skinned and chopped tomatoes and the shelled peas. Cook 3 minutes longer.

At this stage it can be left for several hours if convenient. Otherwise tip into the paella pan – this should be at least 14 inches/36 cm wide – and reheat until simmering. Then stir in the rice and mix well. Reheat the fish stock and pour on all at once, if the pan is large enough to hold it, otherwise it will have to be done in stages. Then add sea salt and black pepper, the saffron, and the mussels and clams. Scatter the giant prawns (unshelled) over the top and cook, either on top of the stove or in the oven. If the pan is large enough to hold all the stock, it is probably best to cook it in the oven: simply cover the pan with foil and place low down in the oven set to 180°C/350°F/Gas Mark 4, and cook for 45 minutes, by which time the stock should all be absorbed and the rice tender. Alternatively, continue to cook on top of the stove, adding the extra stock by degrees, as if making a risotto. This method will only take about 20 minutes, but there is a danger that the centre of the pan will get too hot and the rice will catch, since paella pans are quite thin.

While it is cooking, grill the half red pepper until the skin is charred and blackened; peel it off and cut the flesh in strips. When the paella has finished cooking, lay the strips of red pepper over the top, cover with a cloth or with foil, and stand for 10 minutes before serving. Serves 6; no other accompaniments are necessary, nor even any first course.

The paella pan must be washed and dried very carefully, then rubbed with oil before putting away, or it will rust. Always wash and dry again just before using.

PAELLA VALENCIANA   Spain

This is the best known of all the paellas, in fact the only one that is ever found outside Spain. The ingredients can vary widely but a mixture of chicken, squid and shellfish is usual; pork is often added, although I prefer it without. The mixture of meat and fish is simmered with onion, garlic, tomatoes, peppers and peas with a short-grain rice from Valencia, flavoured with saffron. In Spain, the paella is often cooked outside, on a wood fire, either in the garden or, in a simpler form, on picnics. (The Spaniards are great picnickers, and are to be seen in large numbers on Sundays, even on grey cool days, building bonfires and making paellas in the woods near any large town.)

We have two alternatives, neither of which is ideal. One is to cook the paella, like a risotto, on top of the stove; the other is to cover the pan with foil and cook it in the bottom of the oven. The first has the disadvantage that the paella pan inevitably overlaps the normal hotplate by a large radius, meaning that the centre cooks much more quickly than the outside. The second method is probably better, but only if the pan is large enough, since all the liquid must be added at one go and the pan left untouched for the rest of the cooking. Paella pans need to be really huge; mine is 14 inches/35 cm, and this is barely large enough to hold 1 lb/450 g rice, which my Spanish daily considers only enough for 4 people. As always, the only answer is to experiment, but if buying a pan specially, do buy a really large one, since half the fun of a paella is to make it in large quantities, which permits one to have a wide variety of ingredients.

2½ lb/1·15 kg chicken, cut in 12
    small joints (4 breast, 4 leg
    and 4 wing), plus carcase
1½ medium Spanish onions
1 carrot
1 stalk celery
1 bay leaf
sea salt and black peppercorns
1 pint/350 g unshelled prawns
12 mussels or small clams (or
    both)
½ lb/225 g small squid, cut in
    rings
6 tablespoons olive oil
2 cloves garlic, minced
2 thin pork chops, cut off the
    bone (optional)

10 oz/275 g tomatoes, skinned
    and chopped
1 lb/450 g peas (in the pod), or
    ¼ lb/100 g frozen peas
½ green pepper, chopped
1 lb/450 g Valencia rice, or
    Italian risotto rice, washed
2 packets saffron
1¾ pints/1 litre stock: prawn,
    mussel and chicken, mixed
½ red pepper, grilled and
    skinned
6 giant prawns, unshelled
    (optional)

Put the chicken carcase in a pressure cooker with ½ onion, 1 carrot, 1 stalk celery and ½ bay leaf. Add 2 pints/1·2 litres water, sea salt and peppercorns, and cook for 1 hour under pressure; strain. Shell the prawns (not the giant ones) and put the shells in a pan with 1½ pints/900 ml water; bring to the boil and cook for 30 minutes, then strain. Put the mussels or clams in a heavy pan with 2 tablespoons water; cover and steam until they open. Strain the juice. Clean the squid as usual (see *risotto alla pescara*, page 189), cut the bodies in thin rings and the tentacles in short lengths, using scissors. (If really small, the tentacles can be left undivided.)

Heat the oil in a large saucepan and cook the remaining onion, chopped. Add the minced garlic, then the chicken joints. Cook slowly in the oil, turning until they are golden all over. Cut the pork (if used), in small cubes and add to the pan; brown also. Then add the squid and cook for another 5 minutes, stirring now and then. Finally add the chopped tomatoes, the shelled peas, if fresh, and the chopped green pepper. Cover the pan and simmer slowly for 10 minutes; if it shows signs of sticking, add ¼ pint/150 ml of the chicken stock. The stocks should now be mixed; pour the prawn stock and the mussel or clam juice into a measuring jug, and make up to 1¾ pints/1 litre with the chicken stock, taking into account any that you have already added to the saucepan.

Now heat the paella pan on top of the stove and pour the contents of the pan into it, adding the rice, unshelled mussels or clams, the saffron, ½ bay leaf, and sea salt and black pepper. (If forced to use frozen peas, thaw them and add with the mussels, clams and saffron.) Heat the stock and add gradually; if the pan is large enough to hold it all, pour it all in, otherwise only add as much as it will hold comfortably. If all has fitted into the paella pan, stir it well, and simmer for a moment or two on top of the stove. Cut the skinned red pepper in strips and lay over the rice like the spokes of a wheel, with the giant prawns, either unshelled, or with just the tails left on, in between. (I only add these if there are no mussels or clams about, to add interest.) Cover with foil, transfer to the bottom shelf of the oven, and cook for 45 minutes at 180°C/350°F/Gas Mark 4, by which time all the stock should be absorbed, and the rice tender. Alternatively, cook on top of the stove like a risotto, adding more stock as the first lot is absorbed, and only adding the strips of red pepper and giant prawns towards the end. In either case, the pan must be allowed to stand for 8–10 minutes before serving, covered with a cloth, or with foil. Serves 6, unless they are Spaniards.

BULGUR PILAV   Turkey

Bulgur is a form of cracked wheat, known as *burghul* in the Middle East. It is extremely nourishing and can be delicious, either hot, or cold in salads. (See *tabbouleh*, in Salads, page 76.) It can be bought as *burghul* from some health food shops, but be sure that it is the right thing, for English cracked or kibbled wheat is another thing entirely. Serve this dish as an accompaniment to meat or poultry, or alone with a bowl of yogurt.

¼ lb/100 g butter
1 medium onion, chopped
½ lb/225 g burghul

approx. ¾ pint/350 ml chicken
    stock
sea salt

Melt the butter and cook the chopped onion until it is pale golden. Add the burghul and cook gently over low heat for 10 minutes. Heat the stock and pour on enough to cover. Add sea salt, bring to boiling point and cover the pan. Simmer until the stock is almost absorbed – about 10 minutes – then test to see if the burghul is tender. If not, add a little more stock and continue cooking. Serves 3–4.

BURGHUL AND VERMICELLI PILAV   Cyprus

The Turkish habit of adding vermicelli to pilav seems to have spread to Cyprus, for I was given this recipe for a cracked wheat – called burghul in Cyprus – pilav with vermicelli by a Greek Cypriot. The vermicelli gives an added texture to the burghul. It can be served as a dish on its own, with yogurt, or as part of a vegetarian meal, or with chicken or lamb.

3 oz/75 g butter
1 medium onion, chopped
2 oz/50 g vermicelli, broken up
6 oz/175 g burghul

sea salt and black pepper
approx. ¾ pint/350 ml chicken
    stock

Heat the butter in a sauté pen with a lid and cook the onion until it starts to colour, then add the vermicelli which you have broken up into short lengths. Stir round in the fat for 3 minutes, then add the burghul with some sea salt and black pepper and cook gently for 8–10 minutes, stirring often. Heat the stock and add enough barely to cover the contents of the pan; cover, and simmer gently until it is almost absorbed, about 10 minutes. Test the burghul to see if it is tender; if not, add the remaining stock and continue to simmer until it also is absorbed. When all is tender, turn off the heat, cover the pan with a cloth under the lid, and stand for 10 minutes. Serves 3–4.

CHICKEN PILAV   Turkey

¾ lb/350 g raw chicken, boned,
   with bones separately (½ a
   3 lb/1·35 kg chicken, boned)
juice of ½ lemon
½ large onion
½ carrot
1 stalk celery
½ bay leaf
1 medium onion, finely
   chopped

1 oz/25 g butter
2 tablespoons pine kernels
2 tablespoons currants
½ teaspoon allspice
½ lb/225 g risotto rice, washed
   (see page 184)
1 pint/600 ml light chicken
   stock
sea salt and black pepper

Cut the chicken in small pieces and squeeze the lemon juice over it. Make a stock with the bones and flavouring vegetables in a pressure cooker. Strain and measure 1 pint/600 ml. Cook the chopped onion in the butter till it starts to colour, then add the chicken. Cook gently for 8–10 minutes, stirring often, then add the pine kernels, currants and allspice. Stir around for a few moments, then add the washed rice and cook gently for 2 minutes, stirring often. Pour on half the heated stock, add sea salt and black pepper and cover. Simmer until the stock is absorbed, then add the remaining stock and continue to cook gently until the rice is cooked and the stock all absorbed. Serves 4.

CHICKEN LIVER PILAV   Turkey

Chicken livers make a good basis for a Turkish pilav, especially when combined with nuts and currants. This makes an inexpensive and nutritious dish which only needs a green salad as accompaniment.

½ lb/225 g chicken livers
½ oz/15 g butter
1 tablespoon olive oil
1 clove garlic, finely chopped
1 ½ tablespoons pine kernels
1 ½ tablespoons currants

½ teaspoon allspice
½ lb/225 g risotto rice, washed
   (see page 184)
1 pint/600 ml chicken stock
sea salt and black pepper
1 tablespoon chopped parsley

Chop the chicken livers, discarding any discoloured bits. Heat the butter and oil and cook the finely chopped garlic for 1 minute, stirring, then add the livers. Stir round over brisk heat for 3 minutes, until they have lost their pink colour, then lift out with a slotted spoon and keep warm in a covered dish. Add the pine kernels and currants to the pan, also the allspice and the washed rice. Stir round for a few minutes, then add the heated stock. Cover the pan and simmer gently for 15–18 minutes, till the rice is cooked and the stock all absorbed. Add sea salt and black pepper, then stir the chicken livers back into the rice. Turn onto a hot dish, sprinkle with chopped parsley, and serve. Serves 3–4.

LAMB PILAV   Turkey

For this and other Turkish rice dishes it is important to have the right sort of rice. It must be a short-grained risotto-type rice; although Uncle Ben rice works perfectly well, it doesn't look right. I buy Italian Arborio, Cristallo or Lupa rice, or Valencia rice from Spanish shops. All these need careful washing before using, otherwise the finished dish will be sticky.

*¾ lb/350 g tender lamb, from
  the shoulder or leg
1 medium onion, finely
  chopped
1 oz/25 g butter
2 tablespoons shelled
  pistachios*

*2 tablespoons currants
½ teaspoon allspice
½ lb/225 g risotto rice, washed
1 pint/600 ml water or light
  stock
sea salt and black pepper*

Cut the meat in square pieces the size of a walnut. Cook the chopped onion in the butter for a couple of minutes, then add the lamb. Cook slowly until browned all over, stirring, then continue to cook gently, uncovered, until the lamb is all but cooked – about 20 minutes. Then add the nuts, currants, allspice and rice. Stir around for a few moments, then add the hot water or stock; add sea salt and black pepper to taste, cover the pan and simmer until the rice is cooked and the liquid absorbed – about 15 minutes. Turn out on a hot plate to serve. Serves 4.

VERMICELLI PILAV   **Turkey**

Broken vermicelli is often mixed with the rice in Turkish pilavs, and I find this makes an interesting combination of textures.

2 oz/50 g vermicelli
¼ lb/100 g butter
6 oz/175 g risotto rice, washed

1 pint/600 ml chicken stock
sea salt and black pepper

Break the vermicelli into small pieces. Melt half the butter in a sauté pan and cook the vermicelli for 5 minutes, stirring constantly, till pale golden. Add the rice and stir around for another 3–4 minutes. Heat the stock and add to the pan with the remaining butter, sea salt and black pepper. Boil for 1 minute, then stir and lower the heat as much as possible. Cover the pan and cook gently for 15 minutes, till all the stock is absorbed and the rice is cooked. Turn off the heat, cover with a cloth under the lid, and stand for 20 minutes in a warm place before serving. Serves 4–5.

POLENTA, BOILED   **Italy**

This is a favourite Venetian dish, especially in winter time, when it is served as an accompaniment to almost anything you can think of, ranging from game to fish. It is also sometimes served as a main dish in its own right, with a thick tomato sauce. The Venetians have round wooden boards about 18 inches/47 cm in diameter, onto which the polenta is poured. It sets in a round mass about 1½ inches/3·5 cm thick, like a huge yellow sun.

2½ pints/1·5 litres water
½ tablespoon salt

½ lb/225 g cornmeal

Bring the water to the boil with the salt and shake in the cornmeal, stirring continuously. Stir for 10 minutes, then stand over an asbestos mat or transfer to a double boiler and cook gently for 25–30 minutes, stirring now and then. Beat thoroughly before serving. Pour into a shallow dish, or onto a bread board to serve. If in a dish, pieces of chicken, game or rabbit can be laid on it, and the whole covered with a rich tomato sauce. If serving on its own, make a good coarse tomato sauce, unsieved, to go with it. (See *coulis de tomates*, or *pizzaiola* sauce.) Serves 5–6.

POLENTA, FRIED   Italy

This is a most delicious way of serving polenta, either as an accompaniment to meat dishes, or as a hot snack to eat with drinks, as is done in Harry's Bar, in Venice. It is the traditional accompaniment to *fegato alla Veneziana*, the Venetian dish of calves' liver with onions, and is also served with a wide range of other dishes: game, poultry, and even fish.

2½ pints/1·5 litres water   ½ oz/15 g butter
½ tablespoon salt   1 tablespoon olive oil
½ lb/225 g cornmeal

Make as for Boiled Polenta (see previous recipe), then pour into a shallow baking tin rinsed with cold water. Spread with a palette knife to form an even mass about ¼ inch/5 mm thick, then leave for several hours, or overnight. Then cut into rectangles about 3 inches × 1½ inches/7·5 cm × 3·5 cm (smaller if serving with drinks). Heat the butter and oil in a heavy flat frying pan and fry the little cakes until they are very brown, moving them round so that they brown evenly, and on both sides. They should be crisp and slightly blackened on the outside, and soft and creamy within. For a good effect, they can be finished off in a very hot grill pan, to give a stripy finish. Serve on a flat dish. Serves 5–6.

RISI E BISI   Italy

This seasonal dish is a Venetian speciality and is made in early summer with young peas. When made with these and a good chicken stock it is quite delicious, like a moist risotto. Chopped prosciutto (raw smoked ham) is usually added, but it is sometimes made just with peas and rice. It is best eaten in soup plates, with a fork.

1 small onion, chopped
3 oz/75 g butter
2 oz/50 g chopped prosciutto
  (optional)
2 lb/900 g peas (in pod)

½ lb/225 g risotto rice, washed
1½ pints/900 ml chicken stock
sea salt and black pepper
1 oz/25 g grated parmesan

Cook the chopped onion in 2 oz/50 g of the butter until it starts to change colour, then add the chopped prosciutto, if used. Cook for 2 minutes, stirring once or twice, then add the shelled peas. Leave to cook gently for 4 minutes, covered, then add the washed rice and cook for another 2 minutes. Heat the stock and add to the pan. Stir well, add sea salt and black pepper, and cover the pan. Cook for about 15 minutes, until the rice and peas are tender and all the stock absorbed. Stir once or twice towards the end of the cooking, then stir in the grated cheese and the remaining butter. Serve at once, as a first course. Serves 4.

RISOTTO DI CARCIOFI   Italy

This artichoke risotto is a popular winter dish in Venice, where tender tiny artichokes can be bought in the market already shredded for making this and other dishes. The nutty taste of the artichokes goes perfectly with rice, and makes a most appealing dish.

2 artichokes
½ lemon
2 tablespoons olive oil
1 oz/25 g butter
4 shallots
½ lb/255 g Italian Arborio rice,
  washed

1 pint/600 ml chicken stock
sea salt and black pepper
4 tablespoons freshly grated
  parmesan

Remove the coarse outer leaves of the artichokes, and cut the remaining ones down by about half, discarding the pointed ends and leaving only the pale tender parts. Cut in quarters and discard the innermost pinkish leaves with spiky tops, then scrape out the hairy choke. Rub all the cut surfaces with the half lemon or they will discolour. Heat the oil and butter in a sauté pan, and while it is heating, slice the quartered hearts across in thin shreds. Cook these in the oil and butter until tender, about 6 minutes, stirring often. Then lift them out with a slotted spoon, leaving the fat in the pan, and keep them warm while you cook the rice. Chop the shallots and cook in the same fat until pale golden, then add the washed and drained rice. Heat the stock and pour on a third; cover the pan and simmer until the stock is almost absorbed. Then add another third, and cook again till absorbed. Continue in this way until the rice is tender, then stir in the artichokes, adding sea salt and black pepper to taste. Stir in half the grated cheese, and scatter the remainder over the top. Serves 3–4 as a first course.

HERB RISOTTO   Italy

I had this aromatic risotto in a trattoria in Florence one winter, and it seemed to me typical of Tuscan food – full of character and flavour, but less 'fine' than a similar dish would be in a French restaurant.

1 shallot	12 leaves sage
1½ oz/40 g butter	12 sprigs thyme
½ lb/225 g Italian Arborio rice,	12 leaves tarragon
washed	12 leaves oregano
1¼ pints/750 ml chicken stock	sea salt and black pepper
1 bay leaf	

Chop the shallot and soften in the butter. Add the rice after washing and draining well. Stir around until coated in fat, then pour on half the heated stock. Cover and simmer gently until almost absorbed. Meanwhile, crumble the bay leaf and chop the other herbs finely. Add with most of the remaining stock and simmer again until absorbed. Add more stock if needed, otherwise serve as soon as the rice is tender and the stock absorbed. Add sea salt and black pepper to taste. Serves 3–4.

RISOTTO ALLA PESCARA   Italy

This recipe comes from the Gulf of Naples, as might be deduced by the inclusion of tomatoes. It makes an excellent first course for a dinner, or a light main dish for luncheon.

2–3 *small squid, about 6 oz/175 g*
12 *small mussels*
12 *small clams*
½ *lb/225 g prawns, unshelled*
1 *small onion*
3 *tablespoons olive oil*

1 *clove garlic, chopped*
6 *oz/175 g tinned tomatoes*
10 *oz/275 g Italian Arborio rice,*
    washed
6 *fl. oz/175 ml dry white wine*
sea salt and black pepper

Prepare the squid. Holding the head and body in each hand, pull gently but firmly to separate them. Discard the triangular 'fin' inside the body, and anything else. Pull off the pinkish-red membrane that covers the body sac, and wash the sac well under running cold water, turning it inside out and back again. Dry with soft paper and cut in rings about ¼ inch/5 mm. Cut the tentacles off the head just above the eyes, and discard the rest. Wash the tentacles well, and separate them, cutting them in half if they are more than 1½ inches/3·5 cm long. Pat dry and set aside with the rings.

Clean the mussels and clams and put them in a heavy covered pan with ¼ pint/150 ml water. Bring to the boil and cook for 2–3 minutes, till they open. Lift them out with a slotted spoon and keep warm; strain the juice. If the prawns are cooked, shell them and put the shells in a pan with about 1 pint/600 ml water. Cover and cook slowly for 30 minutes, then strain into a measuring jug. Add the shellfish liquor and make up to 1 pint/600 ml. If using uncooked prawns, drop them into ¾ pint/450 ml simmering water, lightly salted, and cook for 2 minutes. Lift them out and cool, then shell and keep the prawns warm. Strain the stock and mix with the shellfish juice, making up to 1 pint/600 ml if necessary with water.

Chop the onion and cook gently in the oil until it starts to colour. Add the chopped garlic, then the sliced squid. Stir around and cook gently for about 4 minutes, then add the tinned tomatoes, drained of their juice and pulped or chopped, and the washed rice. Heat the mixed fish stock and pour on half of it; stir well, then cover the pan and cook slowly until it is mostly absorbed. Mix the wine with half the remaining stock and add it to the pan; stir, cover and simmer again until almost absorbed. Test the rice; if still slightly hard, add the remaining stock and cook as before; if the rice seems tender, stop at this stage. Add the shelled prawns to the risotto and mix; cook for a minute or two, adding salt and pepper. Then add the mussels and clams, unshelled, and cook a moment or two longer. Serve immediately. Serves 4 as a first course, or 3–4 as a light main dish.

SPANAKORISO   Greece

This Lenten dish of spinach and rice is excellent for a vegetarian meal, either as a first course or a light main one. It is usually eaten hot, but is also good sprinkled with lemon juice and eaten after cooling.

2 bunches spring onions
2 lb/900 g spinach
4 fl. oz/120 ml olive oil
2 tablespoons chopped dill,
  when available

½ lb/225 g risotto rice, washed
18 fl. oz/500 ml hot water
sea salt and black pepper
juice of ½ lemon, if serving
  cold

Slice the spring onions across in ¼-inch/5-mm slices, using the best part of the green leaves as well as the bulbs. Boil the spinach in lightly salted water for 5 minutes; drain, cool, and squeeze out all the moisture. Chop roughly by hand. Heat the oil and cook the sliced spring onions for about 5 minutes, until they start to soften. Add the chopped spinach and dill and cook gently for another 5 minutes, stirring now and then. Add the washed and drained rice, stir round for a few minutes until it is coated with oil, then add the hot water. Bring to the boil, cover the pan, and simmer until the rice is cooked and the water absorbed – about 18 minutes. Add sea salt and black pepper to taste. Serves 4–5.

9

COOKED VEGETABLE DISHES

Mediterranean vegetable cookery is extremely varied, for a number of reasons. Since meat is comparatively rare, and correspondingly expensive, the vegetable dishes are designed to replace meat rather than to accompany it, so that many of them are quite substantial. Another reason is that most of the countries on the northern shore of the sea are obliged to abstain from eating meat, and indeed many other foods, during the Lenten fast. Throughout the Roman Catholic countries of Spain, France, and Italy this annual fast is strictly observed, especially in rural areas, and is particularly rigorous during Holy Week when no meat, fresh fish, eggs or oil are allowed. (I read an account of Holy Week on an island in the Gulf of Naples; one large simple dish, either of spaghetti or of vegetables, was cooked each morning throughout the week and eaten for both meals on that day, without even reheating. It is easy to understand how such austere habits lend significance to the festive meals that follow.)

In Greece fasting is even more rigorous: the Greek Orthodox Church imposes several lengthy fasts on its followers throughout the year, and most Greeks are very devout. There are four long fasts in the Orthodox Church, apart from the many one-day fasts, which include every Wednesday and Friday, when meat is forbidden. The long fasts are Advent, the forty days leading up to Christmas; Great Lent, the forty days preceding Easter; the first fortnight in August, preceding the feast of the Assumption of the Virgin Mary; and one week in June, in honour of St Peter and St Paul. During Great Lent, the forbidden foods vary from week to week, and during Holy Week itself not only meat, fresh fish, eggs and oil are prohibited, but also all dairy foods, so that the people live mainly on vegetables and pasta simply boiled in water. Some dishes, like the much-loved spinach pie called *spanakopita*, exist in two versions: one called *nystysimos*, meaning Lenten, which consists simply of chopped spinach and herbs in pastry, while the more usual version, enriched with eggs and feta cheese, is eaten on all other occasions.

Since the vegetables that grow around the Mediterranean are so similar, for reasons we have discussed before, it is not surprising that many of the dishes from the various countries resemble each other. Almost every country has a version of ratatouille, for instance, and many also include eggs to make a form of *piperade*. In Spain and Tunisia an added refinement consists of first charring the vegetables over an open flame, or under the grill; this adds a curious and delicious smoky flavour to *escalibada* and *salat meschoui* respectively. Stuffed vegetables exist almost throughout, especially in Greece and Turkey, but the best I have eaten were in Genoa.

The Spanish are very fond of bean dishes, made either with green beans, *judias verdes*, or white beans, *habas*. Vegetable fritters are popular in France, Italy, and Turkey; usually made with sliced aubergines or courgettes dipped in batter or simply in flour, they are fried briefly in deep oil and served, sometimes with a garlic sauce or just with cut lemons. In Italy, the flowers of the courgette are also treated in this way, either alone, or stuffed with a rice filling. Italy also has a tradition of steamed vegetable dishes called *sformati*; baked slowly in a bain marie, these are like a more solid form of soufflé.

ARTICHOKES À LA POLITA   Greece

This dish is easily made with tinned artichoke hearts but is even more delicious when fresh artichokes are cheap and plentiful. It can be eaten as a first course, or as a separate vegetable dish after a light main course.

¼ lb/100 g small pickling onions
2 oz/50 g carrots, cut in
　½ inch/1 cm cubes
½ pint/300 ml lightly salted water
¼ lb/100 g tiny new potatoes, or
　slightly larger ones cut in
　quarters
1 tin (14 oz/400 g) artichoke
　hearts (or 6 small artichokes)

4 tablespoons olive oil
½ tablespoon flour mixed with
　2 tablespoons water
sea salt and black pepper
6 tablespoons lemon juice (plus
　2 lemons if using fresh
　artichokes)
2 tablespoons chopped dill,
　when available

Peel the onions and put in a pan with the carrots and lightly salted water. Bring to the boil and simmer; after 10 minutes, add the potatoes. When the potatoes are cooked, another 10–12 minutes, add the drained and rinsed artichoke hearts, the olive oil, flour and water paste, sea salt, black pepper and lemon juice. Cook another 5 minutes, then stir in the chopped dill and leave to cool. Serve lukewarm or cold, but never chilled. Serves 3–4.

If using fresh artichokes, discard the outside leaves and cut the inner ones down to within 1 inch/2·5 cm of the bottom. Cut the heart in half lengthways and scoop out the choke with a small teaspoon. Soak in a bowl of cold water with the juice of 2 lemons for an hour before cooking, then par-boil them for 15 minutes and drain before adding to the onions and carrots.

CARCIOFI STUFATI   Italy

This is one of the many delicious Italian artichoke dishes which should really be made with the tender Italian artichokes, in season during the winter and early spring. If using English artichokes, we must take care to cut away all but the most tender parts, or the dish will be tough and fibrous

2 oz/50 g bacon (or pancetta)
2 tablespoons olive oil
4–5 small tender artichokes
1 lemon
6 tablespoons water
6–8 oz/175–225 g shelled peas,
   fresh or frozen

6–8 oz/175–225 g shelled broad
   beans, fresh or frozen
2 tablespoons chopped parsley
sea salt and black pepper

Chop the bacon coarsely; ideally this should be the Italian *pancetta*. Cook gently in the oil in a heavy casserole while you prepare the artichokes. Cut off all the outside leaves and about half or two-thirds of the ends of the leaves, so that you are left with the stumpy inner part. Cut this in half, then in quarters or sixths depending on size, and scrape out the choke. Rub each one with a cut lemon to prevent discoloration. Add the artichokes to the bacon and cook in the oil, turning over and over. Add 6 tablespoons water, cover the pan, and cook for 15 minutes, stirring occasionally. Then add the shelled peas and beans, chopped parsley, sea salt and black pepper, and cook for another 15 minutes, or till the vegetables are tender. (Pierce the artichokes with a skewer to test them.) You may need to add a little more water. If using frozen peas and beans, cook the artichokes alone for 25 minutes, and only add the frozen vegetables for the last 5 minutes. Serves 4.

BEIGNETS D'AUBERGINES   France

Vegetable fritters made by dipping slices of aubergine or courgette in a light batter and deep frying are popular all along the Côte Niçoise, in Italy, Greece and Turkey. Any good frying batter can be used: I like this one made without either egg yolks or milk.

batter:
¼ lb/100 g flour
a pinch of salt
2 tablespoons light oil
6 fl. oz/175 ml tepid water
1 egg white, beaten

2 smallish aubergines
salt
frying oil
2 lemons, or a sauce (see below)

Make the batter 1 hour in advance if possible. Sift the flour with the salt into a food processor or large bowl. Add the oil and process or beat by hand, adding the water gradually and continuing to process or beat until it is a smooth thick cream. Stand for 1 hour, then beat again and fold in the stiffly beaten egg white.

The aubergines should also be prepared in advance: cut them, unpeeled, in slices ¼ inch/5 mm thick. Sprinkle with salt and leave for 30 minutes to drain, then pat them dry in a cloth or soft paper. Dip each slice in batter, then drop, a few at a time, into a pan of hot oil. Fry for 2 minutes on each side, turning once, or until they are puffy and golden brown. Drain on soft paper while you fry the next lot, then transfer to a hot flat dish. Serve immediately, either with lemon quarters or with a sauce: *aïoli*, *skordalia* and yogurt sauce all go well with this. Serves 4–6 as a first course.

HUNKAR BEYENDI (AUBERGINE PURÉE)   Turkey

This purée of aubergines is one of the best things I have eaten in Turkey. It was served – at room temperature – with little joints of chicken, in a beautiful old house on the Asian side of the Bosphorus, looking over towards the Topkapi Saray.

2 lb/900 g aubergines	½ pint/300 ml milk, heated
juice of 1 large lemon	sea salt and black pepper
1 tablespoon olive oil	2 tablespoons grated parmesan,
1½ oz/40 g butter	or gruyère
2 tablespoons flour	

Grill the aubergines slowly, turning often, for about 30 minutes, until the skin is blistered all over. Skin them and chop in large pieces. Mix the lemon juice and olive oil in a shallow dish and put in the chopped aubergines, one at a time. Using two forks, shred them by pulling in different directions, and mashing them into the oil and lemon. Do not try to make it smooth, and on no account use a food processor, blender or vegetable mill. It should be lumpy, and the seeds must remain. Make a béchamel sauce with the butter, flour and heated milk; there should be slightly more purée than sauce. Add sea salt and black pepper to the sauce, then mix with the purée. Check the seasoning, then add the grated cheese. Cool for an hour before serving. Serves 4. Serve with roast or grilled chicken, either hot or cold, or grilled steaks or lamb, or beef or lamb stew.

GREEK STUFFED AUBERGINES   Greece

This is a Greek version of the Turkish imam bayeldi, simpler, but also good. The orange filling looks very pretty, forming diagonal patterns on the dark purple skins of the aubergines.

4 oval aubergines weighing	1 large clove garlic, minced
about ½ lb/225 g each	1 lb/450 g tomatoes, skinned
frying oil	and chopped
2 medium onions, chopped	sea salt and black pepper
4 tablespoons olive oil	

Make 3 deep diagonal cuts on each side of the aubergines, as if preparing a fish for grilling. Heat some oil – enough to come halfway up the aubergines – in a pan and lay them in it. Cook for 10 minutes on each side, until softened, then drain on soft paper; cool. Chop the onions and fry gently in the 4 tablespoons olive oil; when they start to colour, add the minced garlic and the skinned and chopped tomatoes. Add sea salt and black pepper and simmer slowly for about 15 minutes, or until thickened like jam. Cool.

Open up the 3 cuts on one side of each of the aubergines, sprinkle with salt and pepper, and fill with some of the stuffing. (It is best to do this when they are already lying in their oiled baking dish.) Bake for 30 minutes at 180°C/350°F/Gas Mark 4. Serves 4, as a substantial first course or a light main dish. It can be served hot, warm, or after cooling; do not chill.

IMAM BAYELDI   Turkey

This most delicious of all stuffed vegetable dishes can be served as a first course, or as the accompaniment to a simple meat dish. It should be eaten cool, but not chilled. The name – 'The Imam fainted' – is somewhat obscure, since it is not known whether he fainted from delight, or horror at the cost of the dish. (It is quite extravagant in terms of oil.)

3 medium aubergines
salt
olive oil
½ lb/225 g onions, chopped
1½ lb/675 g tomatoes, skinned,
deseeded and chopped

1 green pepper, finely chopped
1 tablespoon raisins
sea salt and black pepper
a pinch of sugar

Cut the aubergines in half and scoop out most of the inside with a sharp teaspoon, leaving a thick wall. Sprinkle the inside with salt and stand upside down to drain for 30 minutes. Rinse and pat dry with a cloth. Cover the bottom of a broad heavy pan with a layer of olive oil and fry the aubergines, cut side down, quite briefly, until they start to soften. Put aside.

Heat 4 tablespoons olive oil in a sauté pan and cook the chopped onion until golden. Add the peeled, deseeded and chopped tomatoes, also the finely chopped pepper and the raisins. Add sea salt and black pepper and a pinch of sugar. Stir for a moment, then remove from the heat. Spoon into the aubergines, filling them quite tightly. Lay them in a broad pan, pouring any extra juice between them, also a couple of tablespoons of hot water, or just enough to cover the bottom of the pan. Cook for 30 minutes, covered, or till the aubergines are soft and the juice evaporated. Cool before eating, but do not chill. Serves 6 as a first course, or an accompaniment to a main dish.

MELANZANE ALLA PARMIGIANA   Italy

Often known simply as *parmigiana*, this dish is widely popular in Naples and the surrounding area. Like all dishes using mozzarella, the timing is vital, since it quickly becomes tough and leathery if left too long in the oven.

1½ lb/675 g aubergines
salt
frying oil
1½ mozzarella cheeses
   (8–9 oz/225–250 g)
1 oz/25 g grated parmesan

tomato sauce:
1 small onion
1 tablespoon olive oil

1 oz/25 g butter
2 cloves garlic, crushed
2 medium tins (14 oz/396 g
   each) tomatoes
sea salt and black pepper
1 teaspoon sugar
½ bay leaf
2 sprigs fresh oregano (or
   marjoram)

Cut the unpeeled aubergines in thin diagonal slices; sprinkle them with salt and leave for 1 hour to drain. Meanwhile make the sauce: chop the onion and cook in the oil and butter till it starts to soften, adding the crushed garlic halfway through. Add the tinned tomatoes, roughly chopped, or squeezed to a pulp, and simmer gently for 45 minutes, till quite thick, adding sea salt, black pepper, sugar, bay leaf, and oregano. Stir now and then to prevent sticking.

Dry the aubergine slices and fry in a sauté pan in oil 1 inch/2·5 cm deep. Turn the slices once so they become light golden on both sides. Drain on soft paper while you fry the rest; do not do too many at once. When all are done, the final dish can be assembled. Make a thin layer of sauce in a large shallow dish, preferably one of brown earthenware. Slice the cheese thinly, and make sandwiches of the aubergine slices, filling them with mozzarella. Keep back a little cheese for the top. Lay the sandwiches overlapping in the dish, and pour the sauce over all. Scatter a few slices of mozzarella over the top, and sprinkle with grated parmesan. Bake for 20 minutes at 180°C/350°F/Gas Mark 4, or just until the mozzarella has melted – the aubergines are already cooked. Serve as soon as possible. Serves 5–6 as a first course, or 4 as a main course, with a green salad. It can be made in advance and frozen (before baking).

PAPETON D'AUBERGINES France

This is an excellent dish, like a mould of aubergines, that originated in Avignon at the time of the Popes' residence. It is quite rich, and not to be eaten in large quantities. It makes an exquisite first course for a small luncheon or dinner.

1 ½ lb/675 g aubergines
salt
1 small onion
approx. 4 tablespoons olive oil
1 clove garlic, crushed
1 sprig thyme
sea salt and black pepper
3 eggs
4 tablespoons milk

tomato sauce:
1 small onion
1 tablespoon olive oil
½ oz/15 g butter
1 medium (14 oz/396 g) tin
tomatoes
sea salt and black pepper
½ teaspoon sugar

Peel the aubergines and cut in cubes about ½ inch/1 cm square. Pile them in a colander, sprinkling with salt, and leave for 1 hour. Then rinse and pat dry in a cloth. Chop the onion and cook gently in the oil for 5 minutes in a sauté pan. Then add the cubed aubergines, the crushed garlic, thyme, sea salt and black pepper. Cook for 15–20 minutes, till all is soft, adding more oil as needed. Using a slotted spoon, lift the vegetables into a food processor, discarding the thyme and leaving behind excess oil. Purée till totally smooth. (This can also be done in a blender, in small batches.) Pour the purée into a bowl and add more salt and pepper if needed. Beat the eggs with the milk and fold into the purée. Spoon into a butter charlotte mould or soufflé dish and bake in a bain marie (a baking tin half filled with water) for 45–50

Cooked Vegetable Dishes · 199

minutes at 180°C/350°F/Gas Mark 4 till firm when pressed lightly in the centre. Turn out on a flat dish to serve.

While it is baking, make a thick tomato sauce. Chop the onion finely and soften in the oil and butter. Add the tinned tomatoes, chopped roughly or crushed, and simmer for about 15 minutes, adding sea salt, black pepper and sugar. Since the only weakness of this delicious dish is its strange colour, I like to pour some of the tomato sauce over the top to mask it, and serve the rest separately. Alternatively, it can be baked for a slightly shorter time, 35–40 minutes, in a ring mould and served with the sauce in the centre. Serves 4.

BROAD BEANS WITH DILL   Greece

This dish can be made either with very young broad beans, before the inner bean has formed, when the pods may still be eaten, or with shelled beans. In the former case, the pods must very fresh, with a soft fluffy surface.

4 fl. oz/120 ml olive oil
2 bunches large spring onions, sliced
1½ lb/675 g very young broad beans, or 2½ lb/1·15 kg slightly older beans

2–3 tablespoons chopped dill
sea salt and black pepper

Heat the oil in a heavy pan and cook the sliced spring onions gently, until starting to colour. If the beans are very young simply cut the pods in 1 inch/2·5-cm pieces; if older, shell and use only the inner beans. Add the pods or beans to the pan and cook gently in the oil for 2–3 minutes, then add a little hot water, just enough to come level with the beans. Add the chopped dill, sea salt and black pepper, and cover the pan. Cook gently until the beans are tender. This is sometimes served with yogurt, handed separately. Serves 4–5.

CAULIFLOWER FRITTERS

Egypt

This is a popular Egyptian dish; there the batter would probably be a simple one of flour and water, but I prefer to use a lighter one made as follows.

batter:
¼ lb/100 g flour
a pinch of salt
2 tablespoons light oil

6 fl. oz/175 ml tepid water
1 egg white, beaten

1 small cauliflower, cut in sprigs
2 lemons, cut in quarters

Make the batter an hour in advance, if possible. (See *beignets d'aubergines*, page 194.) Just before using, beat again and fold in the beaten egg white. The small cauliflower sprigs, washed and patted dry, can be fried raw or partly cooked. I usually parboil them for 5 minutes in lightly salted water, then cool and pat dry before dipping in the batter and dropping into a pan of hot oil. In this case, they will need only 4–5 minutes frying; if fried raw, they will probably take 7–8 minutes. Serve with lemon quarters, as a first course or a vegetable accompaniment. Serves 4–5.

BRAISED CHICORY

Greece

This recipe was given to me by a Greek friend, to go with the Mediterranean Chicken recipe. It is good, with an unusual, slightly bitter taste that is not generally liked by children.

1 ½ lb/675 g chicory
1 ½ oz/40 g butter
1 tablespoon water

juice of 1 lemon
sea salt and black pepper

Cut the chicory in quarters lengthwise. Melt the butter in a sauté pan with the water and lemon juice; add the chicory and cover the pan. Cook for 20 minutes, add sea salt and black pepper, and continue cooking uncovered for another 20 minutes, until well browned and smoky, almost slightly burnt. Serves 4–5.

GRATIN DE COURGE   **France**

Although this recipe actually comes from the Limousin, similar dishes are often found in Provence. It is a delicious way of using pumpkin, and also works well with a vegetable marrow, or large courgettes.

1½ lb/675 g piece of pumpkin	*grated nutmeg*
¾ lb/350 g dry white bread,	*¼ pint/150 ml thick cream*
crusts removed	*2 tablespoons grated parmesan*
3 eggs, lightly beaten	*2 tablespoons grated gruyère*
sea salt and black pepper	

Cut the pumpkin in cubes, discarding seeds, and skin. Cut the bread in cubes also, and lay in a shallow dish. Steam the pumpkin until tender – about 12–15 minutes. Drain it, then lay on top of the bread and leave for 30 minutes. Put pumpkin and bread together in a food processor and blend briefly, or chop and mix thoroughly by hand. Stir in the lightly beaten eggs, add plenty of sea salt and black pepper, and a little grated nutmeg. Stir in the cream, and spoon into a buttered baking dish. Sprinkle the grated cheese over the top and bake for 35 minutes at 190°C/375°F/Gas Mark 5, till golden brown. Serves 5–6. This can be reheated very successfully.

BEIGNETS DE COURGETTES   **France**

These are made exactly as for *beignets d'aubergines*, substituting 5 or 6 courgettes, slightly larger than usual if possible, for the aubergines. If on the small side, they can be cut on the diagonal to give larger slices. Omit the salting, and serve with lemon quarters or a sauce.

STUFFED COURGETTES   **Greece**

I first had these delicious courgettes several years ago, while sailing round the southern coast of Crete. They are not hard to make and would make a good dish to serve friends who are convinced that Greek cooking has nothing more to offer than stuffed tomatoes and *moussaka*.

1½ lb/675 g smallish courgettes
2 oz/50 g butter
1 small onion, chopped
½ pint/300 ml soft white
  breadcrumbs
sea salt and black pepper
2 tablespoons chopped dill,
  when available

sauce:
1½ oz/40 g butter
2 tablespoons flour
½ pint/300 ml milk, heated
4 tablespoons grated gruyère
sea salt and black pepper
1 egg, separated

Wash the courgettes and cut off the stalk ends. Throw into a pan of boiling water and cook for 8–10 minutes, depending on size. Drain and cool. Then cut a thin strip off the top side of each courgette and hollow out the inside with a small teaspoon, leaving shells like little canoes. Chop the centres of the courgettes. Heat the butter and cook the chopped onion until it starts to colour, then add the chopped insides of the courgettes. Cook gently for 4–5 minutes, stirring often, then add the breadcrumbs and cook a minute or two longer, stirring well to mix. Remove from the heat and stir in sea salt and black pepper to taste, and the chopped dill, when available. Leave to cool, then fill the courgette shells with the mixture, laying them in a buttered baking dish, or in small individual dishes.

To make the sauce melt the butter, stir in the flour and cook for 1 minute. Heat the milk and pour on; stir till blended, and simmer for 3 minutes. Add the grated cheese and stir until it has melted. When smooth and well blended, add sea salt and black pepper to taste and remove from the heat. Separate the egg and beat the yolk; stir a little of the hot sauce into the yolk, then return it to the pan, beating well. Cool further, then whip the white until stiff and fold into the sauce. Spoon it over the stuffed courgettes and bake for 12–15 minutes at 190°C/375°F/Gas Mark 5, until puffed up and golden brown. Serves 4, as a first course.

ZUCCHINI E FAGIOLI   Italy

This unusual combination of courgettes with haricot beans comes from the south of Italy, where it is often served with ham dishes. It is particularly good when made in mid to late summer with fresh haricots.

2 lb/900 g fresh haricot beans
  (in their pods) or 6 oz/175 g
  dried cannelini beans
sea salt
3–4 tablespoons olive oil

¾ lb/350 g courgettes
1–1½ tablespoons white wine
  vinegar
black pepper

If using fresh haricots, shell them and cook until tender in boiling salted water. Drain. If using dried cannelini beans, start some hours in advance. Either soak for 3–4 hours in cold water, or bring to the boil, turn off the heat, and leave for 1 hour, covered. After whichever method you prefer, cover them with fresh cold water and bring slowly to the boil, unsalted. Simmer until they are tender; this may take anything from 25–60 minutes, depending on the quality of the beans. When soft, drain, add sea salt to taste and moisten with 1 teaspoon olive oil.

Cut the unpeeled courgettes in ½-inch/1-cm slices and drop into lightly salted boiling water. Poach for 10 minutes, then drain. Cool for a few minutes, then mix lightly with the beans and add more olive oil and wine vinegar, roughly three parts of oil to one of vinegar, until they are nicely moistened without swimming in the dressing. Add more sea salt and black pepper to taste. Serve at room temperature, either as a first course or as an accompaniment to baked ham. Serves 4–5.

COURGETTE FLOWERS IN FRITTATA   Italy

Courgette flowers can be bought in the markets in Italy and southern France, but in England only those with their own sizable vegetable gardens will be able to procure them. It is important to pick only the male flowers until the fruit has formed, when the female flowers may also be cut.

batter:
¼ lb/100 g flour
a pinch of salt
2 tablespoons sunflower or nut
  oil

¼ pint/150 ml warm water
1 egg white

6–8 oz/175–225 g courgette
  flowers, or marrow flowers
lemon quarters

Make the batter in a food processor or by hand. If using a food processor, simply put the sifted flour in it with the salt and oil, and add the water while processing. If making by hand sift the flour into a bowl and add the salt. Stir in the oil and then the water, beating well with a wire whisk or rotary beater until smooth. Stand for an hour or two before using. Then beat the egg white until stiff and fold in by hand, even if made in the food processor.

The flowers should not need washing but if they do, be careful to shake and pat them dry. Dip each one in the batter and drop into deep oil heated to 180°C/360°F. Cook for 2–3 minutes, turning once, until crisp and golden. Do not crowd in the pan but cook in batches. Drain on soft paper and serve immediately all are cooked, with lemon quarters. Serves 3–4 as a truly delicious first course.

STUFFED COURGETTE FLOWERS   Italy

These yellow blossoms, stuffed with a mixture of rice and spinach, make a pretty and unusual dish.

1 medium onion
1½ tablespoon olive oil
1 small clove garlic, minced
2 oz/50 g rice
½ lb/225 g spinach
sea salt and black pepper
1½ oz/40 g grated parmesan
1 egg and 1 yolk, beaten
    together

24 courgette flowers
frying oil
2 lemons, cut in quarters

frying batter:
¼ lb/100 g flour
a pinch of salt
2 tablespoons light oil
¼ pint/150 ml warm water
1 egg white, stiffly beaten

Chop the onion and brown in the oil, adding the minced garlic towards the end. Put aside. Cook the rice till tender in boiling salted water; drain. Boil the spinach in lightly salted water for 5 minutes, drain and chop. When it has cooled, squeeze out excess moisture. Reheat the onion and garlic, stir in the rice and cook for a moment or two, then remove from the heat and stir in the chopped spinach. Add sea salt and black pepper to taste, the grated parmesan, and the egg and egg yolk beaten together. Cool, then spoon carefully into the flowers, folding over the petals to enclose the mixture. Dip each one in batter made 1 hour in advance, shake off any excess, and drop into a pan of hot oil. Fry a few at a time, turning over once, for about 2 minutes on each side. Lift out and drain, then serve on a flat dish with lemon quarters. Serves 4 as a first course.

SFORMATO DI ZUCCHINI   Italy

A *sformato* is a sort of vegetable mould, somewhat more solid than a soufflé. It can be made with a wide variety of vegetables but my favourite is this one, made with courgettes.

1 lb/450 g courgettes	sea salt and black pepper
2 oz/50 g butter	4 eggs
3 tablespoons flour	5–6 slices white bread, slightly
½ pint/300 ml milk, heated	stale
2 oz/50 g grated gruyère	1½ oz/40 g butter, melted
2 oz/50 g chopped ham	

Poach the courgettes for 10 minutes in lightly salted water; drain and cool. Chop them very briefly in the food processor, or roughly by hand; they must not be too fine, and certainly not reduced to a mush. Melt the butter, stir in the flour and cook 1 minute. Heat the milk and pour on, stir till blended and simmer for 3 minutes, until smooth. Stir in the grated cheese, and when that is smoothly incorporated, add the chopped ham. Season to taste with sea salt and black pepper, then stir in the chopped courgettes. Beat the eggs and pour gradually into the mixture, folding in lightly but thoroughly.

Have a soufflé dish prepared beforehand: rub it with butter, then line it with the slices of bread, crusts removed and painted on both sides with melted butter. Pour the courgette mixture into this and stand in a bain marie (a baking tin half full of water). Cook for 40 minutes at 180°C/350°F/Gas Mark 4, until golden brown and set. Serves 4–5 as a first course, or 3–4 as a light main dish.

This can also be made with 1 lb/450 g broccoli or string beans, boiled and chopped, or 1½ lb/675 g spinach, boiled, well drained and chopped.

ELDER FLOWER FRITTERS (SAVOURY)   Yugoslavia

These are identical to the elder flower fritters (sweet) in Desserts and Cheese Dishes, page 222, but omitting the sugar. They make an unusual and delicious vegetable accompaniment to any dry dish of chicken or veal, either roast, grilled or fried.

FASSOULADA   Greece

This Greek bean dish is particularly good when made with fresh haricot beans in midsummer. It is often made in a slightly more liquid form, as a thick soup, but this combination of beans and smoked fish is much more unusual.

1 lb/450 g fresh haricots, or ½ lb/225 g dried haricot (or broad) beans
1 large onion, chopped
3 carrots, chopped
3 stalks celery, chopped

sea salt and black pepper
1 tablespoon tomato purée
6 tablespoons olive oil
1 lb/450 g smoked herring fillets
a little extra olive oil
2 lemons, cut in quarters

Cook the fresh haricots in boiling unsalted water until tender, then drain. If using dried beans, first bring to the boil, then turn off the heat, cover the pan and leave for 1 hour. Then cover with fresh water, bring to the boil, and simmer till tender. Put the other coarsely chopped vegetables in a pan with cold water to cover; add sea salt, bring to the boil and simmer for 25 minutes, or until they are tender. When the beans are cooked, drain off the water – it can be kept for soup – and add them to the fresh vegetables. Reheat, adding the tomato purée, 6 tablespoons olive oil, sea salt and black pepper. Simmer all together for 5 minutes, then cool slightly, and serve with a dish of smoked herring fillets sprinkled with olive oil and garnished with lemon quarters. Serves 4 as a first course. The beans should be fairly hot, but not scalding.

JAMON CON HABAS   **Spain**

Another of the many Spanish bean dishes, this one combines broad beans with raw ham. Serrano ham, from the mountains round Granada, is best; it is similar to Parma ham, and just as good. Raw ham is hard to find in England, and very expensive, so we may be forced to substitute bacon.

2 tablespoons olive oil	3 lb/1·35 kg broad beans in
1 small onion, chopped	their pods
2–3 oz/50–75 g raw smoked	4 tablespoons hot water
ham (or bacon), chopped	black pepper

Heat the oil in a sauté pan and cook the chopped onion until soft. Add the chopped ham (or bacon) and cook for 2 minutes more, stirring, then add the shelled beans. Stir over gentle heat for 2 minutes, then add 4 tablespoons hot water and cover the pan. Cook gently for 20 minutes, or until the beans are cooked, stirring occasionally and adding more water as needed. Add black pepper to taste. Serves 4.

JUDIAS SALTEADES   **Spain**

This dish of green beans, boiled then tossed in olive oil with garlic and chopped onion, is one of many good Spanish vegetable dishes.

1 lb/450 g green beans	1 large clove garlic, finely
2 tablespoons olive oil	chopped
1 small onion, finely chopped	sea salt and black pepper

The Spanish beans are thicker than string beans, and fatter. They are first split in half lengthwise and cooked till only just tender, but still crisp, in boiling salted water. Drain. Heat the oil in a sauté pan and cook the finely chopped onion until it starts to colour, then add the finely chopped garlic. A minute or two later, add the drained beans and toss together, until reheated and well mixed. Add sea salt and black pepper and serve. Serves 5–6.

STEWED OKRA   Greece

This dish of okra and tomatoes stewed in oil makes a good cold hors d'oeuvre, or a hot accompaniment to grilled or roast meat or poultry.

1 lb/450 g small okra
¼ pint/150 ml olive oil
1 large onion, chopped

1 lb/450 g tomatoes, skinned
 and chopped
sea salt and black pepper
1 teaspoon sugar

Trim the okra, wash, drain and pat dry in a cloth. Heat the oil in a heavy pan, add the chopped onion and cook slowly until lightly coloured. Add the okra, stir around, then leave to cook for 5 minutes. Add the chopped tomatoes, with sea salt, black pepper and sugar, and cover the pan. Simmer gently for about 20 minutes, or until the okra are tender. Check to see they are not in danger of boiling dry; if so, add 2 tablespoons boiling water. Serve hot or cool, never chilled. Serves 4–5.

MUSHROOM PURÉE   Italy

This makes an excellent vegetable dish to serve with dry meat dishes, especially roast game or guinea fowl.

1 lb/450 g mushrooms
3 oz/75 g butter
1 tablespoon flour
¼ pint/150 ml milk
¼ bay leaf

1 slice onion
sea salt and black pepper
freshly grated nutmeg
¼ pint/150 ml thick cream

Chop the mushrooms roughly in a food processor or by hand. Heat 2 oz/50 g of the butter and cook the chopped mushrooms for 10–12 minutes, until most of their liquid has evaporated. In a separate pan, make a béchamel sauce with the remaining butter, flour, and the milk which has been brought to the boil beforehand with the bay leaf, onion, sea salt, black pepper and nutmeg, and left for 20 minutes to infuse. Strain before adding to the roux. When all is smooth and well seasoned, stir into the chopped mushrooms and cook for 2–3 minutes, until blended. Add the cream, stir well, and simmer again for a moment. Add more sea salt, black pepper or grated nutmeg as desired. Serves 4.

PEPERONATA   **Italy**

1 large onion, chopped
¼ pint/150 ml olive oil
2 cloves garlic, minced
2 lb/900 g mixed red, green and
  yellow peppers, cut in strips

1 lb/450 g tomatoes, skinned
  and chopped
sea salt and black pepper

Chop the onion and stew gently in the oil in a heavy pan. After 5 minutes add the minced garlic and the peppers, cut in strips. Cover and cook slowly for 15 minutes, stirring now and then, then add the peeled and chopped tomatoes. Cook gently for another 10–15 minutes, stirring occasionally. Add sea salt and black pepper to taste. Cool for an hour before serving, or leave until quite cold, but do not chill. Serve as a first course, with bread. Serves 4–5.

PEPPERONI IN TORTIERA   **Italy**

This recipe for grilled and baked peppers comes from the Gulf of Naples. It makes a pretty dish to serve as a first course, either alone or with other cooked vegetable dishes. It makes quite a small dish, but peppers are a concentrated food and should not be eaten in great quantities.

1 lb/450 g yellow or red
  peppers, or mixed
4 heaped tablespoons fresh
  white breadcrumbs
1 clove garlic, minced

6 black olives, stoned and
  chopped
2 tablespoons chopped parsley
4–5 tablespoons olive oil
sea salt and black pepper
½ tablespoon lemon juice

Char the peppers under the grill or over an open flame until the skin is blackened all over. Scrape it away carefully, and discard the stalks and seeds. Cut the flesh in long strips and lay in an oiled gratin dish. Mix the breadcrumbs with the minced garlic, chopped olives and parsley, and 2 tablespoons of the olive oil. Add salt, pepper and lemon juice and spread over the peppers in their dish. Dribble a further 2 tablespoons olive oil over all and bake for 15 minutes at 190°C/375°F/Gas Mark 5 till the surface is lightly browned and crisp. Serve hot. Serves 3 alone, or 4–5 with other dishes.

STUFFED PEPPERS   Italy

This recipe for stuffed peppers comes from the Gulf of Naples; the peppers would be yellow ones since these are the most popular ones in Italy, but the recipe works equally well with red or green peppers. A simple dish, it makes a good accompaniment to roast or grilled meat, roast chicken, etc. rather than as a dish in its own right.

6 peppers: yellow, red or green
1 medium onion
3 tablespoons olive oil
1 large clove garlic, crushed
6 black olives, stoned and
  chopped
1 heaped tablespoon capers,
  drained and chopped

4 oz/100 g soft white
  breadcrumbs
sea salt and black pepper
2 tablespoons grated parmesan
1 oz/25 g butter
¼ pint/150 ml chicken stock

Cook the peppers briefly under a grill or over an open flame until the skin has blackened and blistered all over. Cool, then scrape off the skin with a small knife. Cut off the stalk end and carefully remove any small peppers and seeds from the inside. Chop the onion and cook slowly in the oil till pale golden. Add the crushed garlic and cook another minute, then the stoned chopped olives and the capers, drained and roughly chopped. After a few minutes stir in the breadcrumbs and stir well for a couple of minutes, till lightly cooked in the oil. Add plenty of sea salt and black pepper and stir in the grated parmesan. Fill the peppers carefully with the mixture and replace the tops. Stand them upright in a casserole that just fits them nicely. Heat the butter and stock together, and pour over the peppers. Cover and bake for 20 minutes at 180°C/350°F/Gas Mark 4 basting two or three times. Serves 6.

PISTO   Spain

This Spanish dish, called *samfaina* in Catalan, is not to be confused with the Provençal *pistou*. It is a simple vegetable stew, very similar to the Turkish *menemen*, sometimes served with beaten eggs blended in with it, like a *piperade*. I ate it twice in Catalonia, once with eggs and once with a *picada* – a Catalan paste of pounded pine nuts and garlic

– added at the end. Both were delicious. I had this version in a restaurant in Barcelona.

½ *large Spanish onion, about*	½ *lb/225 g courgettes*
6 oz/175 g	½ *lb/225 g tomatoes*
4 tablespoons olive oil	*sea salt and black pepper*
½ *lb/225 g red peppers, cut in*	*a pinch of sugar*
strips	*2 eggs (optional)*

Cut the onion in large square chunks about 1 inch/2·5 cm across, then divide each chunk into layers, so that you have large thin pieces. Heat the oil in a sauté pan and cook the onion gently for 10 minutes, without allowing it to brown. Add the red peppers cut in strips and cook another 10 minutes. Cut the unpeeled courgettes in 1-inch/2·5-cm slices, then halve them. Add to the pan and cook for 10 minutes, then add the tomatoes, skinned and cut in chunks. Stew gently, adding sea salt, black pepper and sugar, for another 10 minutes, covered. (The sugar would not be necessary in Spain as their tomatoes are well ripened by the sun.) When the cooking time is up, the vegetables should be soft and gently amalgamated, without being mushy. Cool for 15 minutes before serving. Serves 4–5 as a first course, or as part of a vegetarian meal.

If adding eggs, cool the pistu for a few minutes, then beat the eggs and stir in. Replace over gentle heat and cook slowly, stirring constantly, until they have set, thickening the juices. If serving with *picada* (see Sauces, page 249), spoon into individual heatproof bowls and spread a spoonful of *picada* over the top. Cook under the grill for a few minutes, till lightly browned, before serving.

RATATOUILLE   France

This is not the traditional way of making ratatouille, but I have found that by frying the sliced aubergines in deep oil they absorb much less of it. If preferred, they can be cooked with the peppers in the usual way.

1 lb/450 g aubergines
salt
frying oil
4 tablespoons sunflower seed
   oil
1 large mild onion, chopped
½ lb/225 g red peppers
½ lb/225 g green peppers

3 cloves garlic, minced
¾ lb/350 g tomatoes
sea salt and black pepper
½ teaspoon sugar
6 leaves basil, cut in strips
   (optional)

Cut the unpeeled aubergines in slices lengthwise, about ½ inch/1 cm thick. Sprinkle with salt and leave to drain for 30 minutes. Then pat dry in a cloth or soft paper. Heat a 1-inch/2-cm layer of frying oil in a sauté pan; when it is very hot, drop in a few of the aubergine slices and cook until golden brown on both sides, turning once. Lift them out and drain on soft paper while you fry the next batch.

When all are done, heat the sunflower seed oil in a clean pan and cook the chopped onion until it starts to colour. Then add the red and green peppers cut in ½ inch/1 cm square dice; cover the pan and cook gently for 10 minutes, stirring occasionally. Then add the minced garlic and the skinned and coarsely chopped tomatoes, sea salt and black pepper to taste, and a little sugar. Cook gently for 5 minutes stirring frequently. Cut the fried aubergine slices across in strips about ½ inch/1 cm wide and stir gently into the ratatouille. Cook for another 4 minutes, then pour into a serving dish.

This is best served warm, or cold; unlike most Mediterranean dishes, it is also good chilled, in hot weather. Some fresh basil leaves cut in strips can be stirred in when it is still hot, but after cooking. Serves 5–6.

CATALAN SPINACH   Spain

A purée of spinach with pine kernels and currants, garnished with croûtons rubbed with garlic, this vegetable dish is best served alone, either as a first course, or after a main dish.

2 lb/900 g spinach
2 tablespoons olive oil
2 cloves garlic
2 tablespoons pine kernels

1 tablespoon currants
sea salt and black pepper
2 slices dry white bread
1 oz/25 g butter

Cook the spinach until tender – about 5 minutes – in boiling water to cover, then drain. Leave to cool, then squeeze out all the moisture and chop as finely as possible. Heat the oil and cook 1 chopped clove of garlic for 1–2 minutes, being very careful not to let it burn. Add the pine kernels, then the currants, and cook gently, stirring often, until all are golden. Put the chopped spinach in the pan and stir well, adding sea salt and black pepper. Cook for 5 minutes, stirring often. Cut the crusts off the bread and cut each slice in four triangles. Heat the butter and fry the bread until golden on both sides. Drain on soft paper, then rub all over with the remaining clove of garlic cut in half. Tip the spinach into a dish and surround with the croûtons. Serves 4–6.

TIAN

France

This Provençal dish can be made with any mixture of vegetables, but I find the combination of courgettes and chard, or spinach, one of the best. It is good hot, warm or even cold. If making for a picnic, bake in a round pie tin.

1 small onion	2 oz/50 g rice
3 tablespoons olive oil	sea salt and black pepper
2 cloves garlic, crushed	3 eggs
1 lb/450 g courgettes	2 oz/50 g grated gruyère
¾ lb/350 g chard, spinach beet,	1 oz/25 g grated parmesan, or
or spinach (leaves only of	extra gruyère
chard or spinach beet)	

Chop the onion and cook in the oil until it starts to colour; add the crushed garlic. Chop the unpeeled courgettes coarsely in a food processor or by hand, or grate them on a coarse grater. Add them to the onion and cook for 5 minutes, stirring often. Cook the chard or spinach beet for 10 minutes, or the spinach for 5 minutes, in boiling salted water; drain and rinse in cold water. Squeeze out the moisture between the hands and chop with a long knife. Add to the courgettes and cook for another 2–3 minutes. Boil the rice, drain well and stir into the vegetables, adding plenty of sea salt and black pepper. Beat the eggs and stir in, with the grated gruyère. Tip into an oiled gratin dish and sprinkle the grated parmesan, or extra gruyère, over the top. Bake for

35 minutes at 180°C/350°F/Gas Mark 4, till puffy and golden brown on top. Serves 5.

GRATIN DE TOMATES   France

This is one of those useful dishes which can serve as a first course, a separate vegetable course or a light main dish accompanied by a green salad.

1 lb/450 g potatoes	3 oz/75 g grated gruyère or
4 tablespoons olive oil	emmenthal
1 lb/450 g onions	1½ lb/675 g tomatoes
sea salt and black pepper	2 branches thyme

Boil the potatoes in their skins; drain well and skin as soon as they are cool enough to handle. Cut them in thickish slices and make a layer of half of them in a broad shallow dish which you have rubbed with a little of the oil. (The traditional Provençal *tian* dishes are of brown earthenware, glazed inside, some 12–18 inches/30–45 cm across and about 2 inches/5 cm deep.) Slice the onions thinly and lay half of them over the potatoes. Sprinkle with sea salt and black pepper and half the grated cheese. Slice the unpeeled tomatoes and lay half of them over the cheese. Pull the leaves off the thyme and scatter half over the tomatoes. Add more salt and pepper, then repeat the layers, finishing with tomatoes and thyme. Dribble the 3½–4 tablespoons olive oil over all and bake for 45 minutes at 220°C/425°F/Gas Mark 7. Serve hot, with French bread. Serves 5–6 as a first course, or 4 as a main dish with a green salad.

TUMBET   Mallorca

This dish of mixed baked vegetables is slightly like a Lenten form of *moussaka*, with breadcrumbs replacing the meat. It is quite filling, and serves as a main dish in its own right, or as an accompaniment to cold meat.

thick tomato sauce:
1 tablespoon olive oil
1 oz/25 g butter
1 small onion, chopped
1 clove garlic, crushed
1 medium (14 oz/396 g) and 1
    small (6 oz/175 g) tin tomatoes
1 tablespoon tomato purée
sea salt and black pepper
½ teaspoon sugar
3 sprigs fresh marjoram

¾ lb/350 g aubergines
salt
1 large Spanish onion
¾ lb/350 g green peppers
¾ lb/350 g courgettes
frying oil
2 thick slices white bread,
    toasted
sea salt and black pepper
½ oz/15 g butter

First make the sauce. Heat the oil and butter in a sauté pan and cook the chopped onion until pale golden. Add the crushed garlic, then the roughly chopped or pulped tomatoes with their juice. Add the tomato purée, sea salt, black pepper, sugar and marjoram. Simmer gently, partly covered, for 45 minutes, stirring often, until it becomes quite thick.

Meanwhile prepare the vegetables: cut the unpeeled aubergines in diagonal slices, fairly thin, and sprinkle with salt. Leave for 30–45 minutes to drain, then rinse and pat dry. Cut the onion in half, then slice each half – not too thin. Cut the peppers in strips about ¼ inch/5 mm thick. Cut the unpeeled courgettes in slices lengthwise or diagonally, depending on size. Heat some oil in a sauté pan, enough to come about ¾ inch/1·5 cm up the side of the pan. When it is hot, put in the dried aubergine slices, a few at a time, and fry until golden, turning once. Drain on soft paper. Pour off most of the oil and cook the sliced onions in about 4 tablespoons of oil, adding the pepper strips after a few moments. Cook both together till soft, stirring often. Fry the sliced courgettes in a little fresh oil, turning once, then drain.

Cut the crusts off the toast and tear in pieces. Reduce to coarse crumbs in a food processor or blender. Put one third of them in a buttered gratin dish and cover with the aubergines. Sprinkle with sea salt and black pepper and spread a third of the tomato sauce over them. Cover with the onions and peppers, sprinkle with salt and pepper, then cover with a second layer of toast crumbs and tomato sauce. Top with the courgettes, more salt and pepper, then the remaining tomato sauce. Sprinkle the remaining crumbs over all, dot with the butter, and bake for about 35 minutes at 190°C/375°F/Gas Mark 5 until golden brown on top. Serves 4 as a main dish, or 5–6 as a vegetable accompaniment to a meat dish. It can also be prepared in advance and only baked at the last moment.

10

DESSERTS, CAKES AND
SWEET CHEESE DISHES

The desserts of the Mediterranean do not differ much from those in other parts of the same countries. Thus in Spain the crème caramel known as *flan* is fairly universal, while the tarts with a layer of fruit – apples, pears, apricots, strawberries or blueberries – lying on a bed of crème pâtissière made in the south of France are no different from those in other parts. Mixtures of sponge and fruit, like the *gâteau paysan*, or a form of *clafoutis*, also abound. An excellent cream cake called a *tropézienne* can be found in the south of France, somewhat similar to a Boston cream pie: it is a mixture of feather-light sponge with crème pâtissière. In Nice, however, there is one unique speciality – the *tourte de blea* – a strange combination of two layers of pastry with a sweet filling made from chard, raisins, rum and sugar. It is rarely made at home any more, but is on sale in the market and in many shops in the Old Town. Although it sounds odd, it is rather good, and must be like many medieval English sweet dishes of vegetables in pastry. Somewhat similar is the Genoese *torta pasqualina*, a cake of thin flaky pastry domed high over an air pocket, under which lies a filling of spinach and cream cheese. This is also eaten as a dessert and, like the *tourte de blea*, is rarely made at home or even in restaurants but only in certain shops. This seems to apply to many of the Mediterranean desserts, possibly because they are only successful when made by a professional pastry chef, and are therefore somewhat out of the range of the average housewife.

The same applies to the Italian ices, in my opinion the best in the world. I do not attempt to give recipes for them, for their excellence does not depend on a mere formula, and I for one cannot approach their quality. The best I have ever eaten were in Genoa, in Venice, and in the old-fashioned cafés like Floka's in Athens. In fact they are more often eaten as a light refreshment on their own than as a dessert, either in the afternoon, early evening or after dinner.

Some of my favourite Mediterranean sweet dishes are those based on cream cheese. I spent a night last summer in a small inn frequented by motor mechanics on the outskirts of Lyons, waiting for my car to be fixed; the set dinner, which was pretty good, ended with a most delicious fromage blanc, served in glass goblets with fresh cream poured over it. Another dish of this sort which I love is the Italian *crema alla mascarpone*; this is not as well known as it might be since it is not available during midsummer, partly because the lack of pasture makes the manufacture of cream cheese almost impossible, and the extreme heat prevents its keeping fresh. It is like a lighter and less rich zabaglione, made by whipping up a full cream cheese called *mascarpone* with the yolks and beaten white of eggs. A little kirsch is sometimes added, but I prefer it without; sometimes crumbled *amaretti di saronno* – those tiny macaroons – are folded into it, or occasionally chopped *marrons glacées*. I like it best of all as I first ate it one November, in a restaurant near the Mercado di San Lorenzo in Florence, with nothing added, but two rolled biscuits with which to scoop it up. Another very simple cheese dish, which is found in Tuscany, consists simply of ricotta eaten with a sprinkling of ground coffee beans and sugar.

In and around Trieste the change from Italian/Mediterranean food to the central European flavour of Yugoslavia, until relatively recently part of the Austro-Hungarian Empire, becomes apparent. Here the light Italian confections give way to heartier dishes of fruit dumplings rolled in poppy seeds and browned breadcrumbs, sweet noodle dishes and a variety of cakes. Elder flowers are dipped in batter and made into exquisite scented fritters, while the yogurt is the best I have ever tasted.

As we cross behind Albania into Greece the change is no less noticeable, for now we are entering the range of the Middle East. For four hundred years Greece was occupied by the Turks, and their love of sweet dishes, oriental in the extreme, still persists to a lesser degree in Greece. *Baklava* is a good example: flaky *filo* pastry sandwiched together with ground pistachios subtly flavoured with cinnamon and drenched in a sweet sugar syrup flavoured with rose water. In Turkey there are a myriad such dishes, many of them with highly suggestive names: 'ladies' navels' is one such example. This love of sweet pastries extends all round the Middle East and along the north coast of Africa;

Tunisia especially is famed for the excellence of its pastry shops, and these are now spreading through the many French towns, like Marseilles, with a growing middle-class Algerian population. An unusual Turkish sweet dish is a sweet chicken cream; this is still made in one shop in Athens, as well as many in Istanbul. It is like a very smooth milk pudding, a cross between a cornflour mould and a junket, with pounded breast of chicken incorporated within it. I have tried to make it, but without much success, since it is one of those primitive dishes so common in the Middle East which demand literally hours of pounding and shredding by hand. Some of these have now been made possible with the aid of food processors and blenders, but not this one, alas.

Were I to live in a Mediterranean country I would rarely bother to make sweet dishes, since I have a passion for their fruit, which is unequalled in quality and variety. I also love yogurt, and the innumerable cheeses of France and Italy, especially the goats' milk cheeses we rarely find in England.

AMARDINE FOOL   Syria

A paste of dried apricots called *amardine* is much used in the Middle East, for making into drinks and desserts, and for eating on its own. It can be bought in many shops in England selling Eastern goods, and is useful in that it needs no cooking.

¼ lb/100 g apricot paste	½ pint/300 ml yogurt
½ pint/300 ml water	2 tablespoons orange juice

Using kitchen scissors, cut the paste into pieces and cover with the water. Leave to soak for 2 hours, by which time it will have become quite soft. Put in a food processor or blender and blend, then add the yogurt and blend again. Stir in the orange juice, pour into 4 glasses and chill for 2–3 hours before serving. This makes a thin fool, extremely nourishing without being fattening. Serves 4.

ARTEMIS CAKE   Greece

This is a most delicious cake – light and moist – which keeps well for a day or two.

14 oz/400 g plain chocolate (4
* bars Chocolat Menier)*
½ lb/225 g soft margarine

¼ lb/100 g icing sugar, sifted
5 eggs, separated
2 tablespoons flour, sifted

Break the chocolate in small bits and stand in a large bowl over a pan of very hot water. Stir once or twice only, until smooth and runny, then leave to cool till almost room temperature. Cream the margarine with the icing sugar, then beat in the egg yolks. (This can be done in a mixer or food processor or by hand.) Then stir in the chocolate – this should be done by hand – and mix lightly; it does not need to be too thoroughly mixed. Stir in the flour, and finally fold in the egg whites, beaten until they stand in peaks. Have a buttered cake tin about 8 inches/20 cm across – if it does not have a removable bottom it must be lined with buttered greaseproof paper – and pour in the cake mixture. Bake at 180°C/350°F/Gas Mark 4 for about 45 minutes, until the edges of the cracks that form in the top are just beginning to burn. Do not test with a skewer as it will certainly be moist, even when ready. Leave in its tin till almost cool, then lift out carefully and stand on a rack. Just before serving sprinkle with a little icing sugar. Serves 8.

BAKLAVA   Greece

This is a modified version of *baklava*, which in its usual form – literally dripping with sugar syrup – is really too sweet for most Western tastes. It is also made in smaller quantities than usual, since a little goes a very long way. In Greece and Turkey, *baklava* is often made with pistachio nuts, but these are too expensive here to be practicable.

2 oz/50 g butter
3 oz/75 g sugar
¼ pint/150 ml water
½ lb/225 g chopped walnuts, or
* walnuts and almonds mixed*
¼ teaspoon ground cinnamon
* (optional)*

2 oz/50 g melted butter
½ lb/225 g filo pastry

syrup:
7 oz/200 g sugar
¼ pint/150 ml water
1 tablespoon lemon juice

Melt the butter, sugar and water in a pan and stir in the chopped nuts. Mix well, add cinnamon if used, and set aside. Have a square or rectangular baking tin measuring roughly 8 inches/20 cm across, and 1¼ inches/3 cm deep. Brush it with melted butter and line it with 4 sheets of filo, trimming them to fit and brushing each one with melted butter. Spread half the nut filling over this, then cover with 2 more sheets filo, each brushed with melted butter. Cover with the rest of the nuts, and then 4 more sheets filo, each brushed with butter, and brush butter over the whole top surface. Cut in diamond shapes with the point of a knife, deep enough to penetrate the top layers of the pastry, and bake for 40 minutes at 180°C/350°F/Gas Mark 4.

Just before it has finished cooking, make the syrup. Put the sugar, water and lemon juice in a pan and bring to the boil. Boil gently for 5 minutes, until thick enough to coat the back of a wooden spoon. When the baklava has finished cooking, pour the hot syrup over it and set aside to cool. Stand for 2–3 hours before serving, but do not chill. Although small, this will serve 8–10 people easily, since it is eaten in very small portions.

SWEET CHICKEN CREAM   Turkey

This unusual dessert, like a cross between a cornflour pudding and a junket with pounded breast of chicken added, is a Turkish dish which is also made in one shop in Athens. It is seldom made at home, since it involves literally hours of pounding. I have tried making it with the aid of a food processor but the result was a far cry from the original. I include the recipe nonetheless, for interest's sake.

1 poached breast of a small chicken, about 5 oz/150 g	1½ pints/900 ml milk
3 oz/75 g rice flour	1 teaspoon rose water
3 oz/75 g castor sugar	almond oil
	a little ground cinnamon

First chop very finely, then pound the breast of chicken until reduced to a smooth paste. (It can be started off in a food processor, but must be pounded as well. Some recipes give alternative instructions, which I find even more difficult, namely to shred the chicken meat and rub it between the fingers until reduced to shreds as fine as a hair!) Put the rice flour and sugar in a pan and mix to a paste with the cold milk.

Bring to the boil, stirring, and cook for 10 minutes, stirring almost constantly. Soak the pounded or shredded chicken in cold water for 10 minutes, then pat dry. Stir into the pudding with the rose water and simmer steadily for 10 minutes, until thick and slightly glutinous. Pour into small dishes or moulds rubbed with almond oil and cool, then chill. Turn out and sprinkle with cinnamon. The cream should be almost as smooth as junket. Serves 5–6.

CHOCOLATE SALAMI   Italy

This easily made chocolate roll is always popular with children, and can be prepared several days in advance.

6 oz/175 g unsalted butter
3 tablespoons castor sugar
4 tablespoons unsweetened
  chocolate powder

2 egg yolks
7 Marie biscuits or 6 rich tea
  biscuits, crumbled

Cream the butter with the sugar in a food processor or mixer. Add the chocolate powder and cream again. Stir in the egg yolks and mix till smoothly blended. Turn into a bowl and stir in the crumbled biscuits (I prefer to break them up by hand, as the processor quickly reduces them to dust.) Oil a piece of foil (use a tasteless oil – arachide or sunflower seed) and lay the chocolate mixture on it. Form roughly into a roll, chill for a little to firm, then roll out evenly into a fat sausage. Chill for several hours, then cut in slices. Serves 4–5.

CLAFOUTIS   France

This dish actually comes from the Limousin, but is to be found in all the Nice shops where it is sometimes made with a sponge mixture instead of the batter which is the true *clafoutis*.

1½ lb/675 g black cherries,
  stoned
½ oz/15 g butter
a little castor sugar

batter:
3 eggs
a pinch of salt
3 tablespoons sifted flour
3 tablespoons sugar
1 pint/600 ml milk, heated

Butter a shallow fireproof dish large enough to hold the cherries in one layer. Lay the cherries in it (if you do not have time to stone them it doesn't really matter). Make the batter in a food processor or by hand: beat the eggs with the salt, add the flour and beat again, then the sugar, and finally the hot milk, beating (or processing) until smooth. Pour over the cherries, dot with butter, and bake for 30 minutes at 200°C/400°F/Gas Mark 6, until set and golden brown. Sprinkle with castor sugar and serve warm, with cream. Serves 5–6.

ELDER FLOWER FRITTERS (SWEET)   Yugoslavia

In parts of Yugoslavia, as in Czechoslovakia and Austria, elder flowers are made into both sweet and savoury fritters, for serving either as a dessert or a vegetable. They cost little to make and are light and delicious.

batter:
¼ lb/100 g flour
a pinch of sea salt
2 tablespoons sunflower seed
   oil
¼ pint/150 ml warm water
1 egg white

12 elder flowers
frying oil
castor sugar

If making the batter by hand, sift the flour with the salt into a large bowl. Stir in the oil and enough water to give the consistency of a fairly thick cream. Stand for 1–2 hours, covered, in a cool place. Just before using, beat the egg white until stiff and fold in.

Have the elder flowers rinsed and shaken dry, then patted in a cloth. Dip each one in batter, shaking off any excess. Drop them, a few at a time, into a large pan of oil heated to 180°C/360°F. Do not crowd them. Cook for about 3 minutes, turning once, until golden. Drain on soft paper while you fry the next batch. Serve at once, sprinkled with castor sugar and laid on a flat dish. Serves 4.

FLAN   **Spain**

This is the Spanish version of crème caramel, and is widely popular all over Spain.

caramel:
3 oz/75 g sugar
3 tablespoons water

cream:
1 pint/600 ml milk

1 small stick cinnamon
1 strip lemon peel
3 large eggs
3 tablespoons vanilla sugar or
  plain sugar

Make the caramel by heating the sugar and water together in a heavy pan until the sugar first melts, then turns a light golden. Tip into a small soufflé dish which you have rinsed with cold water, and turn it round and round quickly, so that it is coated all over with caramel.

Then heat the milk with the cinnamon stick and lemon peel, bringing it very slowly to boiling point. Beat the eggs with the vanilla (or plain) sugar in a bowl and pour the almost boiling milk over them, having discarded the flavourings, beating continuously. Pour through a strainer into the caramel-lined mould, stand in a baking tin half full of water, and bake for 40 minutes at 150°C/310°F/Gas Mark 2. Cool completely, then turn out onto a shallow dish before serving. Serves 4.

PESCHE RIPIENE   **Italy**

This dish of stuffed peaches is a popular Italian dessert. The stuffing varies according to different recipes; this is a light version which makes a good end to a summer dinner.

5 peaches
2 large macaroons, slightly
  stale
6 almonds, peeled and
  chopped

1 oz/25 g candied lemon peel,
  chopped
1½ oz/40 g castor sugar
⅛ pint/75 ml white wine

Skin the peaches, cut them in half, and remove the stones. (If you have the patience, the stones can be split and the chopped kernels added to the stuffing.) Crumble the macaroons and put in the food processor or blender with the chopped almonds, peach kernels if used, chopped peel and 1 oz/25 g of the sugar. Process until blended, then tip into a mortar and pound until smooth. Pulp one of the peaches and add to the mixture; pound until blended, then spoon the stuffing into the halved peaches. Lay them in a buttered baking dish, pour over the wine and sprinkle with the remaining sugar. Bake for 30 minutes at 180°C/350°F/Gas Mark 4. Cool slightly before serving, but do not chill; serve either warm or at room temperature. Serves 4.

PLUM DUMPLINGS   Yugoslavia

These little fruit dumplings are typical of the Austrian/Hungarian cuisine which extends over much of Yugoslavia. They make a good and unusual conclusion to a light meal on a cool day. Small peaches, apricots or cherries can be substituted for the plums.

½ lb/225 g self-raising flour
1 level teaspoon salt
8 fl. oz/250 ml milk
3 tablespoons melted butter
1 medium egg
1 egg yolk
12 small purple plums, stoned

¼ lb/100 g butter
1 oz/25 g dry breadcrumbs
2 tablespoons poppy seeds
   (optional)
¼ lb/100 g ricotta cheese
   (optional)

Sift the flour with the salt into a large bowl. Scald the milk with the butter and pour over the flour. Mix well, then add the egg and egg yolk and beat well with a wire whisk or rotary beater. When smooth, divide into 12 pieces and roll each one out thinly in a circle big enough to encompass a plum. Holding the circle of dough in one floured hand, lay a stoned plum in it and wrap the dough all round it, sealing it carefully. Drop them, a few at a time, into a pan of boiling water and cook steadily for about 6 minutes, turning over from time to time. While they are cooking, heat 4 tablespoons butter in a frying pan until very hot, and brown the breadcrumbs, turning them until they are golden all over. Roll the dumplings in the crumbs and pile on a serving dish. Hand the rest of the butter, melted, in a small jug. Alternatively, serve the simply boiled dumplings in a dish with a jug of melted butter separately, and small bowls of browned breadcrumbs, poppy seeds and ricotta cheese. Serves 5–6.

RIZOGALO Greece

Greek rice pudding is quite unlike the English variety; it is thicker and creamier, and can be very good indeed. It is often eaten for breakfast. It is sometimes flavoured with *mastic*, the strange resinous gum of a species of pine which grows mainly on the island of Chios, and is highly valued as a flavouring in Greece, Turkey and much of the Middle East. *Mastic* is supposed to be good for the teeth, and is chewed, like chewing gum, by the children.

2 oz/50 g rice
4 fl. oz/120 ml water
1 pint/600 ml milk, plus 1
  tablespoon
3 tablespoons vanilla sugar or
  plain sugar
2 teaspoons cornflour
1 egg yolk

optional flavourings:
1 pellet mastic about the size of
  a piece of chewing gum and a
  pinch sugar and 2 teaspoons
  rose water
or
ground cinnamon

Wash the rice and soak in the water. Bring 1 pint/600 ml milk to the boil with the vanilla (or plain) sugar, then stir in the rice and water. Bring back to the boil and simmer steadily for 40 minutes, covered, until most of the milk, but not all, has been absorbed. Stir the cornflour into 1 tablespoon water, then add to the rice and cook for a further 5 minutes, stirring. Beat the egg yolk with the 1 tablespoon of milk and stir into the rice; cook over low heat for 2–3 minutes, stirring.

If using *mastic* as a flavouring, it should be added now. Pound it in a mortar with a pinch of sugar and stir into the pudding, adding the rose water at the same time. Simmer for 2 minutes, then pour into a shallow dish and leave to cool. If using cinnamon instead of *mastic*, simply sprinkle it over the pudding in its serving dish. *Rizogalo* is always served cold, but not chilled. Serves 4.

TIRREMAZÚ Italy

This is based on memories of a delicious dessert eaten in a small restaurant in Venice; it is probably far removed from the original, but nonetheless good. It is typical of many Italian desserts made with sponge cake, crème pâtissière and cream.

1 plain sponge cake (measuring
roughly 8 × 3 × 2½
inches/20 × 7·5 × 6 cm) or 3
packets soft sponge fingers
¼ pint/150 ml dry white wine
¼ pint/150 ml peach juice
⅓ pint/200 ml thick cream,
whipped
3 tablespoons grated bitter
chocolate

crème pâtissière:
1 egg yolk
½ tablespoon flour
1 tablespoon home-made
vanilla sugar or plain sugar
⅓ pint/200 ml milk
¼ vanilla pod, if no vanilla
sugar

The sponge cake (or fingers) should be slightly stale. If using the cake, cut it in 3 equal parts horizontally. Mix the peach juice and white wine and sprinkle it over the 3 slices of cake. If using the sponge fingers, mix the wine and peach juice in a shallow dish and dip each finger in it briefly, doing one packet at a time, and assembling in rectangular form on a flat dish.

Have the crème pâtissière made in advance and left to cool. Beat the egg yolk, flour and sugar together; pour on the cold milk and stir till blended. Pour into a pan and stir over gentle heat until boiling point is reached. Simmer gently for 3 minutes, then pour through a strainer and cool in a sink half full of cold water, stirring frequently to prevent a skin forming. (If you have no home-made vanilla sugar, infuse the milk with ¼ vanilla pod for 20 minutes beforehand.)

Fold the whipped cream into the cool crème pâtissière, and spread one third of it over the first layer of cake or fingers. Cover with a second layer of sponge, more of the cream mixture, and so on, finishing with a layer of the cream. Chill for several hours, or better still overnight, in the refrigerator. Before serving, sprinkle the grated chocolate over all. Serves 6.

WALNUT CAKE   Turkey

This recipe came from a Turkish lady living in Izmir; it makes a somewhat moist heavy cake, not unlike a carrot cake, which I find rather delicious. I like to cover it with a cream cheese frosting, although this is certainly not authentic since cream cheese does not exist in Turkey. It is best made a day or two before eating, and I often serve it as a dessert, sometimes with a fruit fool or ice cream.

6 large eggs, separated
5 oz/150 g castor sugar
1½ oz/40 g soft white
   breadcrumbs
3 oz/75 g shelled walnuts,
   chopped (not too fine)
3–4 extra walnuts

cream cheese frosting:
¼ lb/100 g cream cheese
2 oz/50 g unsalted butter
2 oz/50 g castor sugar

Separate the eggs and beat the yolks with the castor sugar until they are pale yellow, thick and creamy. Mix the breadcrumbs with the chopped walnuts – this can all be done in the food processor – then stir them into the egg yolks. Beat the whites until stiff and fold in. Spoon into a buttered cake tin, preferably one with a removable base, or lined with buttered greaseproof paper. Bake for about 1 hour and 10 minutes at 180°C/350°F/Gas Mark 4, till the cake has shrunk away from the sides of the tin, and a skewer inserted in the centre comes out clean. Cool on a wire rack before attempting to remove the paper.

While it is baking, make the frosting. Put all the ingredients in the food processor or blender and blend. Chill for an hour or so to firm. When the cake has completely cooled, cover it with the frosting. Sometimes I cover the top and sides completely, other times I cut the cake in half and make a filling, then cover the top, leaving the sides uncovered. Chop the extra walnuts by hand, quite coarsely, and scatter over the top. Serves 6–8.

ZRIGA Tunisia

This is a typically Eastern dish, flavoured with pistachios and rose water.

pastry rolls:
2 oz/50 g hazelnuts, skinned
2 oz/50 g shelled pistachios
3 tablespoons castor sugar
2–3 tablespoons rose water
1–2 sheets filo pastry
1 oz/25 g butter, melted

custard sauce:
4 egg yolks
4 heaped tablespoons home-
   made vanilla sugar or plain
   sugar
1¼ pints/750 ml milk
1 tablespoon rose water

Roast the hazelnuts in the oven to skin them. Grate them in a cheese mill, then grate the pistachios also. Reserve 1½ tablespoons pistachios, mix the rest of the nuts together, blend with the sugar and stir in enough rose water to make a thick paste.

Spread out the *filo* and cut in strips about 10 × 4 inches/25 × 10 cm. Form the nut filling into long thin rolls, and lay lengthwise along one edge of the *filo*. Roll up, sealing the edges with melted butter, so that you have a long roll not much thicker than a cigarette. You should have enough for about 6 rolls. Lay them on a greased baking sheet and bake for 15 minutes at 180°C/350°F/Gas Mark 4, turning over once or twice so that they colour evenly. Lift out and leave to cool.

To make the custard sauce, beat the egg yolks with the vanilla sugar, then heat the milk to boiling point and pour on, beating constantly. Stand over a pan of boiling water and stir until thickened, about 10 minutes. Cool quickly in a sink half full of cold water, stirring frequently to prevent a skin forming. Stir in the rose water, then chill in the refrigerator.

An hour before serving, cut the pastry rolls with scissors into pieces about 1 inch/2·5 cm long. Pile them, about 8 at a time, into large wine glasses, and pour over the custard sauce. (If by any chance it is on the thin side, only assemble just before serving.) Sprinkle with the reserved grated pistachios and chill for 2–3 hours before serving. Serves 6.

ZUPPA INGLESE   Italy

This is very similar to a good trifle, made with sponge fingers soaked in Marsala, sandwiched between layers of crème pâtissière, and covered all over with whipped cream.

2 egg yolks	6 tablespoons Marsala
1 tablespoon sugar	½ pint/300 ml thick cream
1 ½ tablespoons flour	½ tablespoon chocolate coffee
1 pint/600 ml milk	beans (dip freshly roasted
½ vanilla pod	coffee beans in melted
2 strips lemon rind	chocolate) or chocolate
1 ½ packets crisp sponge	vermicelli or coarsely ground
fingers, preferably Savoiardi	coffee

Put the egg yolks in the food processor or blender with the sugar, flour and milk which has been flavoured beforehand by bringing slowly to the boil with the piece of vanilla pod and strips of lemon rind. When it reaches boiling point, cover the pan and remove from the heat; stand 20 minutes, then strain and cool before using. After processing the ingredients for the crème pâtissière, pour into a thick pan (or double boiler) and stir constantly over low heat until thickened. Cool and chill.

Soak the sponge fingers briefly in the Marsala and make a layer of them in a glass bowl, or on a flat dish. Cover with a layer of crème pâtissière, then another layer of soaked sponge fingers, until all is used, ending with sponge. Whip the cream and spread over all. Chill for several hours – it must be very cold – and sprinkle with a chocolate or coffee garnish just before serving. Serves 6.

CREMA ALLA MASCARPONE Italy

Mascarpone is a delicate cream cheese, a speciality of Tuscany, that is only made during the cooler months since the shortage of rich grazing during the summer makes its production impossible. We have no real equivalent in this country, but I have made a version of this dessert using a double cream cheese which was quite successful. *Amaretti di saronno* are exquisite little macaroon-type biscuits which can be bought here; failing these, use ordinary macaroons. It is also delicious served quite simply, with nothing added. A more extravagant version is sometimes made by adding chopped *marrons glacées*.

2 eggs, separated
3 oz/75 g castor sugar
½ lb/225 g mascarpone or
    double cream cheese

1 tablespoon kirsch (optional)
2 tablespoons crushed amaretti
    di saronno or macaroons or
    marrons glacées (optional)

Beat the egg yolks and shake in the sifted sugar. Beat again, then add the cream cheese and continue beating until smooth. Beat the egg whites until stiff, then fold in. I like to stop at this stage, and serve it with a simple biscuit, like a tuile. The spoonful of kirsch may be added at this stage, or the crumbled *amaretti* folded in or, for those who like them, chopped *marrons glacées*. Serves 4, in small glasses.

LABNEH   Lebanon

This is a soft cheese made from drained yogurt, eaten for breakfast in the Lebanon, but equally good at any other meal. Wild thyme can be bought at L'Herbier de Provence, 341 Fulham Road, London SW10, under its French name, *serpolet*.

1½ pints/900 ml firm yogurt	½ tablespoon wild thyme
½ tablespoon sesame seeds,	(serpolet)
toasted	a little olive oil

Tip the yogurt into a colander lined with muslin, tie with string and hang from the kitchen tap overnight so that it drains into the sink. Next day, turn onto a dish, and serve for breakfast (or lunch) with a small bowl of toasted sesame seeds and wild thyme pounded together in a mortar, and a little jug of olive oil. Each person helps himself, and sprinkles a little herb mixture and oil over it. Serve with flat (or pitta) bread. Serves 4.

RICOTTA WITH COFFEE   Italy

This very simple cheese dessert comes from Tuscany. It consists of ricotta cheese on a large dish, served with little bowls of castor sugar and medium ground coffee beans. Each person helps themselves to ricotta, and sprinkles it with a mixture of sugar and coffee.

11

BREADS, DISHES OF BREAD DOUGH AND BISCUITS

Bread is made of only three basic ingredients – flour, yeast and water – yet it is fascinating to see how many forms it can take. I am not speaking now of the enriched breads of France, the croissants and brioches, which are in no sense typical of the Mediterranean, although they are to be found in the south of France, but the regular *pain ordinaire* of the different countries: the simple round loaves of Spain and Italy, the baguettes and flutes of France, the flat breads of Cyprus and the Middle East, the *carta di musica* of Sardinia and the breads of the Arab countries of North Africa.

An interesting recent development is the growing popularity of wholemeal bread in both France and Italy. Not only in specialized 'health food' shops but even in the daily markets in France one now finds *pain de campagne* in both wholemeal and rye flour, while in Italy even the grissini are now sold in two forms, those baked with white flour and the wholemeal ones called *integrale*.

In some of the poorer countries the baker's oven still fills a general need, especially in the country villages. Since few of the houses have ovens, the large pittas (huge round pies of flaky pastry baked in metal trays as big as a cartwheel) are sent to the baker to be cooked. In Italy, the same ovens are used for baking pizzas, and the aroma of burning wood gives a special flavour that no domestic oven can duplicate. Even in big cities like Naples, Genoa, Nice and Marseilles, many of the commercial bakers still use wood-fired ovens, and do not hesitate to advertise the fact. In France, the bread is still baked regularly twice a day, so that it can be bought fresh for the evening meal; it is illegal to use the agent common in England and America that prevents bread going stale.

There are some interesting local specialities in breads, like the *focaccia* of Genoa and Tuscany, which is also found in Toulon as *fougace*. This is baked in a shallow tin, with a glaze of salt and olive oil which bakes to a salty golden crust. It makes a good accompaniment to a pre-prandial drink, since it encourages a huge thirst. In some areas bread and cake are closely intermingled. The *pannetone* of Genoa, for example, unlike its better-known Siennese namesake, is a solid cake of leavened bread flour, not unlike a large rock cake, spiced and studded with currants.

In Syria, Lebanon and Israel the flat bread similar to that of Cyprus is eaten; this is now well known to English and Americans, at least those living in cities, since it is widely available even in supermarkets. In Egypt, Tunisia and Morocco the Arab bread is rather different, with more substance, and lacking the empty pouch which makes such a useful container for doner kebab and other foods. Bread is doubly important in Morocco, not only as a food in itself, but as an aid to eating *tagine*, couscous and *bisteeya*, since these are traditionally eaten with the fingers, and bread forms a useful scoop. In Egypt, spiced rolls in sweet or salted versions are made in the form of small circles, studded with sesame seeds.

Dishes made with bread dough are best known in Italy, in the various forms of pizza, but dough is also used in Nice for making pissaladière, and a French version of pizza baked in rectangular tins. The Greeks also use bread dough to make *penyeli*: boat-shaped pieces of dough are filled with a feta cheese mixture similar to that used for *tiropitakia*, and baked until golden brown and melting.

FOCACCIA   Italy

This bread baked in a thin cake with a salty crust is a speciality of both Genoa and Tuscany. It is widely sold in small shops throughout the *sotto ripa* of Genoa, the old part near the port, and is often served in restaurants, both in Genoa and Florence, as an aperitif with drinks before a meal, since its high salt content encourages thirst. It is also sold in Toulon, in the vegetable market for instance, under the name *fougace*.

1 lb/450 g white bread flour   **crust:**
½ oz/15 g fresh yeast   1 tablespoon olive oil
½ teaspoon salt   1 teaspoon fine salt
approx. ½ pint/300 ml tepid water

Make the dough as usual, knead, and leave to rise until doubled in bulk. Punch down, turn out and knead again for 4–5 minutes, then roll out to fill a shallow baking tin about 10 inches/25 cm square which has been well oiled, so that it makes a cake about ½ inch/1 cm thick. Leave on the back of the stove for about 15 minutes, until starting to rise, then brush the top with olive oil and sprinkle evenly with fine salt. Bake for 15 minutes at 230°C/450°F/Gas Mark 8, then a further 20 minutes at 220°C/425°F/Gas Mark 7. It should be a nice golden brown, and give a hollow sound when tapped on the bottom with a knuckle. I often make this in half quantities, using a tin 8 inches/20 cm square and 1 inch/2·5 cm deep, since one only eats it in small amounts.

FOCACCIA CON LA CIPOLLA   Italy

This is a version of *focaccia* made with onions. Make exactly as for ordinary *focaccia*, adding at the last moment a layer of sliced onions, cooked (but not browned) in olive oil, over the dough. For a 1 lb/450 g loaf, use ½ lb/225 g onions softened in 3 tablespoons olive oil.

GRISSINI   Italy

Far nicer than the dry as-dust grissini in packets, these can be made at home and eaten still warm from the oven. Grissini can be made with ordinary bread or pizza dough, and are useful for using up extra pieces, but these are particularly good. Another form of bread stick can be made by simply making unfilled pizzas, and cutting them in strips about 1 inch/2·5 cm wide after baking.

¼ oz/8 g fresh yeast	½ lb/225 g white bread flour
2 teaspoons sugar	1 tablespoon olive oil
5–6 fl. oz/150–175 ml tepid water	1 egg, beaten
1 teaspoon sea salt	sesame seeds

Put the yeast and sugar in a cup with 3 tablespoons of the warm water. Leave in a warm place for 10 minutes. Dissolve the sea salt in a little very hot water, then make up to the required amount with warm water. Have the flour in a warm bowl, make a well in the centre, and pour in the yeast mixture followed by the oil. Add enough of the salty water to make it all cling together, stirring until mixed, then turn out and knead for 3–4 minutes, until smooth and elastic. Cover with a cloth and leave for 5 minutes, then knead once or twice more. Divide into 16 pieces and roll each one out as thick as your middle finger. Lay on oiled baking sheets and stand on top of the stove until they start to swell – about 12–15 minutes. Brush with beaten egg, sprinkle with sesame seeds, and bake for about 35 minutes at 150°C/300°F/Gas Mark 2 until crisp and golden brown. Cool on a wire rack for about 10 minutes before serving; alternatively, they can be kept warm or rewarmed. But they are best eaten soon after baking. They also freeze very well; in this case pack into plastic bags as soon as cool and put in the freezer.

To make grissini *integrale*, or wholemeal grissini, substitute 100 per cent wholewheat flour for the white flour, and use slightly more water. Omit the sesame seeds; simply brush with beaten egg and sprinkle with a little extra wholewheat flour just before baking.

MANAKEESH BI KISSHIK   Lebanon

In most Lebanese villages, people send their bread to the local baker's oven for baking, since few houses have their own oven. Sometimes a fragrant mixture is spread over the dough before baking; the most usual is *manakeesh bi zaatar*, but a particularly delicious version called *manakeesh bi kisshik* is made in villages in the hills near Beirut. If you prefer, you can simply send along your own *kisshik* mixture and the baker will spread it on his own dough and bake it for you. The same mixture can be spread on small pieces of flat bread (pitta) and heated in a quick oven for a snack to eat with drinks.

dough:
½ lb/225 g white bread flour
¼ oz/8 g fresh yeast
approx. 6 fl. oz/175 ml tepid water
½ teaspoon sea salt
½ tablespoon oil

kisshik spread:
6 oz/175 g kisshik or powdered trahanas (see Pickles, Preserves and Spice Mixtures, page 269)

2 oz/50 g chopped walnuts
6 tablespoons lightly toasted sesame seeds
6 dried chillies, chopped
1 small onion, chopped
1 tablespoon dibis ruman or tamarind syrup (see Pickles, Preserves and Spice Mixtures, page 268)
5–6 fl. oz/150–175 ml olive oil
sea salt and black pepper

Make the dough as usual: put the flour in a large bowl in a warm place, put the crumbled yeast in a cup with 2 tablespoons of the tepid water and stand this in a warm place for 10 minutes. Dissolve the salt in a little hot water, then make up to the desired amount (of water) with warm water. Make a well in the centre of the flour, pour in the yeast mixture, followed by the oil, and cover with flour. Pour on the water, stirring constantly with a wooden spoon, and mix till all is absorbed. When all clings together nicely, turn out and knead for 5 minutes, then put back in the clean bowl, rubbed with a little oil, and cover with cling-film wrap. Stand in a warm place until it has doubled in bulk – about 1½ hours – then turn out and knead again for about 4 minutes. Divide it in half, and roll and pull it out as evenly as possible, without tearing, until you have a thin round shape like a small pizza. Have 2 oiled baking sheets very hot, by putting in the oven for 5 minutes beforehand. Lay the flat bread on them, one on each. Cover with the spread which you have made while the bread was rising (simply combine all the dry ingredients in a food processor and blend, adding enough oil to make an oily spread) and bake for 8–10 minutes in a very hot oven. Have it preheated to 260°C/500°F/Gas Mark 9, then as soon as you put the bread in, turn down the heat to 230°C/450°F/Gas Mark 8. Makes 2 *manakeesh*.

For a simpler version, simply warm bought pitta, split them in half, and cut in diamond shapes. Spread the *kisshik* mixture on the soft inside, lay on a baking tray, and put in the oven for 4–5 minutes at 200°C/400°F/Gas Mark 6 until brown and crisp. Serve immediately, with drinks.

MANAKEESH BI ZAATAR   Lebanon

This is a popular snack in Lebanon, where it can be bought from most bakers. It is round flat bread, like a slightly smaller than usual pizza, covered with an oily herb mixture before baking.

dough:
½ lb/225 g white bread flour
¼ oz/8 g fresh yeast
approx. 6 fl. oz/175 ml tepid water
½ teaspoon sea salt
½ tablespoon oil

zaatar spread:
3 tablespoons lightly toasted sesame seeds
3 tablespoons sumac (see page 267)
3 tablespoons wild thyme
approx. ¼ pint/150 ml olive oil

Make the dough as for manakeesh bi kisshik (see page 234). While it is rising, make the zaatar spread. Put the dry ingredients in the food processor and add enough oil to make an oily paste (or pound together in a mortar and pestle). Spread on the dough and bake as for manakeesh bi kisshik. Alternatively, spread on small pieces of bought pitta bread as for manakeesh bi kisshik, and simply heat through in the oven. Makes 2 manakeesh, or 2 bought pitta.

PAN BAGNA   France

The original version of pan bagna must have been very similar to the first gazpacho: both were simply salads with pieces of bread soaked in them, not unlike the Arab fattoush. The Spanish form gradually developed into a liquid soup, while the Provençal one became a sandwich – a sort of salade niçoise in a roll. The last one I ate was bought in the pretty market at Antibes, and it appeared identical to those sold in the Old Town at Nice. Enclosed in a large soft roll measuring about 8 inches/20 cm across, it included slices of mild raw onion, celery, radish, strips of red and green pepper, sliced tomato, hard-boiled egg, anchovy fillets and black olives. The whole was dressed with olive oil so that the bottom half of the roll was quite moist. Outside the immediate environs of Nice, the pan bagna is usually made in a piece of baguette, but in and around Nice these large rolls are baked specially for this purpose.

PENYELI   Greece

This recipe comes from southern Greece where these hot cheese breads, like small thick pizzas, are made for weddings, parties and other festivities.

dough:
12 oz/350 g white bread flour
½ oz/15 g fresh yeast
approx. 9 fl. oz/275 ml warm
   water
½ teaspoon salt
1 scant tablespoon oil

filling:
6 oz/175 g feta cheese
2 eggs, beaten
black pepper
2 tablespoons chopped fresh
   mint or 2 teaspoons dried mint
2 tablespoons melted butter

Make the dough as for pizzas (see page 238). When it has been kneaded for the second time, divide in 4 equal pieces and form each into an oval shape about 6 inches/15 cm long. Make the dough into canoe shapes, raising the edges and pinching the ends together to form a sort of prow, and lay them on an oiled baking sheet.

To make the filling, mash the feta with a fork – if very salty, it should have been soaked for 1–2 hours in cold water – and mix in the beaten eggs to make a soupy mixture. Add black pepper and the chopped or powdered mint and spoon into the little boats. Bake them for 15 minutes at 200°C/400°F/Gas Mark 6, then a further 15–20 minutes at 180°C/350°F/Gas Mark 4. Test by tapping on the bottom to see if they give the desired hollow sound. Take out of the oven and brush all over with melted butter. Serve immediately. Serves 4.

PISSALADIÈRE   France

This Niçois dish is redolent of the many years Nice was part of Italy, or at least the kingdom of Sardinia, for it is closer to an Italian pizza than to any French dish. Made with a base of bread dough it was originally covered with sliced onions mixed with a little *pissalat*, a salty paste made from small preserved fish. Nowadays it usually has a lattice of anchovy fillets enclosing black olives (over the sliced onions), but in Nice itself it is often made simply with onions and olives. With the sweet onions of the region this is utterly delicious, but when made with ordinary onions it can be dull, and benefits from the addition of anchovies.

dough:
10 oz/275 g white bread flour
¼ oz/8 g yeast
1 teaspoon salt
1 teaspoon sugar
8 fl. oz/250 ml tepid water

filling:
2½ lb/1·15 kg onions
6 fl. oz/175 ml olive oil
1–2 cloves garlic, minced
6 anchovy fillets
2 tablespoons milk
8 black olives

Make the dough as usual and leave to rise until doubled in bulk – about 1½ hours. Then punch down, knead briefly, and roll and pull out to line a rectangular baking sheet measuring approximately 12 × 9 inches/30 × 23 cm.

While it is rising make the filling: slice the onions and cook very slowly in ¼ pint/150 ml of the olive oil in a covered sauté pan, stirring now and then. Allow about 40 minutes for them to become soft without browning, adding the minced garlic halfway through. Soak the anchovy fillets in milk for 10 minutes, then rinse and pat dry. When the dough is ready on the baking sheet, spread the sliced onions over it, draining off any excess liquid that might remain. Make a lattice pattern of anchovy fillets over the top, and put an olive in each square. (Omit the anchovies if you prefer.) Dribble the remaining 2 tablespoons oil over all and bake for 40–45 minutes at 190°C/375°F/Gas Mark 5. Cut into squares to serve. Serves 6. This is best eaten hot or warm.

PIZZAS   Italy

Home-made pizzas are never quite so delicious as those baked in an Italian wood-fired pizza oven, especially those made in Naples. They are fun to make, however, and always popular with children. I find it best to make only two at one time, since this is all the normal domestic oven can take, and they must be eaten immediately.

pizza dough:
½ lb/225 g white bread flour
¼ oz/8 g fresh yeast
approx. 6 fl. oz/175 ml tepid
   water
½ teaspoon salt
½ tablespoon oil

filling:
approx. ½ pint/300 ml
   pizzaiola sauce (see Sauces,
   page 249)
1 Italian mozzarella cheese,
   coarsely grated
8 black olives
3 anchovy fillets, soaked in
   milk
½ teaspoon dried oregano
4 tablespoons olive oil
a few drops chilli oil (optional)

Have the flour in a large warm bowl. Put the yeast in a cup with 2 tablespoons of the warm water and put in a warm place for 10 minutes. Dissolve the salt in a little very hot water, then make up to the desired quantity with cooler water. When the yeast has had time to prove, make a well in the centre of the flour and pour it in. Cover with some of the flour, pour the oil over it, then the rest of the water, stirring. You may need a little more or less water, so add the last drops gradually.

When the dough clings together nicely, turn out onto a floured surface and knead for 5 minutes, then replace in the bowl, which you have washed and rubbed with oil. Cover with cling-film wrap, and leave in a warm place until it has doubled in bulk, about 1½ hours. While it is rising, make the *pizzaiola* sauce. When the dough has risen sufficiently, punch down and turn out. Knead again for 3–4 minutes, then divide in half.

The problem is now to stretch the dough out as thin as possible in a perfect circle, without tearing it. Unless you are as skilled as the Italian pizza-makers, it is probably easiest to use a combination of rolling and stretching, patching up any tears as you go. When you have a thin circle approximately 10 inches/25 cm across – ideally it should be slightly thicker round the rim – lay it on an oiled baking sheet. When both are made, cover each with a thin layer of the sauce, about 5–6 tablespoons, and half the grated mozzarella. Dot with the black olives and the rinsed dried anchovy fillets cut in pieces. Sprinkle with dried oregano and pour 2 tablespoons of the olive oil over each. Have the oven heated to 260°C/500°F/Gas Mark 9, put in the pizzas and turn down immediately to 230°C/450°F/Gas Mark 8. Cook until light golden brown and crisp round the edges, and bubbling in the centre, about 12 minutes. Serve immediately, with a little jug of chilli oil (see preserved chillies in Pickles, Preserves and Spice Mixtures, page 259) to sprinkle over them as desired. Sliced pepperoni sausage can be substituted for the olives and anchovies, or these can be omitted altogether if preferred.

CALZONE   Italy

These filled pizzas looking like a filled sock – hence the name – are very popular in Venice. They need a very hot oven to cook the dough to a golden brown while the egg inside remains soft. They take a bit of practice to achieve even moderately successfully, and are never so good as in Italy, but they are fun to try. Once the knack has been learnt, you can make four at a time, since two will fit – just – on one baking sheet.

dough:
1 lb/450 g white bread flour
approx. 12 fl. oz/350 ml tepid
    water
½ oz/15 g fresh yeast
1 teaspoon salt
1 tablespoon oil

filling:
approx. ½ pint/300 ml
    pizzaiola sauce (see Sauces,
    page 249)
¼ lb/100 g smoked raw ham,
    chopped
1 Italian mozzarella cheese,
    coarsely grated
black pepper
½ teaspoon dried oregano
4 eggs

Make the dough, knead, rise and knead again as for pizzas. Divide it in 4 pieces and roll and stretch each one exactly as if making an ordinary pizza. Cover half of each circle with *pizzaiola* sauce, then scatter a quarter of the chopped ham and the grated mozzarella over the sauce. Sprinkle with black pepper and dried oregano, and dampen the edges of the dough. Break a raw egg on top of the filling, then quickly fold the dough over it to make a semi-circle, sealing the edges by pressing them together. Lift carefully onto an oiled baking sheet. Have the oven heated to 260°C/500°F/Gas Mark 9, with both oven racks near the top. Put in the *calzone*, turn down to 230°C/450°F/Gas Mark 8, and cook until the dough has coloured nicely, about 10–12 minutes. Serve immediately; the eggs should still be runny. Serves 4.

SPICED ROLLS   Egypt

These little rolls sprinkled with sesame seeds are very popular in Egypt and the Middle East, where they are served with drinks or at buffet parties.

½ lb/225 g white bread flour
1 heaped teaspoon sea salt
½ teaspoon ground cumin
½ teaspoon ground coriander
½ oz/15 g fresh yeast

4 fl. oz/120 ml tepid water
a pinch of sugar
4 tablespoons light oil
1 egg white, beaten
1½ tablespoons sesame seeds

Sift the flour with the salt into a large warm bowl. Stir in the ground cumin and coriander. Crumble the yeast into the water with the sugar. Put yeast and flour in a warm place for 10 minutes, then make a well in the centre of the flour and pour in the yeast mixture. Cover with flour, then pour on the oil, mixing with a wooden spoon. Stir till it all clings together, then turn out and knead briefly. Wash out the bowl, dry it and rub with a little oil. Put back the dough, cover with a cloth, and leave in a warm place until doubled in volume – about 1½ hours. Then punch down, turn out, and knead again for a minute. Divide into small balls and roll out in a thin sausage, about as thick as your little finger and slightly longer than your middle finger. Form them into a circle, pinching the ends together, and lay on buttered baking sheets. Leave in a warm place for about 12 minutes, until starting to rise, then brush them with beaten egg white and sprinkle with sesame seeds. Bake for 30 minutes at 180°C/350°F/Gas Mark 4, then turn off the heat and leave them for a further 10–15 minutes in the oven as it cools. Makes about 30; serve the same day, or pack in an airtight tin.

BRIKS AUX NOIX   Tunisia

These are little sweet pastries, filled with a mixture of hazelnuts and pistachios, then deep fried or baked in the oven.

2 oz/50 g hazelnuts
2 oz/50 g pistachios, shelled
3 tablespoons castor sugar
2–3 tablespoons rose water

2–3 sheets filo pastry
approx. 1½ oz/40 g butter, melted
frying oil (optional: see below)

Roast the hazelnuts in the oven, then rub off the skins. Grate them in a cheese grater, then grate the pistachios also and mix the two together. Add the sugar, and enough rose water to make a thick paste. Spread out a sheet of filo at a time, leaving the rest covered with a damp cloth, and cut in strips 10 × 2 inches/25 × 5 cm. Brush with melted butter and lay a teaspoonful of the nut filling in one corner of each strip. Fold up to form triangular packets (see diagram on page 161), sealing the ends with melted butter. Either drop into hot oil and deep fry very briefly, just until golden, or brush all over with melted butter, lay on a greased baking sheet and bake for 15 minutes at 180°C/350°F/Gas Mark 4, until light golden brown. Makes about 16 pastries. Serve soon after cooling.

ELIANE'S BISCUITS   **Greece**

These little biscuits are quite delicious, but as I don't like the taste of cloves, I leave them out, and mix a little ground cinnamon with the icing sugar.

¼ lb/100 g unsalted butter
1 tablespoon castor sugar
1 tablespoon ouzo or vodka
4½–5 oz/125–150 g flour, sifted

approx. 20 cloves or ground
    cinnamon
icing sugar

Cream the butter and sugar. Add the ouzo (or vodka) and mix to a soft cream. Work in the sifted flour gradually, stopping when you have a soft but firm dough. (Do not knead, just mix lightly.) Roll into a sausage shape about 1½ inches/3·5 cm in diameter, and cut in slices about ½ inch/1 cm thick. Flatten each one slightly in the palm of the hand and press with your thumb to make a hollow in the centre. Push a clove in the centre, and lay them on a greased baking sheet. Bake for 20 minutes at 150°C/310°F/Gas Mark 2. They should be quite pale, but firm and crisp. While still hot, sprinkle with icing sugar through a tiny sieve. Leave on the baking sheet until cool. Makes about 20 biscuits; serve soon after cooling.

The sauces that are found in the Mediterranean world are not those of haute cuisine. The delicate *beurre blanc*, the *sauce mousseline*, even the *veloutés* are rarely found except in the three star restaurants, whose cuisine has more in common with other three star restaurants than with their country of origin. The sauces of the Mediterranean are for the most part those based on olive oil, garlic, herbs or nuts. Many of these have a mayonnaise base, like the *aïoli* in its most usual form – although the original *aïoli* was often made with pounded bread or even potato, much like the Greek *skordalia*. Mayonnaise itself is of Mediterranean origin: it is thought to have come from Mahon, the capital of Menorca. Others, like the typically Mediterranean *rouille*, are made in the same manner but without the eggs; *rouille* is simply an emulsion of pounded garlic, chilli peppers and bread with olive oil. Hot sauces of this type are very popular in Spain, possibly as the result of the years of Arab occupation, and a typical Catalan sauce called *romescu* is in fact very similar to *rouille*, with the addition of pounded nuts.

To my mind, the best by far of the Mediterranean sauces is the Genoese *pesto*. This smooth green paste is made of generous quantities of fresh basil pounded with a combination of roughly equal parts of parmesan and *sardo*, with olive oil. *Sardo* is a Sardinian cheese, so this dish is an interesting testimonial to Genoa's past, since up until 1860 it was part of the Sardinian kingdom. Nice, where *pesto* is also enormously popular under its French name *pistou*, was also part of the Sardinian kingdom until it was ceded to France in 1860, just before the unification of Italy. Pounded pine nuts are sometimes added to this Italian/Provençal sauce, but I prefer the simplicity of its original form.

Another excellent Mediterranean sauce is the Greek *avgolemono*.

Basically egg yolks and lemon juice beaten together, this is added to a stock of chicken, veal or fish, and served either as a sauce, or as part of a soup or stew. Fresh dill is often added, and this delicate sauce is at its best poured over poached meatballs made with veal, which have contributed a tasty stock.

Another interesting sauce is the Turkish walnut sauce made from pounded walnuts and breadcrumbs, diluted with chicken stock. Like many of the Middle Eastern sauces of nuts and bread it is somewhat of an acquired taste: its bland flavour and porridge-like colour and consistency take some getting used to. I find an addition of fried onions and a little garlic make it more appealing to Anglo-Saxon palates. This sauce is traditionally served over joints of boiled chicken, while a similar sauce – the sauce *tarator* of Syria and Lebanon – is usually served with a poached bass.

The North African cuisine does not depend much on sauces, the dishes being for the most part quite complex and incorporating the sauce within them. The exception is the hot sauce, *harissa*, which is added in minute quantities to a bland *couscous*, as a *rouille* is added to a fish soup.

AÏOLI OR ALI-OLI   France, Spain

Although this is thought of as a Provençal sauce it probably originated in Valencia, as *ali-oli*. The Spanish version is still sometimes made with breadcrumbs or mashed potato, very like the Greek *skordalia*, but the French form, nowadays at least, is usually a simple mayonnaise incorporating a lot of pounded garlic. I give three versions. Serve with poached fish, boiled vegetables, salt cod, hard-boiled eggs or boiled chicken.

aïoli I:
4–6 *cloves garlic, peeled*
2 *egg yolks*
a pinch of sea salt

½ *pint/300 ml olive oil*
1½–2 *tablespoons white wine*
vinegar or lemon juice or a
mixture of both

Peel the garlic, chop it, then pound in a mortar until reduced to a smooth pulp. Break the egg yolks on top of it and pound till blended. Add a pinch of sea salt. Start to add the oil drop by drop, exactly as for a mayonnaise, until you have used about one third. Thin with a little vinegar if necessary. Start to add the oil a little more quickly, continuing to beat or pound constantly. When all is amalgamated, stir in the remaining vinegar or lemon juice, tasting as you do so. Serves 4–5.

aïoli II:

1 thick slice stale white bread, without crusts
a little milk

4–6 cloves garlic, peeled
a pinch of sea salt
½ pint/300 ml olive oil
1½–2 tablespoons lemon juice

Tear the bread into small pieces and soak in milk for 10 minutes, then squeeze out. Chop the peeled garlic and pound in a mortar until pulpy, adding a pinch of sea salt. Add the moist bread and pound again until amalgamated. Start adding the oil gradually, beating all the time, then a little faster, until all is absorbed. Add lemon juice to taste. Serves 4–5. If the aïoli should separate, it can sometimes be rescued by pounding two more cloves garlic in the clean mortar, and adding the separated sauce to it.

aïoli III:

Substitute 1 medium potato, boiled, peeled and mashed, for the breadcrumbs and milk in the above recipe.

SALSA AVGOLEMONO
Greece

A light sauce that goes well with almost any food that you can think of, ranging from poached fish, chicken, veal, lamb and meatballs to stuffed leaves of vine or cabbage. It can be made with whatever stock is most appropriate to the dish it is to accompany.

1 egg yolk
2 tablespoons lemon juice
½ pint/300 ml stock: fish, chicken, veal, lamb or vegetable

sea salt and black pepper
1–2 tablespoons chopped dill (optional)

Beat the egg yolk with the lemon juice in a small bowl. Heat the strained stock until boiling, then pour a ladleful onto the egg and lemon, beating with a small whisk. Return the contents of the bowl to the saucepan, having lowered the heat as much as possible, and stir constantly for 3 minutes, without allowing it to boil. When very slightly thickened, remove from the heat and add sea salt and black pepper to taste. Add the dill if appropriate, and serve. Serves 4–5.

GARLIC AND ALMOND SAUCE

I found this in an old English cookery book, but it is so obviously Mediterranean in origin that I couldn't resist including it. It is similar to the Middle Eastern sauce *tarator* and the Turkish walnut sauce. Serve with grilled chicken wings (see Mezes and Tapas, page 57), as a light luncheon dish, with a green salad, or as a first course for a dinner, omitting the salad.

1½ oz/40 g blanched almonds
1 large clove garlic, chopped

¼ pint/150 ml olive oil
a large pinch of sea salt

Put the almonds with the chopped garlic in the food processor. When both are finely chopped and blended, start adding the oil in a thin stream through the lid while processing. Add a pinch of sea salt and pour into a small jug to serve. Serves 3–4, or can be made in double quantities.

HARISSA SAUCE   Morocco, Algeria, Tunisia

In the countries of the Mahgreb – Morocco, Algeria and Tunisia – *harissa* is used to add a fiery element to the bland dishes of *couscous*. This is a way of serving it incorporated in a hot sauce, to be sprinkled sparingly over the *couscous*.

½ teaspoon harissa
1 tablespoon tomato purée

2 tablespoons chicken, meat or
   fish stock

Mix the *harissa* (bought or made at home, see Pickles, Preserves and Spice Mixtures, page 262) with the tomato purée in a small bowl. Stir in the hot stock, which can be taken from the dish with which it is to be served. Pour into a tiny dish – an *oeuf en cocotte* dish does well – and serve with *couscous*.

HOT SAUCE   France

This is a French hot sauce, a substitute for *harissa* when that is unavailable, for serving with *couscous*.

1 teaspoon ground cumin	2 tablespoons tomato purée
1 teaspoon ground coriander	2 tablespoons chicken, meat or
½ teaspoon chilli powder	fish stock

Mix the spices and stir into the tomato purée. Dilute with the hot stock, which can be taken from the dish with which the sauce is to be served. Pour into a tiny dish and serve with *couscous*.

MAYONNAISE   Menorca

It is almost impossible to trace the origins of any dish beyond dispute, but since it is generally thought that mayonnaise was invented by the French chef of the Duc de Richelieu while he was besieging Mahon, the capital of Menorca, in 1757, I feel justified in including it here. In any case, it is the basis of many other Mediterranean sauces, such as *aïoli*.

If making in advance, cover with cling-film and store low down in the refrigerator.

2 egg yolks	1 ½ tablespoons white wine
a pinch of salt	vinegar
½ teaspoon Dijon mustard	½ tablespoon lemon juice
½ pint/300 ml olive oil	

Have the eggs, oil and vinegar all at room temperature. Break the yolks into a bowl and beat for a moment or two, adding the salt and mustard. Start adding the oil literally drop by drop, stirring constantly, until about one third of the oil is used. If it gets too thick to work easily, add ½ teaspoon of the vinegar. Then start to add the oil slightly more quickly, finally pouring it in slowly, in a thin stream. When all is absorbed, stir in the remaining vinegar and lemon juice, tasting as you do so.

If at any point the mayonnaise separates it can sometimes be rescued by starting again with a teaspoon of Dijon mustard in a clean bowl.

Add the separated sauce drop by drop, then the remaining oil and vinegar. Otherwise, it means using a fresh egg yolk and increasing the oil and vinegar proportionately. The original amount will serve 4–5.

OIL AND LEMON SAUCE   Turkey, Italy, etc.

This sauce is used along much of the north Mediterranean shore, for basting grilled fish and dressing cooked vegetables or salads. It is sometimes served just as it is, sometimes chopped herbs are added.

6 tablespoons olive oil
3 tablespoons lemon juice
sea salt and black pepper
   (optional)

2 tablespoons chopped parsley
   or other fresh herbs
   (optional)

Beat the oil and lemon juice together thoroughly, until completely amalgamated, using a whisk. Then stir in the sea salt, black pepper and herbs, if used. In Italy, Turkey and the Middle East, this is the classic sauce for grilling fish. Use it to baste them while cooking, then pour more over them just before serving. It can be made just as easily in double quantities.

PESTO   Italy

This is the original version of the basil sauce so beloved of the Genoese. Nowadays pine kernels are usually added, but I find it equally good without. In Genoa it is always made with equal amounts of parmesan and sardo, a hard cheese from Sardinia. Since this is often hard to find outside Italy, it is best to make it with ⅔ parmesan and ⅓ pecorino, or all parmesan. It is utterly delicious served on home-made pasta, potato gnocchi or stirred into a minestrone.

¾ pint/350 ml loosely packed
   basil leaves
1 clove garlic, finely chopped
a pinch of sea salt
2 tablespoons pine kernels
   (optional)

1 oz/30 g each grated parmesan
   and sardo or 1½ oz/40 g
   grated parmesan and
   ½ oz/15 g grated pecorino or
   2 oz/60 g grated parmesan
5 tablespoons olive oil

Chop the basil and pound in a mortar. Add the finely chopped garlic and sea salt and pound again. When reduced to a pulp, add the chopped pine kernels (if used), then the grated cheeses. When all are pulverized and blended, start adding the oil gradually, pounding constantly.

To serve over pasta or gnocchi, stir in a spoonful of the cooking water just before serving to thin it slightly, then spoon onto plates of cooked and drained noodles or gnocchi, and top with a lump of butter and grated parmesan. To serve in a minestrone, stir into the finished soup and stand for 5 minutes before serving. Serves 3–4 on pasta or gnocchi, or 5–6 in a minestrone.

PICADA   Spain

This Catalan sauce is used to give its own special flavour to a variety of dishes – grilled fish, grilled aubergines and a Spanish version of piperade called pisto. I ate it with pisto in a house near Barcelona, and it was quite delicious, served with thin slices of Serrano ham.

2 oz/50 g pine kernels	1 teaspoon sea salt
2 cloves garlic, chopped	3 tablespoons olive oil

Pound the kernels with the chopped garlic in a mortar. Add the sea salt and continue pounding until a smooth mixture is obtained. Stir in the oil gradually, continuing to work until amalgamated. To serve with pisto, simply spoon over the surface of the dish and reheat in the oven or under the grill. Serves 4.

SALSA ALLA PIZZAIOLA   Italy

This is the basic pizza sauce so beloved of the Neapolitans. It can be served not only with pizzas but also with grilled steaks, pasta of all sorts, or incorporated in dishes of braised beef or game. It can, of course, be made with fresh tomatoes, but for much of the year English tomatoes are a pallid – and expensive – replica of the Italian ones.

1 medium onion
1 ½ tablespoons olive oil
2 cloves garlic, crushed
1 lb 6 oz/625 g tinned tomatoes
    or 1 ½ lb/675 g fresh ones
1 tablespoon tomato purée

½ bay leaf
1 teaspoon dried oregano or 3
    sprigs fresh oregano or
    marjoram
1 teaspoon sugar
sea salt and black pepper

Chop the onion and cook gently in the oil in a sauté pan. When it has softened – do not allow it to brown – add the crushed garlic and cook for another minute or two. Then add the tomatoes, skinned if fresh and roughly chopped, or squeezed to a pulp if tinned. Add the tomato purée, herbs and seasoning, bring to the boil and simmer gently, partly covered, for 1 hour, stirring occasionally. Remove the fresh herbs and adjust the seasoning before serving. If preferred, it can be blended briefly or passed through a food mill, but I like a lumpy texture. Makes approximately ½ pint/300 ml.

RAGÚ BOLOGNESE   Italy

I have a great affection for this recipe, for my American grandfather brought it back from a trip to Italy more than fifty years ago; I compared it with a recipe in the most recently published Italian cookbook to find it was identical. It is the classic sauce for *pasta alla Bolognese*, the traditional *sugo di carne*. It is very adaptable, can be made in advance, in double or triple quantities, reheated or frozen and is delicious with all pasta, particularly home-made fettucine.

2 tablespoons finely chopped
    onion
2 tablespoons finely chopped
    celery
2 rashers streaky bacon, finely
    chopped
1 ½ oz/35 g butter
1 tablespoon olive oil

½ lb/225 g lean steak, finely
    chopped or minced
1 teaspoon flour
1 tablespoon tomato purée
⅛ pint/75 ml white wine
½ pint/300 ml meat or chicken
    stock
sea salt and black pepper

Brown the onion, celery and bacon slowly in 1 oz/25 g of the butter and 1 tablespoon olive oil. Add the chopped steak when they are starting to colour, and stir until lightly browned all over. Cook gently for about 12 minutes, stirring now and then. Add the flour, tomato purée, wine and stock. Bring to the boil, adding sea salt and black pepper, and simmer gently for 45 minutes, stirring occasionally for the first half hour and more frequently during the last fifteen minutes. Stir in the remaining ½ oz/15 g butter and serve. If making in advance, only stir in the extra butter just before serving. Serves 3–4.

ROMESCU

Spain

This fiery Catalan sauce is not unlike a *rouille*, but to my mind much more delicious. It is often served together with an *aïoli*, so that each person can mix them according to his taste. I like to eat it with grilled or boiled shellfish, either hot or cold, although I must admit its strong flavour does dominate the dish. In Spain it is also served with grilled meat, and with rabbit, while a friend of mine who lives in Spain eats it with mashed potatoes.

1 dried red chilli
2 tablespoons coarsely
  chopped (nibbed) almonds
1½ tablespoons pine kernels
2 cloves garlic or 1 large clove,
  minced

1 large tomato, skinned and
  chopped
sea salt and black pepper
¼ pint/150 ml olive oil
2 tablespoons wine vinegar, red
  or white

Cut the end off the chilli, split it in half and scrape out the seeds. Soak it in cold water for 10 minutes. Toast the chopped almonds gently in a frying pan, turning them over often until they are an even colour. Remove them and do the same thing with the pine kernels. Put both nuts in the food processor with the chilli, which you have chopped very finely, and the minced garlic. Process until blended, then add the chopped tomato and process again. Add sea salt and black pepper, then add the olive oil and vinegar very gradually, pouring them alternately through the lid in a thin stream while processing. Pour into a bowl to serve. This makes only about ⅓ pint/200 ml, but will serve 5–6, since it is so strong.

SKORDALIA   Greece

This pungent and delicious sauce is the Greek form of *aïoli*. For those who like garlic, it is irresistible. The Greeks sometimes add a drop of evaporated milk at the end, to improve the colour. Evaporated milk is often used in this way in Greece, where cream hardly exists, but since I never have it, I sometimes use a little thin cream instead. Serve with fried fish, salt cod, hard-boiled eggs or vegetable fritters.

½ head of garlic, separated into
   cloves and peeled
1 large potato, freshly boiled
2 slices dry white bread,
   without crusts

¼ pint/150 ml olive oil
1–2 tablespoons lemon juice
1 tablespoon evaporated milk
   or thin cream or top of the
   milk (optional)

Chop the garlic and pound in a mortar. Mash the potato to a smooth purée and add to the garlic. Pound until blended. Soak the bread for 10 minutes in water, then squeeze out. Add the moist crumbs to the mortar and continue to pound until all is amalgamated. Then, very gradually, start adding the oil as if making a mayonnaise. Continue to work continuously with the pestle, or a wooden spoon if you prefer, while you add the oil first drop by drop, and then in a thin stream. If it starts to separate, beat in 1 tablespoon warm water. When all the oil is absorbed, stir in lemon juice to taste. Then, if you wish, add a drop of evaporated milk or thin cream to make it paler in colour and a little smoother. Serves 5–6.

SOUR CREAM SAUCE   Yugoslavia

This is like a slightly richer form of *avgolemono*, and particularly good served as a sauce for stuffed cabbage leaves, made with the stock they have been cooked in.

½ pint/300 ml chicken or
   vegetable stock
1 egg yolk

¼ pint/150 ml sour cream
sea salt and black pepper

Heat the stock, and while it is heating, beat the egg yolk with the sour cream in a bowl. When the stock boils, pour a ladleful of it onto the egg and cream mixture, beating with a small whisk. Pour the contents of the bowl into the pan containing the rest of the stock and whisk constantly for 3–4 minutes over very low heat, without allowing it to boil. Add sea salt and black pepper to taste and serve. Serves 4.

SAUCE TARATOR   Syria, Egypt, Lebanon, Turkey

In the Middle East this is the traditional sauce to serve with cold poached fish, a large bass or *daurade* for example, while in Turkey it is more often served with boiled vegetables or sometimes with fried mussels. I like it as a dip for crudités.

2 thick slices dry white bread (approx. 1 oz/25 g), crusts removed
¼ lb/100 g pine kernels
2 cloves garlic, crushed

4 fl oz/120 ml olive oil
2 good pinches sea salt
4 tablespoons white wine vinegar or lemon juice

Tear the bread in pieces and soak in warm water for 10 minutes. Chop the pine kernels in a food processor; add the bread squeezed dry and process till blended. Add the crushed garlic, the olive oil and sea salt and process again. Finally add the vinegar or lemon juice. (Lemon juice is more commonly used in the Middle East, but I prefer it made with a good wine vinegar.) This sauce can be served at room temperature or chilled. Serves 4–5.

COULIS DE TOMATES   France

This thick tomato sauce, unsieved, is like a simpler version of the Italian *salsa pizzaiola*. I use it constantly, for serving with pasta for a quick meal, with vegetable moulds or as an addition to other dishes. It can also be made in large quantities when tomatoes are cheap, and frozen. It works equally well with fresh or tinned tomatoes.

1 small onion
1 oz/25 g butter
¾ lb/350 g tomatoes, fresh or
  tinned
1 clove garlic, crushed
  (optional)

sea salt and black pepper
½ teaspoon sugar

optional flavourings:
½ bay leaf and/or ¼ teaspoon
  dried oregano or 1
  tablespoon chopped fresh
  basil

Chop the onion and cook slowly in the butter in a sauté pan. If using fresh tomatoes, skin them and chop coarsely. If using tinned ones, simply chop them roughly with the edge of a palette knife, or crush them in the hands. When the onion starts to turn golden, add the tomatoes with the crushed garlic. Cook gently for 8–10 minutes, until slightly thickened, adding sea salt and black pepper, sugar, and the bay leaf and/or dried oregano, if used. If using fresh basil, only add when the cooking is finished. Serves 3–4.

A TURKISH SALAD DRESSING   Turkey

2 oz/50 g almonds, skinned and
  chopped
2 oz/50 g walnuts, chopped
a large pinch sea salt
1 clove garlic, minced
1½ tablespoons soft white
  bread, without crusts

1½ tablespoons lemon juice or
  white wine vinegar
approx. ⅓ pint/200 ml water
a little black pepper
1 tablespoon olive oil

Pound the nuts in a mortar, adding the sea salt and minced garlic. Soak the bread in cold water for 10 minutes, then squeeze dry and add to the nuts. Pound until all is amalgamated to a smooth paste, then add the lemon juice or vinegar gradually, working all the time with the pestle. Add enough water to give the consistency of thin cream, then a little black pepper. Pour over a dish of purslane heads, or peeled sliced cucumber. Dribble the olive oil over all. Serves 4. This sauce can also be served over cooked fillets of mackerel, at room temperature.

SALSA VERDE   Italy

This is the traditional sauce to serve with *bolliti misti*, or with plain boiled beef, or with artichokes. The usual ingredients consist of parsley, capers, garlic, olive oil and lemon juice; anchovy fillets are sometimes added. Over the years, I have taken to including a soft-boiled egg, stirring the yolk into the sauce, and adding the finely chopped white at the end. I find this delicious, especially when serving with cold boiled artichokes, but I must admit I have never had it in Italy.

4 tablespoons chopped parsley	1 clove garlic, minced
2 tablespoons capers, drained, rinsed and chopped	sea salt and black pepper
	8 tablespoons olive oil
4 fillets anchovy, drained and chopped (optional)	½ tablespoon lemon juice

Mix the chopped parsley, capers, anchovies, if used (I find they add a subtle flavour to the sauce, especially when used in small quantities) and garlic. Chop all finely together, either in a food processor or by hand. Turn into a bowl and add sea salt and black pepper. Stir in the olive oil very gradually, beating all the time with a wooden spoon, then the lemon juice. Serves 5.

variation:
Make as above, either with or without anchovies, and adding 1 egg, boiled for exactly 4½ minutes and cooled immediately under the cold tap. Shell carefully and cut in half over the sauce. Stir the yolk into the sauce, beating until smooth, then chop the white very finely and stir in. Serves 6.

WALNUT SAUCE   Turkey

This typically Turkish sauce is usually served in conjunction with boiled chicken – see Circassian chicken, page 116 – but it is also good with grilled chicken wings (see Mezes and Tapas, page 57), hard-boiled eggs and raw vegetables. It is quickly made in a food processor.

1 thick slice dry white bread,
  crusts removed (about
  ½ oz/15 g)
⅓ pint/200 ml chicken stock
3 oz/75 g shelled walnuts,
  roughly chopped

1 clove garlic, crushed
sea salt and black pepper
a pinch of paprika

Tear the bread in pieces and soak in 3 tablespoons of the chicken stock for 10 minutes. Then put it, without squeezing out, in the food processor with the roughly chopped walnuts and the remaining stock. Process briefly, then add the crushed garlic, sea salt and black pepper. Process again till fairly smooth. Serve either warmed, or at room temperature, if possible soon after making, sprinkled with paprika. Do not chill. This sauce can be made in conjunction with grilled chicken joints, using the back, neck, etc. to make a small amount of good flavoured stock.

YOGURT SAUCE   Lebanon

This is a useful sauce, very quickly made and delicious with roast or grilled lamb, vegetable fritters or stuffed vegetables. It is particularly good served with meat dishes, since it merges with the juices in a most delicious way.

½ pint/300 ml yogurt
2 cloves garlic
½ teaspoon sea salt

1 tablespoon chopped fresh
  mint, or ½ teaspoon dried
  mint (optional)

Beat the yogurt until smooth. Stir in the crushed or pounded garlic and the sea salt. Add mint or not, as desired. Chill before serving.

PICKLES, PRESERVES
AND SPICE MIXTURES

The art of pickling and preserving is an extremely important one in the Mediterranean world, since the abundance of cheap fruit and vegetables in the summer is in direct contrast to the hard winters, when food is scarce, except at high prices. In some cases, pickled food has become almost a luxury, as has happened with smoked fish in England, since the rising cost of the raw product has put it out of reach of all but the most affluent. This has happened with the pressed roe of the grey mullet, once common fare in Greece, Turkey and the south of France, but now only seen in the best restaurants. The salt or dried cod which was for hundreds of years the staple winter diet of the poor, particularly in Spain, has now reached a high price due to the dramatic rise in the price of cod, but its popularity is such that people continue to buy it, when they can afford it. Bacalao is the salted cod which is widely popular in Spain, France and parts of Italy. It needs lengthy soaking in running water to desalt it before use, and figures in many of the Catholic Mediterranean countries as a maigre dish for fast days. Stockfish, on the other hand, is dried but not salted, this needs soaking for even longer periods, since the extraction of water is even higher than in the case of bacalao, but it does not need running water, since it has not been salted. The greater degree of concentration makes it even more expensive than bacalao, but in some parts, such as Genoa and Nice, it is the more popular of the two and figures in many of the local specialities.

These expensive preserves are, however, the exception rather than the rule, and in the case of bacalao and stockfish they are of course already imported in their preserved form, since cod does not exist in the Mediterranean. As in relatively poor countries everywhere, the pickling and preserving of everyday products still goes on, since few houses possess a deep freeze. The Italian peasants still preserve tomatoes in huge quantities, and put tunny fish by in oil, since it is much cheaper than tinned. In Spain and the Middle East chilli peppers are preserved in various ways; I find this worth doing, even for use in summer time, since few shops will sell less than ¼ lb/100 g chillies, while I rarely want more than one. Anchovies are salted, both commercially and in the home, in France, Italy and Turkey, although *pissalat*, the salty paste made from small fish on the Côte Niçoise, one of the original ingredients of pissaladière, is not much made any more. In Egypt and the North African countries, lemons are pickled in salt and preserved in oil, while a sort of spiced dried meat is put by for lean times, and for taking on trips into the desert. Throughout the Arab countries, a myriad different spice mixtures are mixed and ground during the summer months, the recipes varying according to the locality and family tradition, for flavouring dishes throughout the winter. In Turkey, many fragrant syrups are prepared, from the leaves of the Damask rose, soft fruits and even flowers. These are used for making drinks and sweet dishes during the rest of the year.

As one finds so often in the Mediterranean world, similar processes are going on at widely distant points. The quince paste that is so popular a sweetmeat in Spain turns up in an old Turkish cookery book, the dried orange peel that figures frequently in Provençal dishes also appears in Tunisia and Morocco, and the preserved meat of the Arab countries has a parallel in Turkey.

SALTED ANCHOVIES   Italy, Turkey, etc.

This is a preserve made in large quantities in Italy, in Turkey where anchovies are very much loved, and in many other Mediterranean countries. The anchovies are first washed, then boned and filleted. They are then packed into barrels – or broad jars for domestic use – with alternate layers of coarse salt. When full, they are covered with brine and sealed, but they should not be kept much longer than one month.

BOUTARGUE   **France**

This is the preserved roe of the grey mullet which has been first salted, then pressed. It is a speciality of Martigues, near Marseilles, and is considered a great delicacy. It is eaten as an hors d'oeuvre, cut in thin slices. In Greece it is called *tarama*, or *avgotaramo*, and was the original ingredient for making *taramasalata*. It has now been generally superseded for this purpose by smoked cod's roe, which is cheaper – though not very much – and both easier to buy and to work. This explains the old recipes for making *taramasalata* which call for hours of pounding, since the genuine *tarama* is very hard to work, unlike the fairly soft cod's roe.

DRIED CHILLIES   **Spain**

In Spain and in the Middle East where hot dishes flavoured with chilli peppers are much eaten, red chillies are often preserved in a practical and decorative way. They are threaded on lengths of knotted string, like a rather barbaric necklace, and left to dry in the sun. After drying, they are hung in a cool dark place, and used as needed. They should be soaked in cold water for an hour before using, and are then similar to a fresh chilli.

PRESERVED CHILLIES   **France**

Chilli peppers are well worth preserving in some form, since it is impossible to buy them in small enough quantities. I think the best way is to preserve them in oil. Simply wash and dry them, trim the stalks and pack them into a small jar with a screw top. Pour over enough oil to cover, and screw the lid on tightly. They will keep well in this way for several months, and the oil can be used, but very sparingly, to sprinkle over pizzas after baking.

SOUR CHERRY SHRUB   Turkey

This syrup is made with the juice of a sour cherry called *vişne*, which is very popular as a drink in Turkey. It can be made with our morello cherries, or any sour fruit such as cranberries or damsons, and can be used throughout the winter as a sauce for puddings and ice creams, or as the basis for a sorbet.

4 lb/1·75 g morello cherries,   *approx. 1 lb/450 g sugar*
    stoned

Press the stoned cherries in a juice extractor. Measure the juice and strain it through a fairly coarse strainer. Add its volume of sugar and bring to the boil slowly, stirring until the sugar has melted. When it boils, remove from the heat and strain again. Cool, then pour into bottles and seal. Makes about 2 pint/1·2 litres.

RED CURRANT SHRUB   Turkey

This is made exactly as the sour cherry shrub (above), and is a useful way of preserving currants when there is a glut in the garden. The resulting syrup is perfectly delicious, and a beautiful colour. It can be made for mixing summer drinks, as the base for sorbets, or for giving to babies or small children, since it is rich in vitamin C. If you have a juice extractor it is very quickly made since the currants do not even need to be pulled from their stalks.

ROSE LEAF SHRUB   Turkey

I make this with blackcurrant leaves or elder flowers, since I don't have enough roses, and am in any case not sure which variety of rose is needed. It makes a delicious scented syrup, useful for making sorbets during the winter.

¼ lb/100 g young rose leaves or   *2 pint/1·2 litres water*
    blackcurrant leaves,   *1 lb/450 g sugar*
    unsprayed, or elder flowers   *1 egg white, stiffly beaten*

Wash the leaves (or flowers) and drain in a colander. Bring the water to the boil in a large pan and throw in the leaves (or flowers). Bring back to the boil, cover the pan, turn off the heat and leave until cool. Then strain into a clean pan and add the sugar and beaten egg white. Bring to the boil, skim off the froth, and pour through a muslin into a jug. Pour into sterilized glass bottles, cool and seal.

To make into a sorbet, add the juice of 1½ lemons to every 1 pint/600 ml syrup and freeze as usual. Halfway through the freezing, fold in 1 stiffly beaten egg white.

DUKKAH   Egypt

This spice mixture is irresistible, and I often eat it with hard-boiled eggs for a light lunch. It is also good eaten on bread and butter, either alone or with *foul medames*. It is usually made with either hazelnuts or roasted chick peas, but I like to use a mixture of both. Sesame seeds can be bought much more cheaply in Eastern and Cypriot shops than in health food stores, and packets of roasted chick peas can also be found in these shops.

6 oz/175 g sesame seeds
1½ oz/40 g hazelnuts
1¼ oz/40 g roasted chick peas
2 oz/50 g ground coriander
1½ oz/40 g ground cumin

2 teaspoons sea salt
½ teaspoon black pepper
3 teaspoons dried wild thyme
 (serpolet), when available

Cook the sesame seeds in a heavy frying pan over gentle heat, turning over and over with a spatula until they are evenly browned. Put aside, and do the same thing with the hazelnuts, removing the skins at the same time. (If you prefer, you can use whole coriander seeds instead of ground coriander, in which case these also should be toasted. I prefer to use ground coriander since it requires less pounding.) When all the seeds and nuts have cooled, put them in a food processor and process till finely chopped, adding the sea salt, black pepper and wild thyme. Then turn into a mortar and pound until a finely ground mixture. (It can be done entirely in the processor, but I think that a degree of pounding gives a better texture: dry and powdery.) Store in tightly sealed jars in a cool dark place, and use as needed. Makes about

1½ pints/900 ml. This makes a good present for any homesick person from the Middle East.

PICKLED GRAPES   Turkey

This can be made with any grapes – black or white, large or small – but it is particularly pretty when made with the small green seedless grapes from Cyprus. They are very refreshing in hot weather.

4 lb/1 ·8 kg small green seedless grapes
2 tablespoons mustard seeds

approx. 1 pint/600 ml white wine vinegar

Take one half of the washed grapes and divide into small bunches. Pack these into broad-mouthed glass jars which have been sterilized, adding the mustard seeds as you go. Make the other half of the grapes into juice and measure it, after straining. Add an equal amount of white wine vinegar and pour into a small pan. Bring to the boil and pour over the grapes. Cool, seal and leave for 1 month before using.

HARISSA   Morocco

I include a recipe for *harissa* largely for interest's sake, since I don't really consider it worthwhile making at home. One's hands become impregnated with the colour and smell of the chillies, and the mortar and pestle also seem to absorb the strong flavour. It can be bought in tins or tubes from shops selling Eastern goods, while in France the spices for making it can be bought already ground and mixed in a dry form, which I prefer, and which keeps much longer. I simply mix this with a little tinned tomato purée, and dilute it with a spoonful or two of the stock from the *couscous*. Alternatively, a substitute can be made, using ground spices mixed with tomato purée (see page 247); this seems perfectly acceptable to me, although it would not satisfy a Moroccan.

2 oz/50 g dried chilli peppers
½ oz/15 g chopped garlic
¼ oz/8 g sea salt

1 oz/25 g caraway seeds
a little olive oil

If possible, use large chillies which you have dried yourself rather than tiny ones bought in packets. Cut off the ends, split them and remove the seeds. Soak them for 3–4 minutes in water, then chop very finely and pound in a mortar until reduced to a paste. Add the chopped garlic with the sea salt, and pound again until reduced to a pulp. Add the caraway seeds and pound again. When all is pulverized, pack into a small jar and cover the surface with olive oil. Seal tightly.

KISSHIK   Lebanon, Syria

This is the Middle Eastern version of the Greek *trahanas*. It is made from coarsely ground wheat and yogurt, similar to *trahanas*, but finer in consistency. It is used for making soup (see *kisshik* soup, page 37), and for thickening stews; it is also mixed to a paste with ground walnuts and spread on flat bread before baking (see *manakeesh bi kisshik*, page 234). The Middle Eastern soup differs from the Greek one in that the dried wheat is first fried in oil with onion and garlic before the stock (or water) is added, while in Greece it is added directly to the liquid. Both versions are good.

PICKLED LEMONS   Egypt

These are also much used in Tunisia, where they are called *limons*, and it is not easy to find substitutes for them in several Tunisian dishes. In Egypt they are often served as a dish in their own right, to accompany a *foul medames* perhaps, or other *mezes*. The very best preserved lemons are pickled in lemon juice instead of brine, but since this would be prohibitively expensive in England, I have not considered it practical for the purposes of this book.

6 lemons with thin skins	**brine:**
3 tablespoons sea salt	½ lb/225 g coarse salt
	4 pints/2·25 litres water

Cut the lemons almost in quarters from top to bottom, stopping about ½ inch/1 cm from the bottom. (Alternatively, they are sometimes simply cut with three or four deep cuts up and down each side, then squeezed to open them enough to push in the salt.) Remove any obvious pips and push the sea salt into the cut surfaces. Pack into a stoneware jar (or glass, but few glass jars are big enough to hold whole lemons). Make the brine by dissolving the salt in a little boiling water, then make up to 4 pints/2·25 litres with cold water. Cool completely, and pour over the lemons so that they are covered. If possible, lay a piece of wood which has been boiled over the lemons, so that they are kept submerged, then cover the jar and leave for at least 10 days before using. To serve, cut in slices and lay on a small dish with assorted *mezes*, or use as one of the ingredients in cooked dishes such as the Tunisian *salat meschoui*.

PRESERVED LEMONS   Turkey

Another lemon preserve with a totally different character from that of the Egyptian pickled lemons.

2 lb/900 g lemons with thin
  skins
4 heaped tablespoons coarse
  salt

¾–1 pint/approx. 1 litre olive
  oil

Wash the lemons and cut them in thin slices. Pack them in a bowl or broad jar, sprinkling the salt between each layer. Leave for 24 hours, then tip into a colander and leave to drain. Later, pack them in layers in broad-mouthed glass jars and fill up with the olive oil. Do not fill too full. Seal, and store in a cool dark place. Leave for 2–3 weeks before eating, but do not keep longer than 3 months.

DRIED ORANGE PEEL   France

This is a very useful preserve, and the easiest of all to make. Strips of dried orange peel give a truly Provençal flavour to a dish, for instance to *daubes* of braised beef. Orange peel also features in Moroccan cooking, and in that of Tunisia, and although it does not have to be dried it is certainly more economical than buying a whole orange for the sake of a strip of peel. The peel of bitter Seville oranges gives another flavour again, and it is useful to have a supply of both, while lemon peel can also be treated in the same way. Simply pare the skin finely, avoiding the white pith, and lay in the sun – or in a warm dry place – until quite dry, then store in glass jars with airtight lids. One, or at the most two, pieces will be enough to give a subtle flavour to a dish.

QUADDID   Tunisia

This is a sort of preserved meat used in Tunisia to replace fresh meat in many dishes. It is first salted, then rubbed with garlic and spices, then marinated in a strong brine for 1–2 days. After drying, it is again rubbed with spices and dried in the sun for several days. It is then cut in strips, cooked in oil and bottled. It can be kept for a year and was much used in former times for trips into the desert.

A Moroccan version, called *khelea*, is prepared by first salting the meat, then rubbing it with garlic and spices before leaving it to dry in the sun. It is then cooked in boiling oil and sealed with a layer of melted fat.

Most of the Arab and Middle Eastern countries have some version of this preserve, since it is extremely useful; in Turkey it is called *bastourma*. It has little appeal to Europeans however, unless they find themselves stranded in the Sahara perhaps, when they might view it with a more indulgent eye.

QUATRES ÉPICES   France, Tunisia

In France this is usually taken to mean a blend of nutmeg, cloves, cinnamon and white pepper, although ginger can replace either the cinnamon or the pepper. Sometimes, however, it means simply allspice, the berry of a tree called *Pimenta officinalis*. This spice, sometimes called Jamaica pepper in England, and *toute-épice*, or *poivre de la Jamaique* in France, confuses many people, since it does seem to contain within itself the blended flavours of several different spices, notably cinnamon, pepper, nutmeg and cloves.

In Tunisia, however, the term *quatres épices* means a blend of four different spices entirely, namely, white pepper, paprika, cinnamon and powdered *coeurs de roses*. The last adds a typically Tunisian flavour.

QUINCE JELLY   Turkey

Quinces are very popular in Turkey, where they are used both in meat dishes and sweet ones, like this jelly.

3 lb/1·35 kg quinces   approx. 1½ lb/675 g sugar
water to cover

Do not peel or core the quinces; simply wash them, cut in quarters, and put in a large pan. Cover with cold water and bring slowly to the boil. Boil steadily for about 30 minutes, or until they are soft when pressed against the side of the pan with a wooden spoon. Pour into a jelly bag, or a strainer lined with muslin, and leave to drain overnight.

Next day, measure the juice and put it in a clean pan. Add 1 lb/450 g sugar to every 1 pint/600 ml juice. Bring to the boil quickly, skim until the surface is clear, and continue to boil until setting point is reached – about 20 minutes. (Test by pouring a tablespoonful into a saucer and placing in the freezer to set; if it wrinkles when pushed with a finger, it will set.) Skim again, pour into sterilized glass jars and cover tightly when cool. Makes about 1½ lb/675 g.

QUINCE PASTE   Spain, Turkey

This is a most popular Spanish sweetmeat which is also found in Turkey and in parts of the Middle East. It is generally served with coffee, after a meal. It makes a good Christmas present, since quinces are in season in the autumn.

2–3 lb/1–1·25 kg quinces   *a few blanched almonds, split*
approx. 1 lb/450 g sugar   *(optional)*
2–3 tablespoons lemon juice

Wash the quinces but do not peel them; cut them in quarters and remove the cores. Put ½ inch/1 cm water in the bottom of a heavy pan and add the fruit. Cover and cook slowly until very soft. Push through a fine food mill and weigh the resulting purée. Then put in a clean pan with roughly the same weight of sugar, adding lemon juice to taste. Cook gently for about 1 hour, skimming and stirring often, until it is thick enough to come away from the sides of the pan. Turn into a shallow baking tin rinsed in cold water, and spread evenly to form a rectangular cake about ½ inch/1 cm thick. Leave behind the stove – or in a warm dry place – for several days to dry out; in the Mediterranean this would be done in the sun. Then cut in small diamond shapes and store in an airtight container, wrapped in foil, cling-film wrap, or greaseproof paper. If you like, a halved (blanched) almond can be pressed into the centre of each diamond. Keeps well; makes about 2 lb/900 g.

RAS IL HANOUT   **Tunisia, Morocco**

This is a very ancient and complex mixture of spices, much used in the cookery of the North African countries. In Tunisia it is usually a combination of black pepper, *coeurs de roses*, cinnamon, cloves and *cubeb* peppers – the latter being a sort of pepper much used in medieval English cookery, but now unknown in England. In Morocco, however, *ras il hanout* appears to be an even more complex blend, sometimes including as many as fifteen or twenty different spices.

SHATAH   **Egypt**

This is a pounded chilli pepper much used in Egyptian cookery (see Arab salad, page 70), which can be replaced, in some dishes, by a dash of Tabasco, and in others by a pinch of chilli powder.

SUMAC

A herb much used in Middle Eastern dishes, this is made from the chopped dried leaves of a plant called *Rhus coriara*. It is also used medicinally, as an astringent.

TABIL   **Tunisia**

This is a specifically Tunisian spice mixture, much used to flavour dishes of *couscous*, ragouts and other meat dishes. The word *tabil* may mean coriander alone, but more generally means this combination.

2 oz/50 g whole coriander seeds   *¼ oz/8 g minced garlic*
½ oz/15 g caraway seeds   *¼ teaspoon chilli powder*

I have come across two different versions of making this spice mixture. The first is probably better suited to Tunisia than England since it involves laying out all the spices for several hours to dry in the hot sun, then grinding them in a coffee mill and bottling. The second, which can be done on the greyest of English days, involves first pounding them in a mortar, then drying them in a cool oven, then grinding to a fine powder and bottling. The chilli powder can be replaced by a small piece of dried chilli, but it must not be allowed to dominate the flavour of the coriander.

TAMARIND SYRUP   **Turkey**

Tamarind can be bought from shops selling Eastern foods, and this delicious syrup is easily made. I find it invaluable for adding to sweet and sour dishes of all descriptions, and curries; it also makes a good substitute for the *dibis ruman* (pomegranate syrup) in the Syrian recipe for stuffed aubergines on page 131. This is an old Turkish recipe.

6 oz/175 g tamarind   *1 lb/450 g sugar*
2 pints/1·2 litres water

Put the chopped tamarind in a pan with the water; bring to the boil and boil steadily until reduced to 1 pint/600 ml. Strain into a clean pan and add the sugar. Bring back to the boil and boil for 2 minutes, just until the sugar has dissolved. Remove from the heat, cool, then pour into a jelly bag (or a strainer lined with muslin) and leave to drip overnight. The result will be a beautiful pink syrup of an exquisite taste. Pour into a wide-necked jar and seal.

PRESERVED TOMATOES   France, Italy, etc.

Since tomatoes are relatively cheap for such a short period of time, in midsummer, and so expensive for the rest of the year, they are well worth preserving in some form. There are a number of different ways of doing this. They can be made into a thick purée and frozen (raw tomatoes do not freeze well), or simply bottled as follows. Skin the tomatoes and pack tightly into sterilized broad-mouthed glass jars, sprinkling 1 teaspoon sea salt and 1 teaspoon sugar into each jar. Two or three fresh basil leaves may be added, if you are sure that their use will not be limited by this flavouring. If the tomatoes are really tightly packed, they can be simply left as they are and sealed tightly as usual. Otherwise, fill up with a brine made by dissolving 1 tablespoon sea salt in 1½ pints/900 ml hot water, then leaving to cool.

Another method much used in the Mediterranean countries but less practical here, where the sun is unreliable, is making a sun-dried purée. To do this, you skin and chop the tomatoes, discarding all seeds and juice. Put the chopped tomatoes in a large piece of clean muslin and suspend over a bowl, hanging it from the legs of a chair placed upside down on the seat of another chair. Leave in the sun to drain for several days, without squeezing it, until it has completely stopped dripping. Then tip out the purée into a shallow dish to make a layer about 1 inch/2·5 cm thick, and leave again in the sun for 48 hours to dry. Then cut in squares and pack in an airtight container. Use instead of tinned tomato purée.

TRAHANAS   Greece

Trahanas is a sort of instant soup mix made by Greek peasants in late summer. It is formed from coarsely ground wheat mixed to a dough with goats' milk or yogurt, then left in the sun for several days until as dry as powder. It is then stored, usually in the form of small rolls, and used to make a delicious and nourishing soup which the Greek women carry out to their men working in the fields for their midday meal. It can be found in Greek Cypriot shops, either in powder form in packets with instructions for making into soup, or in the form of small rolls as thick as your thumb looking rather like dogs' biscuits, simply packed in plastic bags. The Greeks prefer the latter sort, but I find the packaged form easier to use, since the rolls must be broken up and soaked for 30 minutes before using, and can become lumpy.

TUNNY FISH IN OIL   Italy

Since tunny fish figures often in Mediterranean dishes, and tinned tunny is expensive, it is well worth buying some fresh fish whenever it appears on the market and preserving it at home.

2 lb/900 g tuna, cut in steaks   about 20 black peppercorns
    about 1 ½ inches/5 cm thick   a branch of fennel
1 tablespoon sea salt   olive oil
4–5 bay leaves

Put the tuna steaks in a broad pan and cover with cold water. Bring slowly to the boil and skim until the surface is clear. Add the sea salt, 2 bay leaves, 10 black peppercorns and the branch of fennel. Cover and simmer for 1 hour, then leave to cool in the liquid. Later, lift out the tuna and remove the skin and bone. Break the flesh up into chunks and pack into broad-mouthed jars (sterilized, of course) leaving as little space between them as possible. Scatter each layer with a few black peppercorns, and lay a small bay leaf on the top. Fill to the brim with olive oil and seal tightly. Keep in a dark cool place.

VERJUICE   Turkey

I cannot resist including this Turkish recipe since it is identical to the verjuice that was so widely used in English medieval cookery. It comes from a one-hundred-year-old Turkish cookery book written in English, which was lent me by a friend living in Athens.

Gather any unripe fruit that may have fallen from the trees, such as peaches, pears, nectarines, plums, apples, apricots, cherries, etc. Mix all together, and place them in bottles or a stone jar, cover them with a very strong wine vinegar, tie up the mouths of the bottles with a piece of leather, and let them remain for thirty or forty days before using.

ZAATAR

This is a popular spice blend in the Lebanon consisting of a mixture of wild thyme, toasted sesame seeds, sumac and salt. The word *zaatar* actually means wild thyme, just as the word *tabil* means coriander; yet in both cases *zaatar* in the Lebanon has come to mean this blend, of which the main ingredient is wild thyme, while in Tunisia *tabil* usually means the spice blend based on coriander. A simpler version of *zaatar* is a combination of equal parts of wild thyme and toasted sesame seeds, used to coat a cheese made from drained yogurt called *labneh*, which is often eaten for breakfast in the Lebanon.

14

SNACKS
AND QUICK FOODS

Snacks, sold for the most part in the street, have always played a prominent part in the life of the Mediterranean, much more than they do in England, with its circumscribed street life. For many people in the Latin and Middle Eastern countries, snacks take the place of a midday meal, and they contribute greatly to the general gaiety of urban life. In some of the poorer countries, the variety of snacks almost equals the range of cooked dishes in the national repertoire, in quality and appeal if not in actual number.

As I write this, I am on a Greek boat halfway between Samos and Piraeus, travelling third-class in the middle of August. With a calm sea and cloudless sky, the uneventful trip is continually enlivened by the cries of vendors offering things to eat. First come little bunches of grapes, weighed on an antique iron scale; then tiny packets of shelled nuts, wrapped in minute cones of paper. Iced beer and toasted cheese sandwiches are constantly on sale, and each time the boat stops at one of the islands, boys run on board to sell the local speciality. At Mykonos, thin round cakes of creamy nougat are brought on; with crisp chopped nuts enclosed in a flaky sort of meringue, it is quite the best I have ever tasted. The lady on my left, a stout Greek matron, is constantly chewing. Each time she opens a new package, according to some obscure rule of etiquette, she apparently feels obliged to offer me some also. By experiment I learn to accept, for only then with a sigh of relief does she feel free to continue eating herself. In this way, I eat a number of interesting things, without having any idea what they are.

Turkey is even richer in the variety of its snacks than Greece. A trip up the Bosphorus a week ago provided a good example. As the ferry plied its way from bank to bank, a boy would circulate every few minutes carrying just a few bottles of icy orangeade and coca cola, while a man would pass in the opposite direction with little glasses of hot tea carefully balanced on a tray over our heads. Sesame seed bars and nuts were constantly offered, while at Kandilis, a village on the Asian shore famed for the excellence of its yogurt, cool tubs were brought aboard. In Bodrum, a small town in south-west Turkey, I found giant mussels being sold on the half-shell, simply steamed and with a squeeze of lemon juice. Ears of corn are boiled and rubbed with salt, then sold from barrows, whereas in Italy and Yugoslavia they are usually grilled. Along the Galatea Bridge in Istanbul, the range of quick foods for sale is wide: small pieces of grilled mackerel are stuffed into flat bread, mussels are fried, lambs' intestines are cooked on a spit, and rounds of bread dough are spread with sliced raw vegetables.

In France and Italy many of the food markets have their own species of quick foods, peculiar to them, which prove invaluable for restoring tired shoppers and stall-holders alike. My favourite is the Genoese *farinata*, called *faina* in Sardinia, *socca* in Nice and *cade* in Toulon. This is a totally delicious dish, like a vast thin cake of chick pea flour, mixed to a thin batter with olive oil and water, poured into a metal tray at least a yard wide and baked in a wood-fired bread (or pizza) oven. It emerges after about twelve minutes, accompanied by a most delicious smell, dark brown and crisp around the edges, and pale creamy yellow in the centre. I first ate this in a small shop in the sotto ripa of Genoa, where a group of old men and women were waiting patiently for the next baking – this happens every hour – for *socca* is at its best immediately after emerging from the oven. Wedges of the thin cake, only about ¼ inch/5 mm thick, are scraped and shovelled into squares of oiled paper, sprinkled with pepper and eaten standing up. Alternatively, you can do as I did and sit by the cosy wood oven, eating my *socca* with a fork. The identical dish is sold from a stall in the market in the old town in Nice, close to the *traiteur* called Julien. This stall is run by a lady who has been there for years, and every half hour or so she receives reinforcements in the shape of another huge metal tray full of *socca* straight from the oven, kept hot under a domed metal lid very like the lid of a Moroccan *tagine*, and transported on the back of a bicycle. Even more delicious, however, is the *socca* baked each evening in a small bar near the harbour in Nice. At 5 p.m. a small group of habitués starts to gather, waiting for the first baking. When enough people are assembled to make a baking worthwhile, the batter is poured into the huge tray and shoved into the oven. When it is done, it stands on a table near the door and passers-by stop to buy some, again wrapped in paper, as they pass, while the addicts like myself sit at tables and consume plate after plate, accompanied by glasses of red wine, as an early evening snack. In Toulon market this same dish is called *cade* and is sold from a barrow. Sadly, many of these quick foods seem to be disappearing. In Toulon there is only one barrow left selling *cade*, while in Genoa it took me three days combing the narrow streets before I could find one – although a Genoese friend described the *sotto ripa* as being full of tiny shops selling *farinata*, *panizza*, *focaccia* and *moscardini fritti* (the tiny local octopi no bigger than a spider).

In Nice market squares of pissaladière are also sold; here they are made without anchovies, simply with the sweet Provençal onions and whole black olives. Another popular Provençal snack is the *pan bagna*; this was originally a sort of salad with bread, rather like the first version of gazpacho, but later developed into a sort of sandwich composed of a simple *salade niçoise* in a soft roll, moistened with olive oil. The rolls, about 8 inches/25 cm across, are baked especially for this purpose in the area round Nice, while in other parts a baguette is used.

Further east, hard-boiled eggs make a popular snack. In the streets of Beirut they are sold from barrows, accompanied by little twists of paper holding a simple spice mixture to eat with them. Here and in Turkey thin slivers of grilled lamb are carved off huge doner kebabs and stuffed into flat bread. In Tunisia, there are many stalls selling eggs which are eaten on the spot; unfortunately I was unable to determine whether they were raw or cooked without actually eating one. Toasted seeds of all sorts are also on sale all over Tunisia and make a nourishing and sustaining snack.

Snacks also play their part in the home, often replacing more conventional meals in hot weather. In a pretty Venetian apartment I was given thin slices of prosciutto wrapped round freshly baked grissini; these were served with a green salad, after a dish of mixed green and white noodles, and made a most excellent light lunch. Another simple dish that is widely popular in Mediterranean countries, especially in hot weather, is a combination of feta cheese and watermelon. The contrast between the salty dry cheese and the crisp juicy fruit is almost unbeatable, especially when accompanied by a glass of ouzo, arak, raki, or whatever form the local version of pernod takes.

15

DRINKS

The first drink that comes to mind in relation to the Mediterranean is of course wine, for the vine is one of the three staple crops of this part of the world, together with wheat and olives. However I am not qualified to write on wine, and such a complex subject would demand a whole book to itself. The other alcoholic drink that is so typical of the Mediterranean countries – I don't think it even exists elsewhere – is pernod, in all its forms. Called ouzo in Greece, arak in the Middle East and raki in Turkey, it differs little if at all (as far as I can see), and is the universally popular aperitif. It is flavoured with aniseed, like the absinthe which is now illegal, and even those who dislike it at first usually grow to love it. It should always be drunk with some little accompaniment – just a few olives or nuts make all the difference Sherry is, of course, the most popular aperitif in Spain, and it tastes better there than it ever does anywhere else. Each time I visit Spain, I make a point of going into a small bar and ordering a glass of medium dry sherry, such as Domecq's La Ina, served ice cold with a little dish of olives.

I give here a few recipes for summer drinks – non-alcoholic for the most part – made from Mediterranean ingredients. These range from the mint tea of Morocco to the Turkish *ayran*, a diluted yogurt drink. They are all refreshing and sustaining for the weary traveller, especially if, like me last year, he has been living in a camping van for several weeks.

AYRAN   **Turkey, Lebanon, etc.**

This refreshing summer drink makes a perfect substitute for a meal in hot weather, since it is nourishing as well as thirst-quenching.

Alternatively, it can be drunk with a meal. It is just yogurt, diluted with iced water, and a little salt. In Lebanon, a few mint leaves are sometimes added, but I like it best quite plain, as it is served in Turkey. Unfortunately it just doesn't work with English or French yogurt which is too bland to dilute. The Turkish yogurt is more like Russian yogurt, quite strong in flavour and more suitable for serving as a sauce with meat or vegetable dishes than eating as a dessert. Some of my friends in England grow this sort of yogurt from culture imported from Russia or the Middle East, so I give a recipe for *ayran* in case you find a source of suitable yogurt.

1 pint/600 ml strong yogurt
½–¾ pint/300–450 ml iced
  water

salt to taste
a few mint leaves, chopped
  (optional)

This is best made in a blender. Otherwise beat the yogurt until smooth and stir in enough iced water to give a good consistency, thin enough to drink easily. Add a very little salt – it wants to be quite bland – and pour into tall glasses. Scatter a little chopped fresh mint on top if you wish. Serves 2–3.

TURKISH, GREEK OR ARAB COFFEE

What we call Turkish coffee is also the coffee drunk in Greece, the Middle East and the North African countries of the Arab world. The method of making it does not vary much, although there are a few slight variations. It is important to have the correct grind of coffee, which should be as fine as flour, and a proper Turkish coffee pot is helpful, although not essential. Any small saucepan with a pouring lip will do. It is always made in small quantities – ⅛ pint/75 ml per person is sufficient – and drunk in minute cups. If using regular demi-tasse cups, they should only be filled half full. The coffee that is grown in the Yemen, a mocha bean, is considered to be one of the best in the world, but as it is so widely drunk throughout the Arab world it is almost all used for home consumption, and little is exported. I use a blend of Mocha and Mysore, pulverized to what is known as 'Turkish grind'. In the Middle East, the beans are roasted – usually over charcoal – and ground immediately prior to making. Since the sugar is cooked with the coffee, the desired degree of sweetness must be decided in advance; in Arab countries, very sweet coffee is served at happy occasions, while a bitter blend is served at funerals. The recipe given here produces a medium sweet blend which is acceptable to most people. In the Lebanon, one or two cardamom seeds are sometimes added to the pot, or even ground up with the coffee.

for each person:
⅛ pint/75 ml water
1 generous teaspoon castor
  sugar

½ tablespoon pulverized
  (Turkish grind) coffee
1–2 cardamom seeds (optional)

Put the water with the sugar into the little coffee pot and bring to the boil. Add the coffee (and the cardamom seeds if used) and stir. Bring back to the boil, when the froth will rise to the top of the pot. Remove from the heat and allow the level to sink, then replace over the heat and boil up again. Remove once more, then boil up for the third time, and pour immediately into cups, a little at a time into each one, so that the froth on the top is evenly distributed. Some people give the pot a little tap to help the foam subside each time they remove it from the heat; others add a few drops of cold water to help settle the grounds just before pouring it into the cups. In any case it must be left for a few moments in the cup before drinking, to allow the sediment to settle; it must never be stirred, so that no spoons are necessary, and the cup should not be drained.

KIR   France

This summer drink is both pleasing to look at and light to drink, especially as a pre-luncheon aperitif. Strictly speaking it should be made with crème de cassis, which is the alcoholic liqueur made from blackcurrants, but many bars cheat by using a cheaper blackcurrant syrup. I have tried using both, and since the proportions of cassis to wine are so small, I find I can hardly tell the difference.

    In the bottom of a large wine glass put a dash – no more than a small teaspoonful – of crème de cassis (or blackcurrant syrup if like me you can't tell the difference). Add a chilled dry white wine until the colour reaches that of a pale vin rosé; it must never be as red as red wine. If the wine is not sufficiently chilled, ice cubes can be added, although this may give purists a second shock.

MINT TEA   Morocco

This is the mint tea which is drunk endlessly in Morocco, light and refreshing in spite of its sweetness. Even if you don't like sweet tea, as I don't, you will grow to love this, for the flavours of the mint, the tea and the sugar blend together in a miraculous way. I have moderated the sugar somewhat – in Morocco it would be much sweeter – but it just does not work if you try to leave it out altogether, or cut it down further than this. I use a tea imported from China called Temple of Heaven; both the special chunmee and the special gunpowder blends make good mint tea.

1 tablespoon green tea,
   chunmee or gunpowder
3–4 tablespoons sugar
about 24 large leaves fresh
   spearmint or ¼ pint/150 ml
   loosely packed

boiling water
3–4 small sprigs or leaves,
   fresh mint

Warm a small pot holding about 1 pint/600 ml, then empty it out. Put in the tea, sugar and mint leaves, then pour over enough boiling water to fill the pot. Stand for 5 minutes, then pour from a height into 3 or 4 small glasses, putting a tiny sprig of fresh mint into each one.

TEA WITH ALMONDS   Tunisia

In the pretty village of Sidi Bou Said, just outside Tunis, they serve tea in all the cafés with a layer of toasted almonds, each one cut in 2 or 3 pieces, floating on the top.

A MONACO   France

Two or three years ago this almost non-alcoholic cocktail was very fashionable in the south of France. For all I know it has now been superseded, but I have grown to love it and make it often, each summer. It is useful for giving to adolescents since the alcohol content is small, yet it has an air of sophistication about it.

In a tall glass, put a dash – about 1 teaspoonful – of sirop de grenadine. (This is made from the juice of pomegranates, and can be bought from good wine merchants; watch out for cheap imitations made from raspberry juice.) Fill up with a mixture of light lager (e.g. Heineken) and fizzy lemonade in equal parts. Stir briefly and add ice cubes. This makes a beautiful cloudy pink drink, perfect for serving before lunch, but too sweet to drink with a meal.

SANGRIA   Spain

This red wine cup is much drunk in Spain in the summer; there are many different versions, but the variations are slight. It makes a good light and relatively inexpensive drink that goes well with almost all summer dishes.

2 oz/50 g sugar	¼ pint/150 ml cheap Spanish
4 tablespoons water	brandy
1 bottle Spanish red wine	2 peaches, sliced
1 lemon, chopped	6 ice cubes
1 orange, chopped	½ pint/300 ml soda water

Heat the sugar with the water in a small pan until it has dissolved. Cool. Pour the wine – it does not need to be a good one – into a large jug and stir in the sugar syrup and the chopped lemon and orange, peel and all. Stir in the brandy and chill for 2–3 hours. Then pour through a strainer into a clean jug, squeezing the orange and lemon pieces between the hands. Stir in the sliced peaches and the ice cubes. Chill again, and just before serving add the soda water.

VIŞNE Turkey

This is the juice of a sour cherry, not unlike our morello cherry, which is widely drunk in Turkey. Since alcohol is prohibited by the Moslem creed, soft drinks play an important part during the long hot summers. I found that by mixing it with the Turkish white wine, rather in the manner of a kir but using slightly more *vişne* than cassis, one could make a pleasant drink, a pretty pinkish colour.

INDEX

References to recipes are in bold type